DATE DUE

3/19/18	

The Politics of Voter Suppression

About The Century Foundation

The Century Foundation is a progressive think tank, founded in 1919 and initially funded by Edward A. Filene. With a strong legacy of research and analysis aimed at addressing a range of important issues related to U.S. economic and social policy and international affairs, its work currently focuses on issues of equity and opportunity in the United States, and how American values can best be sustained and advanced in a world of more diffuse power. With offices in New York City and Washington, D.C., The Century Foundation is nonprofit and nonpartisan.

THE POLITICS OF VOTER SUPPRESSION

*Defending and Expanding Americans'
Right to Vote*

TOVA ANDREA WANG

A CENTURY FOUNDATION BOOK

CORNELL UNIVERSITY PRESS
ITHACA AND LONDON

First published 2012 by Cornell University Press

Printed in the United States of America

Library of Congress Cataloging-in-Publication Data

Wang, Tova Andrea.
    The politics of voter suppression : defending and expanding
Americans' right to vote / Tova Andrea Wang.
        p. cm.
    "A Century Foundation book."
    Includes bibliographical references and index.
    ISBN 978-0-8014-5085-3 (cloth : alk. paper)
    1. Elections—United States—History—20th century.   2. Elections—
Corrupt practices—United States—History—20th century.   3. Voter
registration—United States—History—20th century.   4. Voter
registration—Corrupt practices—United States—History—20th century.
5. Suffrage—United States—History—20th century.   6. Voting—
United States—History—20th century.   7. United States—Politics
and government—20th century.   I. Title.
    JK1976.W36 2012
    324.60973—dc23   2012005954

Cornell University Press strives to use environmentally responsible
suppliers and materials to the fullest extent possible in the publishing
of its books. Such materials include vegetable-based, low-VOC inks
and acid-free papers that are recycled, totally chlorine-free, or partly
composed of nonwood fibers. For further information, visit our website
at www.cornellpress.cornell.edu.

Cloth printing   10 9 8 7 6 5 4 3 2 1

For my father, Robert Wang

Contents

Foreword, by Janice Nittoli   ix

Preface   xiii

1. The Voter Inclusion Principle   1

2. The Early Years of Vote Suppression   16

3. Conditions and Consequences of the Voting Rights Act   29

4. Vote Suppression Goes National—and Republican   42

5. The Battle over Motor Voter   60

6. The Election of 2000 and Its Fallout   75

7. A Slight Upswing   91

8. Effects on Election Outcomes   108

9. How to Increase Participation   126

Epilogue: What Citizens Can Do   156

Notes   161

Acknowledgments   187

Index   189

Foreword

The right to vote is at the heart of American ideals of democracy. The U.S. Constitution places the election of representatives firmly in the hands of "the People," and its amendments enumerate the many ways in which this right to vote cannot be denied. Access to the ballot by American voters not only has been protected; it also has been greatly expanded. U.S. history has been, generally, a tale of increasing suffrage, with the Fifteenth and Nineteenth amendments extending the franchise to blacks and women, respectively.

While the nation's watershed moments have seen numerous hands in Congress raised in support of increasing voting rights, at other times, there have been much less distinguished efforts to claw back these rights. As Tova Wang details in *The Politics of Voter Suppression*, there have been many attempts by members of all political parties to restrict the right to vote throughout American history, typically in ways that satisfy purely partisan aims. And what is particularly distressing is that voter suppression is not just a relic of the past but rather continues today under the guise of election "reform." Wang argues that reforms that increase participation are nearly always legitimate, while activities that suppress voting are almost never legitimate.

In today's political and economic climate, voter suppression should not be viewed as a trivial matter, particularly when it is aimed at Americans whose voices are often ignored, such as the poor, minorities, and the young. As recent elections have shown, nationwide outcomes can hinge on vote numbers in the thousands, so even modest attempts to deny voters access to the ballot can result in a change in direction for the nation. But perhaps more important, the denial of someone's ability to vote is, in itself, a violation of that person's rights and a harm to our democracy, even if it does not change the outcome of an election. It is estimated that legislation enacted in the past year alone—requiring voter identification, making it harder to register or use early or absentee voting, and so on—may make it more difficult for millions of Americans to cast their votes. These laws restricting access to the ballot are very disturbing, particularly as they occur against the backdrop of an equally distressing change in campaign finance law, the U.S. Supreme Court's 2010 ruling in *Citizens United v. Federal Election Commission,* which removed any limits on private contributions to political action committees (PACs). This sudden reversal of the nation's progress in striving toward full electoral participation, combined with the Court's huge boost to private money in political campaigns, significantly tilts the political playing field in favor of the wealthy, the powerful, and the connected.

With over a decade of experience covering voting and election issues as The Century Foundation's democracy fellow, Wang is uniquely qualified to present this perspective. In 2001 she was staff person to the National Commission on Federal Election Reform, co-chaired by former presidents Jimmy Carter and Gerald R. Ford, of which The Century Foundation was a cosponsor. Tasked with making recommendations to Congress for improving the nation's election process, the commission released its report, *To Assure Pride and Confidence in the Electoral Process,* in 2001. The following year, Congress passed the Help America Vote Act, which built on the recommendations made by the commission. Wang was the executive director of The Century Foundation's Post-2004 Election Reform Working Group, composed of many of the most preeminent election law scholars in the country, which released their report, *Balancing Access and Integrity,* in 2005.

She is also coauthor of the widely remarked upon 2006 report on voter fraud and voter intimidation for the U.S. Election Assistance Commission.

Tova Wang's work for The Century Foundation builds on its long history of looking at voting and election issues. For over a quarter century, the foundation has examined the problems with campaign finance, with publications such as *What Price PACS?*, the report of its Task Force on Political Action Committees (1984); Anthony Corrado's *Paying for Presidents: Public Financing in National Elections* (1993); and the more recent volume of essays, *Money, Politics, and the Constitution: Beyond* Citizens United, edited by Monica Youn and cosponsored by the Brennan Center for Justice at the NYU School of Law (2011).

Wang's argument in *The Politics of Voter Suppression* probably will be perceived as controversial, but it should not be. While her criticism of current efforts to manipulate election reform to partisan advantage is leveled mainly at one side of the aisle, it is based on a bedrock assumption of American democracy: that an American's right to vote shall not be denied, but rather full voter participation should be supported by the efforts of the government and of all political parties. On behalf of the Trustees of The Century Foundation, I thank Tova Wang for her work on this important issue.

Janice Nittoli, President
The Century Foundation

April 2012

PREFACE

No single American political party has cornered the market on dirty tricks. Across our country's history, all political parties—from the Whigs to the Democrats to the Republicans—have abused voting laws, procedures, and reforms to suit their own narrow political ends. My concern here is with how election reforms have been used to partisan ends and, critically, how those reforms have often been used to skew and diminish voter participation across the United States. What is needed now is a new reform plan that works through the partisan election system yet results in achieving the overriding American agenda of participatory and representative government.

The time-tested strategy of party operatives for both the Democratic and Republican parties has been to make a vague or dramatically overstated claim about voter fraud and then demand the system be cleaned up through "reform." Very often, the "reform" method chosen by those in power is a change in voting practice that is unlikely to reduce fraud but will make it harder for some segments of society to vote—populations, not coincidentally, expected to vote for political opponents. At other times, well-intentioned reforms that had a real chance to do some good are subsequently manipulated by one party or another so as to gain unfair political advantage by disenfranchising opponents.

Until the second half of the twentieth century, the Democrats were the main culprits. Over the past fifty years, however, Republicans have most frequently and deftly employed election law and procedures to help their party win elections. As the country remains ideologically divided, and outcomes of local, some statewide, and presidential elections have the potential to be close, contemporary Republicans have made it a central part of their election strategy to enact laws and call for practices that will reduce turnout among those who tend to vote Democratic, at least at the margins—where elections can often be won or lost.

In this book I establish a new framework for analyzing election laws and policies and examine the history of election manipulation through this paradigm. I will look at election reforms for partisan advantage from the 1800s to recent times—revealing the alarmingly common use of these tactics today and how the strategies employed to suppress voting in recent times are not novel but build on the strategies used by a variety of actors across more than a century. Political abuses of election reform are a continuous—if admittedly ignoble—feature of American history. This long history of abuse should not, however, lead to political passivity and indifference; it also is possible to pursue reforms that can enhance democracy. Indeed, a key element of this book is the proposal of a number of legitimate and positive reforms that ought to be pursued as a major part of each party's agenda. Legitimate election reform will increase the number of voters who come out to vote in a party's favor. This is a more democratic and beneficial way to win elections. It is also a way to pursue partisan ends without undermining the very participatory basis of representative government.

Politics is, of course, a dirty business, and parties and candidates are given fairly wide leeway in campaign tactics. However, one tactic that should never be considered legitimate is the suppression of votes, whether overt or conducted through subtler means of legal and procedural manipulation. My essential argument is that reforms that increase participation are nearly always legitimate, while activities that suppress voting are almost never legitimate. The gain in registered and active voters encouraged by such positive reforms results in gains for democratic participation.

As I have examined the history of American elections, it has struck me how often my colleagues and I make arguments that we think are creative and novel, but in truth, everything old is new again. The reality is that the fights we voting-rights advocates are engaged in now are disturbingly similar to the ones Americans have fought in this country for decades, if not centuries.

My entry point into the work of advocating for voting rights was the infamous 2000 election. That year I went to work as a staff person for the National Commission for Federal Election Reform, co-chaired by former presidents Carter and Ford and created to identify the problems with that election and provide recommendations for future improvements. This was an irreplaceable on-the-job crash course on the myriad systemic problems in election law and practices at the polls that routinely disenfranchise many Americans. I went on from my work with the National Commission for Federal Election Reform to study our election system and then to hands-on work with academics, advocates, policymakers, and concerned citizens as we sought to establish ways more Americans, particularly those repeatedly left out of the democratic process, might have a voice in our system.

It seems in America we have swayed back and forth over my years in the field between greater access and more restriction. Over the last decade I have seen positive movement toward enabling persons with prior felony convictions to become eligible to register and vote, as well as improvements in the registration system, particularly in the slowly rising number of states allowing citizens to register and vote on the same day. Yet there are worrying signs for the critical 2012 election cycle. In 2011 there was an explosion of states passing highly restrictive requirements for voters. Foremost among these requirements was the demand that an eligible voter provide government-issued photo identification at the polls; these new electoral laws now threaten to disenfranchise thousands upon thousands of Americans in 2012. Not coincidentally, these provisions will hit hardest voters who came out in historic numbers in 2008—a majority for President Obama—including African Americans, Latinos, and young people. Voting rights groups will now face the daunting task of ensuring that these groups—along with the poor, disabled, and elderly—are able to get to departments of motor vehicles with the proper documents to get the IDs they need. Advocates for voting rights are also at work at the level of state legislatures in order to prevent other such restrictive laws from passing and thereby limit the swing of the pendulum toward restriction and, perhaps, encourage a move back toward access.

These swings are found across American electoral history. Of course each era is unique, and since the nineteenth century, circumstances, demographics, and political contexts have changed dramatically in the United States. These changes have shaped the particulars of the strategies employed to change the electoral landscape and suppress votes. But it is nevertheless quite astounding how familiar is some of the language employed in earlier debates. Each era's particular battle over the right to vote has its own unique features, but my consideration of the history of American elections shows that the tactics used by one generation build on those used by others in earlier circumstances. And, of course, there are political epochs of access and epochs of restriction and suppression.

The lessons of history are helpful as advocates of voting rights look ahead to November 2012. In the last two presidential elections, voter registration issues were exacerbated by partisan rule making, long lines, partisan "caging" and challenges to voters' eligibility, vote suppression of students, and deceptive practices. The pendulum has on balance swung even further toward restriction and suppression, and the midterm elections of 2010, as well as the activity around voting issues in the 2011 state legislatures, showed nothing to suggest that the country was ready to sway back toward access and the encouragement of voter registration and participation. The policy prescriptions, legislative lobbying, and legal action undertaken by those who work for voting rights need to be informed by a perspective broader and longer than the election cycle. In 2012 we will meet with many of the same issues, although in different guises, and what we learn from history can and should guide our actions.

If voter suppression has long been a bipartisan affair, our contemporary history shows that the Republican Party has taken the clear lead in working for restriction of access. Accordingly, some of my policy prescriptions and analyses will be highly critical of the Republican Party, Republican Party leadership, and Republican elected officials. So I also want to acknowledge that some Republicans are no doubt sincere in their concerns that there is "rampant" fraud. In addition I want to note that current exaggerated claims of malfeasance in the election system are not limited to Republicans. Particularly in the context of the debate over electronic voting machines, a minority on the left has expressed hyperbolic concerns about manipulation of such machines through nefarious methods, with strongly worded allegations that elections have on several occasions been "stolen" because of criminal interference with the functioning of these systems. There are certainly problems with malfunctioning voting machines, and all types of systems—but especially computerized ones— have serious vulnerabilities that must be addressed. Yet, just as with the Republican charges of massive voter fraud, the claims made on the extreme left end of the spectrum about widespread machine manipulation have been made without solid evidence. There is one enormous distinction between those who attack the election process from the left and the right, however. Those who express alarm about voting machines are not advocating a reform that would potentially make voting more difficult for some people or jeopardize disenfranchisement; they are actually trying to ensure that every person's vote gets counted. Suspicions about the voting process abound, then, on the left and the right. My criticisms focus on the Republican Party because their suspicions have been translated into effective methods to restrict the vote and because Republican advocacy for restriction has been widespread and effective across the United States.

My advocacy for access to the vote does not mean that I claim election fraud does not occur. In particular, there is fraud through absentee balloting and to a lesser degree vote buying (usually through the use of absentee ballots). And the fraud of purposefully providing misinformation to voters so that they do not vote or do not have their vote counted has become increasingly common. But this is not what contemporary Republicans are addressing when they denounce fraud. Republicans talk about fraud taking place at the polling place. They repeat what have practically become mantras about dead people voting, voters voting twice, and noncitizens voting. Yet every bit of evidence shows that these types of activities at this point in the development of our electoral system occur rarely. Republicans and their supporters nonetheless fight vigorously for measures that would address these nonexistent problems, making voting harder for certain constituencies while completely ignoring the real types of fraud and other forms of malfeasance that are perpetrated against voters and the voting system.

My work analyzing democracy and elections both here and abroad has convinced me that most efforts to increase participation, even if just among a particular group or groups of voters, should be encouraged. Because Democrats in recent years have been more favorably inclined toward measures that expand the electorate, many of the recommendations may be more helpful to that party in increasing the number of voters in their column, but many of my suggestions apply to Republican campaigns as well.

It is crucial to the health of our democracy for these measures to be part of the routine political agenda and not merely one-offs raised in response to the latest Election Day travesty. In the midst of predictions that the system would be overwhelmed by historic voter turnout (maybe even as high as 70 percent!) in 2008, I stated in response to an inquiry of the political press, "We have an election system that's exquisitely designed for low rates of participation." This should not be so. Our democracy will only be a true democracy when the full range of voices and interests have an equal opportunity to be heard and heeded.

1

The Voter Inclusion Principle

In 2011 and 2012, following a wave of Republican takeovers of state legislatures and statehouses in the 2010 elections, states across the country saw an extraordinary assault on American citizens' voting rights—the worst in geographic scope in generations, potentially impacting hundreds of thousands of voters. The requirement for voters to have government-issued photo identification at the polls—a favorite tool of some in the Republican Party to disenfranchise constituencies more likely to vote for Democrats—was rammed through and passed into law in eight states across the country, and made it through some part of the legislative process in more than two dozen more states. As these laws were pushed ahead, one heard a lot not about the *right* to vote but about the *privilege* of voting. Since when did a citizen's franchise become a privilege and not a right?

Florida, a state by now infamous for election manipulation by politicians, already had a fairly strict voter ID law in place. Its new conservative Republican governor and state legislature found additional ways to make registering and voting more difficult for particular constituencies.

The state's new voting law, passed in 2011, requires voters challenged at the polls to cast provisional ballots, with no opportunity to contest the challenge and cast a regular ballot. Long experience confirms that provisional ballots frequently go uncounted, because if they are to be tallied, these ballots need to be hand counted by elections officials, who must then determine, often by ill-defined standards, if the voter was eligible to vote. The number of provisional ballots out of the total ballots cast and the number of rejected provisional ballots out of provisional ballots cast vary widely by state and even by county within states, demonstrating a lack of standardization in this area. The Florida law also bars voters from updating a changed address at their polling place on Election Day. Voters who moved within the state of Florida had previously been able to update their information at their polling place and still cast a regular ballot. Under the new law, such a voter has to cast a provisional ballot—often a thrown-away vote. This provision has the biggest impact on more-mobile voters—often low-income, minority, and young people, and especially students—who tend to support Democratic candidates.

The Florida law does not stop with individual voters. It also stymies citizen groups that undertake voter registration drives, which typically seek to reach marginalized communities where people are unlikely to register to vote at motor vehicle offices. New restrictions require volunteers for organizations like the League of Women Voters to travel to local supervisors' offices, register by providing detailed personal information, take an oath, and be held personally and financially liable if they do not deliver the completed forms back to the supervisor within forty-eight hours. If these volunteers fail to return the forms in time, they are subject to fines of up to $1,000. As a result, the league has decided it simply cannot risk conducting voter registration drives in Florida and has ceased operations in the state. According to census data, nationally nearly 9 million citizens reported having registered "at a voter registration drive" in 2008, and 9.4 million citizens reported that they registered "at a school, hospital, or on campus"—all locations where voter registration drives are often conducted. Some portion of the 19.7 million citizens that registered to vote by mail received these applications from third-party organizations.[1] African Americans and Hispanics are twice as likely to register to vote through voter registration drives as white applicants or applicants from English-speaking households.[2]

Finally, Florida's exclusionary law curtails early voting, which in past elections had been highly used by the state's African American voters. Under the old law, the early voting period ran for two weeks, from a Monday through the Sunday before Election Day. Now early voting runs only eight days, from Saturday through Saturday, leaving off the final Sunday. In prior elections, urban districts with the highest African American populations had used the last Sunday before the election to conduct early voting, knowing that many African American church groups would collectively bring out their voters to the polls. In 2008, fully one-third of early voters on the final Sunday were African American.[3]

A member of the Florida state Senate, Republican Michael Bennett, made this rambling argument in support of the bill:

> We all want everybody to vote. But we want an informed voter. . . . Voting is a privilege. How easy should it be? . . . Do you read the stories about the people in Africa? The people in the desert, who literally walk two and three hundred miles so they can have the opportunity to do what we do, and we want to make it more convenient? How much more convenient do you want to make it? Do we want to go to their house? Take the polling booth with us? . . . This is a hard-fought privilege. This is something people die for. You want to make it convenient? The guy who died to give you that right, it was not convenient. Why would we make it any easier? I want 'em to fight for it. I want 'em to know what it's like. I want them to go down there, and have to walk across town to go over and vote.[4]

This is a point of view I fundamentally reject. Voting is not a privilege, and the United States certainly should not emulate election conditions in developing nations. (Incidentally, Bennett grossly exaggerated the hardships facing voters in Africa,[5] presumably taking some poetic license.) Voting is a right that should be as accessible as possible to all American citizens, and should not purposefully be made more difficult just so a voter can somehow prove he or she is "informed" or sufficiently dedicated as defined by some arbitrary measure. Although there is no explicit right to vote in the Constitution, the equal protection clause of the Fourteenth Amendment prohibits states from denying any person within their jurisdiction the equal protection of the laws, including with respect to the right to vote, and the Fifteenth Amendment declares, "The right of citizens of the United States to vote shall not be denied or abridged by the United

States or by any State on account of race, color, or previous condition of servitude."

It is not surprising then that Supreme Court associate justice Hugo Black wrote in explaining the elections provision of the Constitution in the seminal voting rights case *Wesbury v. Sanders*,

> Our Court has held that . . . Article [Art. I, § 2] gives persons qualified to vote a constitutional right to vote and to have their votes counted. *United States v. Mosley*, 238 U.S. 383; *Ex Parte Yarbrough*, 110 U.S. 651. Not only can this right to vote not be denied outright, it cannot, consistently with Article I, be destroyed by alteration of ballots, *see United States v. Classic*, 313 U.S. 299, or diluted by stuffing of the ballot box, *see United States v. Saylor*, 322 U.S. 385. No right is more precious in a free country than that of having a voice in the election of those who make the laws under which, as good citizens, we must live. Other rights, even the most basic, are illusory if the right to vote is undermined. Our Constitution leaves no room for classification of people in a way that unnecessarily abridges this right.[6]

The struggles of the civil rights movement in the 1950s and 1960s were in large part for the right to vote. People died in that effort to secure the right to vote. It was the right to vote that drove suffragette women into the streets in the early twentieth century, until they were finally granted that right in the Nineteenth Amendment to the Constitution in 1920. The key civil rights legislation of 1965 is called the Voting Rights Act.

Rather than making efforts to curtail the rights of groups that might vote a certain way, states should welcome the approach taken in 2008 in North Carolina, where the Obama campaign and nonpartisan voter organizations used early voting and a newly passed same-day registration law to push turnout to historic highs, especially in the African American community. Same-day registration—allowing voters to register and vote at the same time during the early voting period—"was a major focus of the Democratic ground game. The Democrats invested tremendous resources into registering new voters and getting these new voters to the polls during the early voting period."[7] In this way, North Carolina increased its voter participation more than any other state in the nation in 2008, going from 64 percent turnout in the previous presidential election to 70 percent turnout.[8] Some 2.4 million people voted early in North Carolina in 2008. With more locations to vote early, more days and hours to cast an early ballot, and sites on college campuses, the number of those voting early more than doubled from 2004.[9] A quarter of a million voters took advantage of same-day registration, and nearly half of them were first-time voters in their jurisdiction. Most notably, the rate of African American voting increased from 59 percent to 72 percent from 2004 to 2008.[10] A total of 21 percent of the voting-age population in North Carolina is African American, yet these voters made up 35 percent of same-day voter registrants. More than half of African Americans voters used either early voting or same-day registration and voting.[11]

Obama's candidacy was no doubt one motivation for this strong turnout: African Americans voted overwhelmingly for Obama.[12] During early voting the Democratic candidates, including Obama, outpolled opponents by more than 300,000 votes, whereas on Election Day, Republican candidates got far more votes than Democrats—strong evidence of the Democratic Party's successful effort to promote early voting as a tool for increasing participation on their side.[13] Sixty-three percent of Obama's votes came from early or absentee voters, compared with 51 percent of Republican candidate John McCain's votes.[14] Yet a voter is not registered for one election. A registered voter is enfranchised for the future, and his or her participation is a net gain for democracy.

This is how election law should be used: to encourage and boost voter participation, not make it unnecessarily difficult, or serve as a deterrent to any citizen's participation. The sanction for the kind of get-out-the-vote activities the Obama campaign engaged in is the fundamental democratic intuition that more political participation among citizens is always desirable. I take this intuition and develop it into what I call the principle of voter inclusion. This is the normative concept that gathers our democratic intuitions about participation, and the critical framework that I will use to analyze campaign and election practices designed to mobilize or suppress the vote, practices that have emerged throughout our nation's history and continue today. My perspective is not ideological, but relies on a long history of political theories and principles about what makes for a robust and healthy democracy.

The Harms of Vote Suppression

The use and abuse of election laws and policies to suppress votes have detrimental impacts on democracy. In our system, we like to believe that elections express the will of the people—all of the people. Yet our elections are not representative as a result of low voter turnout, partisan redistricting, and the influence of money on elections.[15] Deliberate attempts to prevent some eligible voters from voting distort the democratic process. Willful blindness to the negative impact certain laws have on voting rights is also a subversion of the process.

Over at least the last five decades, the electorate has consistently skewed toward a richer, more educated, whiter, and older demographic.[16] And there are ideological differences between voters and nonvoters. According to a 2006 poll, while Republicans and Democrats are equally regular voters, Democratic constituencies are more likely to be nonvoters: 20 percent of people who identify as Democrats say they are not registered to vote, compared with 14 percent of Republicans. Twenty-nine percent of liberals say they are not registered to vote, compared with 20 percent of moderates and 17 percent of conservatives.[17] It strains logic to believe that, given the closeness of many American elections, these differences in voting behavior do not end up having an impact on electoral outcomes, at least once in a while. This means that election outcomes, while representative of the will of those who voted, are not necessarily the will of the district to be represented. Conversely, the more citizens turn out to vote, the more representative the electorate becomes by definition than when fewer people vote.[18] Although there is some debate over whether an increase in voters would affect policy outcomes,[19] it is clear that voting barriers have meant that certain groups are guiding public policy far more than others.[20] The known active electorate sets the priorities for the nation before the voting, legislating, and policy decision making ever takes place—and nonvoters' voices go unheard and unheeded.[21]

When laws and customary practices make it permissible to deny voting, this atmosphere degrades the strategies political campaigns employ and how they structure and devote resources to their operations. Rather than trying to boost the number of voters who come out to vote for their candidate, campaigns may opt to employ a strategy of suppressing the votes of people they suspect will vote for their opponents. Historically, of course, parties and politicians have used and abused election rules to keep down the voter turnout of the other side, rather than focusing solely on turning out their own supporters and potential supporters and increasing the popularity of their preferred candidate. Campaigns are not a zero-sum game, but resources are limited, and when more is spent on suppression, less may be available for turnout—especially if one strategy seems easier than the other. It is also true that in an election where suppression trumps turnout, the political discourse is narrowed. Efforts are not made to engage with those likely to be undecided about or even predisposed to disagree with a candidate's platform. Rather, a candidate whose campaign emphasizes vote suppression addresses his or her core constituency and works to tamp down the votes of the opposition.

In a 1999 poll about citizens' views of government, the top-ranked proposal for making government work better was simply to "have more people vote in elections." (Seventy-three percent rated that change as likely to be very effective in making government work better.)[22] Despite this apparent consensus, some still argue that lower voter turnout is a good thing. Consider this comment from Tim O'Brien, who writes for the *Albany (NY) Times Union*:

> If you are one of those people who normally stays home on Election Day, who doesn't really pay attention to the issues and isn't sure what anyone stands for, then by all means stay out of the voting booth on Tuesday. . . . If you are too preoccupied with your own daily struggles, or too lazy to take some time to examine the candidate's platforms and make a decision, well then please don't listen to those other commentators. Stay home. Let other people who care more than you do decide.[23]

Or this from Drew Avery, a contributor to the *Seattle Times*:

> Stop talking about voter quantity and start focusing on voter quality. I know people who don't vote and, frankly, I'm glad they don't. Not because their political philosophies don't match mine, but because they don't have passion and they can't be bothered to inform themselves.[24]

A book by economist Bryan Caplan, *The Myth of the Rational Voter: Why Democracies Choose Bad Politics*, provides a more scholarly presentation of the arguments made by O'Brien and Avery. Caplan states that the problem is not that too few Americans vote, but rather that the average 50 percent turnout is too high. He believes that many voters are more than ill-informed: they are downright stupidly misguided about political issues, and their votes prompt bad policies and legislation.[25]

Those who support restrictive voter identification laws are really making the same argument. As a Colorado woman testified at a 2011 state senate hearing about a bill to require documentary proof of citizenship in order to register to vote,

> If you go, "Oh gee, let's see . . . do I wanna buy a 6-pack of beer, or do I wanna go get my birth certificate so I can vote?" I'm pretty sure, you know, that you're gonna get your birth certificate. So, to me, the 7% that can't afford it, then guess what—then they don't have any room to complain how things are run. So the 93% that can and have it, should be allowed to be here.[26]

As one letter to the editor of the *Livingston (MI) Daily Press & Argus* expressed it,

> I went to the Brighton Secretary of State Office on Aug. 6 and, according to a very pleasant and helpful employee, the cost of a state photo ID is $10 and must be renewed every four years. Three very ordinary and common pieces of proof of identity also are required. If someone cannot afford $2.50 per year, they probably cannot afford a newspaper, radio, or TV and are, therefore, unlikely to be well-informed about the election issues anyway.[27]

While many of us instinctively recoil at these sentiments, it is important to spell out exactly why such thinking is wrong. If large segments of the population—the poor, for example—do not vote, representatives will feel little obligation to serve the needs of the whole community. They will be more likely to attend mostly to the needs of the constituencies that voted for them—groups whose interests may not coincide with those of the broader community. Since voter turnout rates are skewed according to income, education, and race, the citizens who depend most on the government may have their concerns neglected, while those who make sizable campaign contributions are heard. This represents a serious flaw in our democracy and process for decision making.

The Means and Benefits of Increasing Turnout

Creating and using election laws and procedures to increase participation of legal, eligible voters is inherently legitimate, as long as no strong countervailing value would be demonstrably and specifically jeopardized. Indeed, it must be considered appropriate for the parties and candidates to use all legal means to increase participation: if the parties and candidates do not do this vital work, civic participation will not reach its full potential. Election reforms passed in a vacuum—without any of the relevant players seizing upon and using them proactively—while necessary and helpful, will not take our country far enough in increasing voter participation. Many reforms are more likely to retain existing voters, or make people who vote sometimes into people who vote often—also necessary and good—than to increase turnout among previous nonvoters. That may be due to the "transient" voter's socioeconomic characteristics and preexisting engagement in politics and the political process.[28] Structural reforms need an assist from the parties and candidates' campaigns, as well civic organizations. Recent studies have noted that when a party, especially the Democratic Party, steps in to use electoral reforms to its advantage to increase base turnout, these laws become much more effective in turning out more voters.

For instance, the use of early voting in itself did not increase voter turnout in Texas. When the Democratic Party made a concerted effort to mobilize its voters to vote early, however, voter turnout in Texas increased.[29] Similarly, it has been found that making absentee ballots a method more voters can use increases turnout only when the reform is combined with party mobilization efforts, such as sending out applications to known supporters.[30] The combination of candidate expenditures, party mobilization efforts, and Election Day registration can lead to a significant increase in voter turnout, as researchers have noted: "Election Day registration can spur turnout as candidate campaign organizations and political parties capitalize on the opportunities it offers them."[31] The 2008 presidential election put these theories into practice in North Carolina with results even more dramatic than might have been predicted. Through party mobilization using early voting and same-day registration, 800,000 more voters cast ballots in North Carolina than in 2004.

If inspiring an interest in politics and political information is the real key to improved participation, as many have suggested and the facts support, the personal attention of parties and campaigns is likely to foster voters' political engagement more effectively than pure structural change. When a potential voter interacts with a party or candidate, the direct interaction reduces the "cost"—the time and energy—of forming political opinions,[32] which reinforces the new voter's engagement.

Beyond these immediate practical considerations about political and policy outcomes, ethical and philosophical arguments also support the notion that any legal act to increase public participation in the system is of tremendous worth. It strengthens the very concept of democracy, both as a collection of institutions and for the individual voter. When more people participate, we as a people make a statement about how we wish to organize our social and political structure. It says something about what our values are. The act of voting also has an impact on voters as individuals, strengthening their connection with fellow citizens and instilling a sense of voice and meaning beyond their immediate community. Finally, the act of voting realizes our core democratic intuitions regarding our agency and responsibility, as well as the representative character of our governing institutions.

Indeed, as public policy scholar Dennis Thompson put it, "Electoral institutions signal not only whose votes should count, but *who* should count."[33] How we as a society treat the right to vote and the voters themselves makes a statement about our relationship to democracy. If the right to vote is the bedrock of our political system (and it is), when political actors seek to block access for some of the citizenry, it says that a so-called democracy that is exclusive, perhaps elitist, is acceptable, even perhaps preferred. It is hard to believe that most of us want our country to drift into a system of rule led by the elite or the wealthy. We are proud of having moved past the days of only landowners, only men, only whites, being allowed to vote. Yet when we allow politicians to rig the rules in a purposeful attempt to disenfranchise certain groups, this justly earned pride is badly tarnished.

On the other hand, using electoral rules in a legal manner to increase the base of those who "count" declares that we are the inclusive and democratic society that we claim to be. When parties increase turnout fairly and legally—even for partisan purposes, to benefit one candidate or party—they are increasing engagement and thus enriching our democratic process and how the citizenry views it. They are sending a message of inclusiveness and signaling the respect that each individual should be accorded in the kind of democracy we aspire to

By the same token, when a citizen votes, it is not solely about choosing a candidate. As Dennis Thompson says, "Elections are not only instruments for choosing governments; they are also media for sending messages about the democratic process." Voting is an expression of participation and membership in the democratic system and American society.[34] This intangible benefit accounts for people who vote—even when it may seem that, rationally speaking, an individual vote is unlikely to make a difference. And the vast majority of American people, despite the politically organized discouragement, do believe that voting is meaningful. A major poll recently found that three-quarters of Americans agree that "voting gives people like me some say about how the government runs things."[35] The act of voting is an expression of support for democracy itself. A vote sends a message that individuals are watching and holding their elected leaders accountable. This in itself is a public good that advances the goal of ethical, responsible, and responsive government.[36]

The full functioning of democratic society requires that people claim their stake in it through the act of voting. Although there are of course many others means of expressing this participatory spirit—for example, through involvement in civic groups and volunteering—voting is the most fundamental. Moreover, voting becomes habitual; once someone votes for the first time, he or she is much more likely to vote in the future. Among voters who voted in 1968 and 1972, for example, only 3 percent failed to vote in 1974 and 1976. Of the respondents who missed voting in the earlier elections, however, more than two-thirds did not vote in the following election.[37] A more recent study of 25,000 voters in New Haven, Connecticut, conducted after voters were targeted with canvassing and direct-mail interventions to raise turnout in 1998, found that those voters who did vote in that 1998 election were much more likely to vote in the 1999 election. Even after taking into account other factors that might cause higher turnout, researchers found that registered voters who did not vote in 1998 had a 16.6 percent chance of voting in 1999, while 63.3 percent of those who voted in 1998 returned for the next election. This difference was attributable solely to the act of having previously voted.[38] This difference is at least in part explained by a very practical issue: voting for the first time has higher costs in terms of registering, learning how to vote, and so on. Once those initial barriers have been overcome, voting becomes easier and more accessible.[39] It becomes a good habit.

Dennis Thompson has offered a central principle of electoral justice, that just elections demand equal respect for all citizens:

The principle rests on the fundamental idea . . . that the democratic process should respect all citizens as free and equal persons. . . . The core of the principle can be simply stated: the electoral process should provide citizens with equal opportunities to have their votes counted equally, unless respectful reasons can be given to justify unequal treatment. The reasons are respectful if they could be mutually accepted by free and equal citizens, and thus only if they affirm, or at least do not deny, the equal civic standing of citizens.[40]

Using the 2000 election as an example of how voters instinctively demand this equal respect, Thompson describes the scenes of protest and outrage outside the Palm Beach Board of Election's operations center just after the election in Florida:

A chanting crowd in the parking lot brandished signs that read "Count my vote" and "Why don't I count?" No doubt some hoped that their votes might determine who would be president, but many also evidently were offended by the prospect that their ballots might be completely ignored. They seemed to feel that a refusal to count their votes would amount to a declaration that they did not count as citizens. It would be an affront to their civic standing. The signs were pointedly personal: count my vote; why don't I count?[41]

By contrast, efforts to promote greater equality in the system through increased participation will, under most circumstances, make elections more just. Inclusion, within reasonable boundaries, promotes the value of equal respect.

The very act of voting seems to have a meaningful impact on voters' perception of government. Voting has substantial impacts on "feelings of system responsiveness, political trust, and diffuse political support."[42] This association holds for voters of all education levels. Participation also leads to voters having more of a "sense that their leaders or institutions are responsive."[43] In a study of thousands of Canadians, researchers found definitively that the act of participating in elections did change people's attitudes toward the democratic process and democratic institutions. People felt much more positively about government, candidates, and political institutions after voting in an election than before. Perhaps surprisingly, this was even more strongly the case for the less educated and those who started out feeling more cynical toward politics. Exposure to the political process through the act of voting tends to instill a sense of satisfaction and legitimacy regarding the system and the major actors in it, bringing stability and strengthening democratic society.

John Stuart Mill argued in 1861 that the very act of civic participation leads an individual toward greater understanding, commitment, and interest in public life and the common good. He wrote:

> Still more salutary is the moral part of the instruction afforded by the participation of the private citizen, if even rarely, in public functions. He is called upon, while so engaged to weigh interests not his own; to be guided, in case of conflicting claims, by another rule than his private partialities; to apply, at every turn, principles and maxims which have for their reason of existence the common good: and he usually finds associated with him in the same work minds more familiarized than his own with these ideas and operations, whose study it will be to supply reasons to his understanding, and stimulation to his feeling for the general interest. He is made to feel himself one of the public, and whatever is for their benefit to be for his benefit.[44]

Mill saw exclusion as a recipe for the national demise: "Let a person have nothing to do for his country, and he will not care for it."[45] That psychological insight is, in itself, a clinching argument for voter participation: our country needs citizens who care.

Conditions and Caveats

The principle of voter inclusion can serve as a useful guideline in analyzing when an election reform that is likely to increase turnout—even one designed to achieve a partisan goal—is of value and pinpointing the rare occasion when there might be legitimate justification for sacrificing the value of increased participation to promote some other end. There is no pure mathematical calculation that can be applied; it is a balancing of the equities that will lead to a policy that is most beneficial for democracy.

As a result, not every policy decision that makes voting slightly more difficult is necessarily illegitimate. And not every measure that might make voting easier is necessarily worthwhile. However, we should err on the side of greater access and equity unless there is a strong reason, based

on demonstrable data and facts—not presumptions or prognostications—
that it is not worth it.

For example, it is possible that the greatly expanded use of absentee
balloting, while making voting easier for some, increases voter turnout
only marginally in most elections. At the same time it can create more
serious opportunities for fraud and lead overall to more inaccurately completed, uncountable ballots. If this group of spoiled and invalid ballots
would outweigh the increase in new voters who would be brought into
the process through absentee voting, that might be an instance where not
pursuing the voter inclusion principle might be justified, because the values of the accuracy and integrity of the vote would outweigh the marginal
participation increase. Similarly, as will be discussed in the next chapter,
the secret ballot was created to make it more difficult for citizens with low
literacy to vote. It succeeded in doing so, and probably a ballot produced
by a party would make voting much simpler for some citizens today. Yet
we have evolved to the point where the balance is clearly on the side of a
secret ballot that prevents against the very real possibility of outside coercion, as once did occur. In a final example, under the recently passed
MOVE Act, election administrators must transmit ballots to military and
overseas voters forty-five days prior to the election. This caused major
challenges for some state and local election officials in 2010, leading the
Department of Justice to intervene. Yet it is a measure worth pursuing
for the improvement it can lead to in the turnout of military and overseas
voters.

The Partisan Issue

The voter inclusion principle is not a new way of expressing what may
seem like the prevailing Democratic-leaning ideology and politics with respect to election reform. It is a means of restoring the concept of voting as a
right. It is both a plea and a plan for bringing greater equity and justice to
our democratic system of elections for the benefit of all Americans.

Moreover, the vision expressed here and its practical applications benefit all Americans as well as strengthen our democratic institutions. Many
of the reforms that emerge from the voter inclusion principle can boost the
participation of Republicans as well as Democrats. While the discussion

is framed within the reality of a highly partisan system, the principle espoused itself is nonpartisan.

An engaged, active electorate makes for a more robust exchange of ideas in which voices from people from all walks of life and all political perspective are heard. When people feel invested in the political system and elected leadership, it makes for a healthier polity and a more accountable government. Opening up the voting process to more Americans, and creating a system as well as a national creed that expressly welcomes full participation, will help make our institutions stronger, our policies more just, and might begin to restore Americans' faith that our politics can be meaningful.

The legitimacy of our election system—the bedrock of our democracy—depends on an active, engaged, robust electorate. It is therefore incumbent upon all of us who care about American democracy to put an end to unjustified, cynical, partisan vote suppression and work together to maximize the political engagement of our citizenry. The health of American democracy depends upon it.

2

THE EARLY YEARS OF VOTE SUPPRESSION

From the mid-nineteenth century until the turn of the twentieth century, Americans in many states witnessed the enactment and implementation of egregiously disenfranchising laws and procedures. Given the amount of power states had (and continue to have) to determine how elections are administered in our voting system, such laws were put into place by state legislatures and governors. Many of these laws and procedures were enacted in the name of fighting alleged fraud, but with largely political ends in mind. Both parties were complicit in these tactics, because they allowed both parties to maintain their spheres of power. Moreover, it was during this period that the framework was set for vote suppression in many elections to come.

Partisanship was by no means the only motivation behind the reform measures. The disenfranchisement taking place during this period was racially motivated in the South, and it was based on ethnicity and class in other parts of the country. However, many of the laws that disenfranchised blacks also served to exclude poor whites who might have shared some of the same political interests. Indeed, politicians at times hardly hid their partisan motives, unabashedly proclaiming them, and these partisan motives coincided well with racist motives.[1]

In the North, great waves of people from other countries landing on America's shores and moving into the cities during this period caused concern among many American elites who did not see them as fit to participate in the democratic process. Again, for many of the participants in this battle, partisanship and ethnic bias overlapped and became intertwined.[2] The role of class cannot be underplayed, either, as class tended to overlap with ethnicity, which overlapped with partisan interests. As was true in the South, one could distinguish but not easily tease apart partisanship and prejudice.

Contemporary popular belief is that this was a period of widespread fraud at the polls and corruption in politics, and therefore such measures were warranted. Indeed, in arguing that it was legitimate for the state of Indiana to be concerned about in-person voter fraud at the polls, the only example Justice John Paul Stevens cited in his 2008 opinion in *Crawford v. Marion County Election Board*, upholding the state's restrictive voter identification law, was "Boss Tweed and elections of 1868."[3] Contemporary conservative writers cite this era frequently in their writings about elections.[4]

Yet while there certainly was vote manipulation during this period, many historians argue the amount and type of fraud have been exaggerated.[5] Like today, to the extent that historical analysis is dependent on news reports, much of the information was filtered through the lens of the reporters doing the writing and what made for a good story. "Reformers" who sought then and seek now to exclude some voters used a few notorious examples over and over again to make it seem like the problem was widespread when they had little evidence to show that this was so.[6] Moreover, as will be explored below, the entire culture around elections was very different from what we experience in modern times, and indeed allowed some forms of corruption to be nearly accepted components of the process. Certainly fraud occurred in many places, "but was the exception, not the rule."[7]

Elections in the Second Half of the Nineteenth Century

Although so many of the suppression tactics have been repeated in recent years, an American traveling back in time to this period would be surprised by the atmosphere around elections during this half century. A very basic picture of the process in the mid-nineteenth century through the late part of that century can be constructed.[8]

During the mid-nineteenth century, voters used tickets printed by the parties containing the names of their candidates and of sizes and colors that made it obvious which party's tickets they were. The ballots were distributed at the polls by partisans, and this "made the voter's choice of party a public act and rendered voters susceptible to various forms of intimidation and influence,"[9] particularly by employers,[10] while facilitating vote buying. In the cities, polls opened early but also closed too early for men working far distances from their homes. As a result, large crowds of voters gathered in the early hours before work time. And unlike today, some election judges were elected right before the polls opened by the men who happened to be at the poll site. Other poll workers were appointed before the election by local government officials in consultation with the parties (which is more like what we would see today).[11] When voters appeared at the polls, the poll workers were expected to record their names. But this process was complicated by the press of large crowds, uncommon names that were dramatically misspelled, a large number of common names, and illiteracy that prevented some voters from telling workers how to spell their names.[12]

Many states had poll taxes. These were not monies collected at the polls, but rather were fees that were due to be paid at the county assessor's office ahead of the election.[13] This meant an extra trip during the day for workers, poor blacks and whites, in addition to the financial burden of having to pay the tax. As a countervailing force, in some cities, the parties and candidates would pick up the tab for their poor loyalists (especially poor whites)[14] whom they wanted to be able to vote, or they went to the county assessor's office for them, with the expectation that the assisted voter would return the favor at the voting booth.[15] Besides poll taxes, another way for the state to control the vote was though literacy tests. By the late nineteenth century, many states had literacy tests that required that a potential voter prove he was able to read in order to register to vote. Often this meant that the voter had to publicly read a section of the state or federal constitution in order to qualify to vote.[16] In the South the tests were often administered in a racially discriminatory manner. For example, in Terrell County, Georgia, when one black applicant who was perfectly able to read and write came to register, the "registrar dictated at such speed that it was impossible for [him] to write down what was being said. . . . Blacks were also tested individually; whites if they were tested at all were tested in a group. Several black school teachers were denied registration as being illiterate. No white was ever denied registration by reason of failure to pass a literacy test."[17] Such voters were blocked from ever getting to the polling place to try to cast a ballot. If a vote could not be bought, then it could be prevented. The poll tax and literacy tests would keep many away on Election Day. But what of those who had secured the right to vote on a given Election Day?

When a person did get to the ballot box, it was easy for party operatives to tell if he had cast the appropriate vote (women, of course, could not vote). The public ballot, again easily identifiable by party, indeed made it possible for both sides to track votes and engage in vote buying. It was almost an unstated understanding among politicians and the public in some places that both sides would participate in such practices, notwithstanding the loud outcries about such activities in the public press by all involved.

Party challengers were a fixture at the polling place, and their confrontational actions were often guided by their being able to see the party preference of a given voter.[18] Allegations of voter intimidation by employers were also frequent. For example, documents have been found indicating that the Republican governor of Wyoming, Francis Warren, encouraged employer intimidation on the part of railroads and other large employers in his state. He wrote to one hotel operator, "I hope you will see your way clear to persuade all the voters at the Pacific Hotels in Wyoming to agree with us."[19]

Blocking African Americans and Immigrants at the Polling Site

Within the context of this tumult of state-imposed restrictions, voting buying, and aggressive vote challenging, a variety of specific methods were developed in order to suppress voting among certain types of people for specific political ends. More often than not during this time, Democratic partisans were the ones manipulating votes in the South and keeping African Americans from the polls. In the North, Republicans targeted immigrants for exclusion.

In the South, while the primary purpose of poll taxes was black disenfranchisement, the partisan gains of suppressing the African American
vote were lost on few Democrats. For example, in Arkansas in the late
nineteenth century, the Populists (the "People's Party") denounced the poll
tax as a partisan ploy, as did the Republicans. But in the legislature the
measure was greatly supported by the Democrats, who saw its potential
advantage.[20] The poll tax harmed poor whites as well, but blacks tended to
be poorer than even poor whites, election administrators would look the
other way at poor whites without their poll-tax receipt, and as mentioned,
the parties would sometimes pay the tax of a poor voter, more often if he
was white.[21] To further avoid impacting whites, as was the case with some
other restrictions, there were also "grandfather clauses" (citizens whose
grandfather had been enfranchised prior to Reconstruction were exempt)
and other such loopholes in some states.[22]

Another tactic that became popular as the Gilded Age came to a close
was the literacy test to disenfranchise black voters in the South. This would
have impacted poor, uneducated whites too, but as described above, registrars wielded great discretion in how the test was administered, making it
easier for poor whites to get by. The degree to which partisanship worked
alongside prejudice, and sometimes overrode it, can be seen by looking at
how literacy tests were used on either side of the Mason-Dixon line. A favored tool of controlling votes in the South, literacy tests did not work to the
Democrats' advantage in the North, where less-educated and immigrant
voters filled Democratic ranks. As a result, while pushing literacy tests in
the South, Democratic partisans decried and resisted literacy tests when
they were used in the North. By the mid-1920s, thirteen states in the North
and West dominated by Republicans were using literacy tests to disenfranchise citizens who met all other eligibility requirements for the vote.[23]

Also during the mid and late nineteenth century, political actors and
everyday voters often acting at the behest of the parties made it a practice
to challenge the voting rights of other voters.[24] Partisans employed two
methods under challenge laws: challenging the legitimacy of voters on the
registration list prior to Election Day and deploying poll "watchers" on
Election Day to challenge the right to vote of voters the watchers deemed
suspect. The easiest and most obvious way to challenge a voter for partisan
goals was, of course, to challenge someone based on his apparent ethnicity.
Across the country,

in communities with large numbers of aliens [immigrants] who were personally unknown to those attending the polls, the physical appearance of men who presented themselves was compared with stereotypes previously constructed for members of the various ethnic communities. As these men approached the voting window, they would be asked which party they were likely to support or where they lived. If a prospective voter belonged to an ethnic group that tended to support the opposition, he would be challenged as to his citizenship at the window and thus compelled to present his papers.[25]

Some voters without papers would try to claim that they were under the age of eighteen when they immigrated. "Left to their own devices, election officials usually projected [age] estimates favorable to their own party's interest."[26]

Working in conjunction with challenges, many states also began disenfranchising immigrants through proof-of-citizenship requirements in the late part of the century. In the states and cities with these requirements, naturalized citizens and naturalized citizens alone had to present their papers to election officials before registering or voting. "Most commonly these [requirements] were supported by some Republicans, opposed by Democrats, and justified on the grounds that they would reduce fraud."[27] In 1888, the *New York Herald* detailed the disenfranchising impact this had in New Jersey:

"Have you got your papers?" was the question that was frequently asked in Jersey City yesterday. It was registry day, and the new law was in operation. Every foreign born voter was forced to produce his naturalization papers. There were many humorous scenes, but a sad feature was that many persons will be deprived of their vote, as their papers are either worn out, lost or mislaid. Men who have voted in the city for a quarter of a century or more walked to the registry places only to be sent home for their papers or to be debarred because of their inability to produce the documents. Many aged papers were so completely worn out that it was a puzzle to put them together. A few were so ancient and completely gone that the officers refused to receive them as a certification of citizenship, unless the applicant brought the indorsement of the United States Commissioner. Old voters who produced their papers had to make a second journey to find some one to identify them.[28]

Finally, Democrats in the South held "white primaries" from which black voters were completely excluded. Since the Democrats were so dominant throughout most of the South, disenfranchisement from the primary was de facto complete disenfranchisement. The general election was a pro forma affair. Although there were many legal challenges to this practice, the Supreme Court upheld it until the 1940s on the basis that there was a lack of state action involved—primaries were the province of private political parties.[29]

Both parties had multiple options at their disposal to skew election results by minimizing the vote of members of certain ethnic groups identified with their opponents.

The Public Ballot

In the late part of the century states passed laws getting rid of the party ballot and required publicly printed ballots. Although the secret ballot is today a mainstay of our democratic process, historians note that the motives behind its introduction were not so pure. Indeed, although it is true that some amount of vote buying was facilitated by public ballots, the prevention of such activities was not the primary cause for changing the system. Secret-ballot laws were enacted primarily in order to prevent the illiterate and uneducated—mostly poor whites and blacks—from voting. As J. Morgan Kousser observes, "The publicly printed ticket required the voter, sometimes without aid from anyone, to scurry quickly through a maze of names of candidates running for everything from presidential elector to county court clerk. . . . Such a task demanded not merely literacy, but fluency in the English language. . . . Many voters who persisted marked their ballots incorrectly."[30]

In the case of the introduction of secret ballots, once more, partisan motivations were not hidden. In Arkansas in 1891, for example, "Democrats openly avowed the partisan purposes of the [secret ballot] bill. A Democratic newspaper termed it 'a partisan measure' which would prove 'beneficial to the Democratic party,' and Sevier [the legislator proposing it] recommended it as 'conceived in the interests of the Democratic party.'"[31] The bill had its intended consequences. "In black belt Pine Bluff, the *Commercial* [newspaper], exulting in the fact that the Democrats in

1892 overcame the normal three-to-one Republican majority to carry Jefferson county for the first time in 31 years, trumpeted that Sevier's was 'A GREAT ELECTION LAW—It Works Like a Charm in the Cause of Intelligent Government.' The Democrats had won 'thanks to the Australian system.' "[32] Indeed, in Arkansas, the secret ballot contracted voting in the 1890s by about 17 percent, and the poll tax curtailed voter participation by an additional 10 percent. The cumulative effect was to diminish the vote sufficiently so as to ensure permanent Democratic domination.[33] The case was similar in Alabama. In explaining his sponsorship of a secret-ballot act, the sponsor in the Alabama legislature said it " 'would restore the [D]emocratic party in Alabama.' "[34]

Similar measures were employed in the North in the latter part of the century. In Vermont, for example, Republicans kept the secret ballot confined to the larger, urban areas populated by Democratic-leaning immigrants who might have difficulty reading and properly marking a ballot. In other areas, Democrats won the ability to "assist" voters in the polls, to get around obstacles created by the secret ballot for illiterate and non-English-speaking voters.[35] But it was clear that, for both those supporting and those resisting the "reform" of the secret ballot, the motivations were partisan and the stakes were potential Democratic or Republican votes.

In the end, the secret ballot did not decrease the amount of voter fraud that occurred during this period; the political players engaged in active fraud just changed their tactics. At the same time, the secret ballot was effective at keeping down the number of poor whites and immigrants who voted in the North, and the number of southern blacks who could vote. The partisans responsible for the laws knew the duplicitous nature of these actions. For example, in the late nineteenth century, "after the bill was first drafted in Tennessee, the Democratic leadership added, as an afterthought, that the bill would also 'stop the cry of fraud,' but not the fraud itself."[36]

Blocking Participation through Voter Registration Procedures

Voter registration requirements enacted in the 1870s through the beginning of the twentieth century provide a rich example of measures pursued in the name of reducing fraud but primarily enacted to control the electorate for political purposes. Requiring voters to register at all put an additional onus on the voter because it was the voter that was responsible for registering, and elections institutions had no responsibility to ensure all eligible voters were on the list. Once the concept of voter registries was adopted in many of the states in the mid- to late nineteenth century, the dominant parties passed a number of measures to manipulate that process for desired ends. Tactics included requiring only voters in the cities to register; requiring in-person registration and only on very circumscribed days and times; and requiring reregistration frequently and whenever the voter moved, even if just a few blocks away.

Although some may have genuinely believed that the use of a voting registry would prevent duplicate voting and other abuses of the franchise, and hence help ensure clean elections, the parties abused the new requirement for their own gain. Reformers claimed the ever-increasingly restrictive registration laws were designed to prevent fraud, but even they conceded at times that registration laws would not be effective in combating the very problem they sought to address.[37] Indeed, the partisan goals of these laws were revealed in many ways. For instance, throughout the states, as such measures were passed, Republicans sought to impose more-onerous registration restrictions in urban areas, claiming these areas were the main sources of fraud—though they were also the primary locus of Democratic support because of the heavy concentration of poor and ethnic voters.[38] New Jersey, after an influx of immigrants into the state and a Republican takeover of the legislature, enacted its first voter registration law in 1866. The Republicans forced through a law creating a voter registration system in which only those who personally appeared before the board of registry and proved their qualifications were registered to vote:

> Arguing that the registry laws made voting "troublesome, inconvenient, and expensive," the Democratic press charged that the laws were being instituted to keep from "the polls the poor working man, who could not afford to take time off from his job to register." When the Democrats returned to power in 1868 they overrode the Republican Governor's veto and abolished registration. But in 1871, the Republicans took control again and reinstated registration, confining it solely to the seven cities in the state with populations of more than twenty thousand people.[39]

The political stakes of reform could not have been more apparent.

Just as this was occurring in the North, registration was being used to curtail voting rights in the South. There, some different tactics were used by partisans. The weapon of choice in the South was granting the registrars great discretion as to what information to accept and when and where it could be accepted so as to make a registration valid and complete. For example, in North Carolina it was up to the local registrar to determine whether a voter had sufficiently proved his age, occupation, place of birth, and residence. Democratic election officials in Florida in the latter part of the century simply erased Republican names and did not allow voters to try to rectify the situation when they discovered they were no longer registered.[40]

The Nineteenth Century and the Voter Inclusion Principle

The second half of the nineteenth century was rife with violations of the voter inclusion principle. The most distressing aspect of this examination of historical practices of voter exclusion is that a number of them are still in use. We can see in this review of practices at the polls of the nineteenth century precursors of tactics used today to disqualify voters and seek partisan gain. The common thread that connects the second half of the nineteenth century with the early twenty-first century is that measures to reform electoral practice are often driven by partisan motivations that see political gain in keeping whole classes of people from casting ballots.

Democrats and Republicans engaged in vote suppression with equal fervor during this period, with the only real distinction being that the Democrats were more active in southern states while Republicans were more active in northern states. Their rallying cries were to protect the purity of the vote. The means they employed to that end usually did more harm than good to the democratic process when assessed by the voter inclusion principle.

Literacy tests quite obviously do not fit in the voter inclusion paradigm. They were clear efforts to disenfranchise voters based on education and, as we saw, also on race, language ability, and, of course, partisan affiliation. At the time there was no countervailing demand of another democratic value that would justify the suppression of some votes. No one in the nineteenth century was able to articulate a rationale that went beyond prejudice and partisanship, although some do still argue even now that only people with a certain knowledge should be allowed to vote. However, in American democracy, we provide the opportunity for all voices to be heard.

Under the voter inclusion principle, the use of challenges by other individual voters, when not curtailed by specific requirements of what such an individual must prove in order to make a challenge, are not useful to democracy. Under wisely crafted laws that foresee trained elections officials as the primary persons eligible to challenge the eligibility of a voter, or that at least include strict evidentiary rules for other types of challengers, such measures could be helpful in keeping the voting system cleaner. But this is so far from the system that existed decades ago—or today—that currently there is no countervailing value that is achieved by allowing such indiscriminate challenges to the rights of certain voters. Challenges are clearly often used for partisan purposes and are designed to suppress votes, not to make the system more effective.

The practice of requiring proof of citizenship, used in the second half of the nineteenth century, has returned in more recent times with the growth of right-wing led anti-immigrant sentiment. Many states in the nineteenth century disenfranchised immigrants by requiring naturalized citizens and naturalized citizens alone to present their papers to elections officials before registering or voting. Similarly, Arizona passed a law requiring voters to provide proof of citizenship in order to register to vote in 2004.[41] In most cases under the law, a voter could send in a copy of his or her documentation—except for naturalization papers. Those alone had to be presented in person. Thousands of eligible American citizens had their registration forms rejected throughout the state because they could not provide the necessary documentation. Requiring documentary proof of citizenship would appear to provide very little service to democracy but instead serves to disenfranchise eligible voters, and this appears to have by and large been the case in the earlier era as well.

Analyzing the secret ballot through the prism of the voter inclusion principle is complicated, and the case for this nineteenth-century reform of voting practices is in today's world stronger than the case for literacy tests, challenges, and requirements to present proof of citizenship. Today we have come to the consensus that the secret ballot does more good than ill, though that seems not to have been the case during this earlier time of more widespread illiteracy and lack of education. The secret ballot still likely makes it harder to vote for some voters, for example those with literacy challenges and persons with cognitive disabilities. The difference between this measure and the others described is that the secret ballot has a demonstrable benefit that the others do not: the right to cast a vote free from outside interference or pressure. A publicly observable ballot, most generally believe, would leave voters more likely to be subject to coercion. While privacy in the voting booth can mean that a voter is left without help when navigating a complicated ballot, the states have attempted to solve these problems by allowing for assistance at the polls for those who have literacy and language challenges. The states, albeit with very mixed success, have attempted to make ballots more user-friendly. We need to continue to find ways to ease the process for these classes of voters and for all voters. Nonetheless, in today's circumstances, we reasonably do not see the secret ballot as a weapon of vote suppression, but rather as a way to protect voters from partisan pressure and manipulation.

With respect to the creation of voter registries, another legacy of the nineteenth century, it is not being disputed that voter registration laws in concept and sometimes in practice did serve to reduce fraud to some degree, especially fake and repeat voters. The question that must be asked is whether more legitimate voters were disenfranchised by these laws than fraudulent voters were prevented from voting. On balance it would seem that the particularly strict and unevenly applied registration laws did little to reduce fraud, while they certainly served to disenfranchise legitimate voters, and thus they distorted both the elections process and the outcomes. Millions of voters were likely wrongly disenfranchised by the manipulation of voter registration systems.[42] It is highly unlikely such laws prevented anywhere near millions of illegitimate votes from being cast, especially considering the way in which the extent of the fraud was exaggerated by those it politically advantaged to do so. The calculus is much the same today. On balance, under the voter inclusion principle, *reasonable* registration procedures are not objectionable. Unfortunately, many current procedures are not reasonable. The registration system needs to be widely accessible to all, easy to navigate, and the rules must be clear regarding how election administrators manage voter registration forms and databases. Certainly measures such as refusing to accept a registration application because the voter used a middle initial in his registration form but did not when using other government services cannot be a basis of exclusion by way of the registration system. Ultimately, the United States must follow the lead of most Western democracies and take responsibility for registering citizens to vote, rather than putting the full onus on the citizen to ensure he or she is on the rolls. That would be the best way to fulfill the promise of the voter inclusion principle.

Ironically, shortly after the close of this era, in 1920 women finally won the right to vote, a tremendous expansion of the franchise and a pure victory for the voter inclusion principle. It took seventy years of activism, and some of the same undercurrents that blocked voting among blacks and immigrants—for example, that they could not possibly be responsible voters—worked against women in the nineteenth century. In any case, this would be a sort of bookend of an era, and it would be some years before any additional major action in voter participation was taken, for good or ill.

3

CONDITIONS AND CONSEQUENCES
OF THE VOTING RIGHTS ACT

After the monumental victory for voting rights that occurred in 1920 with the ratification of the Nineteenth Amendment, the years between the 1920s and the early 1960s were a time of relative stasis in the election process. Alexander Keyssar has called this era the "Quiet Years." "Despite skirmishes large and small, partisan as well as ideological, there were few major changes in the laws governing the right to vote," he writes. "In the South . . . the dense web of restrictions woven between 1890 and 1910 continued to disenfranchise nearly all blacks and many poor whites."[1] For much of this period, immigration decreased, making newcomers less of a lightning rod in the battle for votes. Movements for greater enfranchisement tended to be small and disparate.

One important exception to this trend of stagnation was the elimination of the poll tax in a handful of states. This movement toward inclusion was principally motivated by an understanding on the part of white politicians that poll taxes were having a bigger effect on poor whites than blacks.[2] As the country entered the Depression, there were, on the other hand, new efforts to disenfranchise paupers or people on unemployment relief, although none met with great success.[3]

Another major change in the voting system during the years of World War II was the elimination of the whites-only primary, prevalent throughout the South. In 1944 the U.S. Supreme Court ruled these primaries, exclusively adopted by the Democratic Party, unconstitutional.[4] Because Democratic primaries had been practically a sure ticket to election throughout the South, state laws that stipulated that white citizens alone could participate in primary elections were an extremely effective measure for excluding African Americans from the decision-making process.[5] With the 1944 Supreme Court ruling in *Smith v. Allwright*, however, that barrier was removed. Moreover, because the political allegiance of black voters had switched to the Democratic Party during the New Deal, the legal and political changes established the conditions for a significant change in party politics and electioneering in the South.

Changing Political Alliances and the Consequences of Realignment

The New Deal had a profound impact on the political allegiances of African Americans and southern whites. These changes would serve as precursors to the major realignments in politics to come some thirty years later. In the 1930s, President Franklin Delano Roosevelt, a Democrat, was reluctant to take on civil rights issues directly. Nonetheless, the programs of the New Deal, although often discriminatory in implementation, provided African Americans with direct economic assistance—a kind of opportunity they had never experienced before. As a result of these programs, as well as a series of popular but largely symbolic actions toward the African American community, those blacks who could vote voted overwhelmingly for Roosevelt and, like many working-class Americans, came to revere him. (As a result of the First Great Migration, in which as many as two million African Americans left the South for the industrial cities of the North, many of these African American votes were cast outside the Jim Crow South.)[6] The landslide presidential election of 1936 sealed black voters' allegiance to Roosevelt and the Democratic Party.[7] In that election, Roosevelt carried more than 60 percent of the popular vote—and 71 percent of the black vote.[8] His appeal transcended regions; with 98.5 percent of the electoral vote, Roosevelt took every state but Maine and Vermont against the Republican candidate Alf Landon. Since the New Deal, the ideological split between upper-income and lower-income voters has remained substantial, with the wealthy much more likely to vote Republican and lower-income Americans voting Democratic.[9] In subsequent decades, this demographic difference in voting patterns has, not surprisingly, led to vote suppression tactics targeting low-income voters.

From the New Deal to the Advent of the Great Society

It was in the post–World War II era that the civil rights movement triggered a major transformation in American politics, creating the next big moment in the history of our election system. The conditions for this change had been set up in the New Deal. But it was the impetus of African American citizens, undertaking organized action across the United States, that changed the political landscape. Between the late 1940s and the early 1980s the southern states went from being dominated by the Democratic Party to, for the most part, being a majority Republican region at some levels by the late 1960s and in almost all respects by the early 1980s. There were a number of reasons for this transition, but race and the shifting attitudes of the two parties with respect to civil rights were the most prominent. This fundamental change had a profound impact on the shape, form, and dimensions of manipulation of voting procedures that persists to the present.

Prior to midcentury, the Democrats had been consistently successful in the South in large part because they had long realized that an important key to defeating the party of Lincoln was race: appealing to traditional white voters while keeping black voters out of the process. As the South's political dynamics shifted, Republicans learned to be masters of this same strategy.

As the civil rights movement grew—and grew more bloody—social unrest forced the federal government increasingly, though incrementally, to intervene in blocking the discriminatory activities taking place in the South. The federal intervention started in 1954 with the Supreme Court decision *Brown v. Board of Education*, which found segregation in public schools to be unconstitutional, and continued via actions such as the intervention of National Guard troops, at the order of President Dwight D. Eisenhower, to safeguard school integration in Little Rock, Arkansas, in 1957. Federal action continued and intensified somewhat during the John F. Kennedy years when, in response to civil rights leaders' growing frustration with the new president, the administration came to strongly support efforts to register black voters. (The Kennedy administration continued to disappoint black leaders, however, with its cautious approach to civil rights and limited willingness to protect civil rights protestors against violence.)

Shortly before Kennedy's death, due to the pressure of the civil rights movement, he and his advisers crafted what would become the Civil Rights Act of 1964. This legislation, along with the Voting Rights Act of 1965, would be enacted under President Lyndon B. Johnson and trigger a massive transformation in American parties and politics. The Civil Rights Act declared racial segregation in public schools, places of work, and any public accommodations illegal. These provisions all drew their authority from the equal protection clause of the Fourteenth Amendment. Looking to the same constitutional source, the 1964 legislation also banned any uneven application of voter registration requirements (for example, poll taxes and literacy tests). In order to put the teeth of enforcement on the matter of voting into the Civil Rights Act, Johnson signed the Voting Rights Act just a year later. That act banned many of the disenfranchising Jim Crow practices and provided the federal Department of Justice authority to screen, prior to implementation, any change in elections procedures in some states. While the laws were national in scope, the southern states were the clear targets of these legislative actions.

These two measures marked a major new federal involvement in desegregating the states of the South. They effectively put an end to practices that had disenfranchised black voters for decades and created a white backlash against the Democratic Party in the South, changing the political equation in that region. The transformation in party politics was significant, but it was not linear and not total.[10] While African Americans, with their Democratic Party leanings, were added to the voting rolls, large demographic shifts were also under way, with some five million African Americans leaving for points north and west from the 1940s to the 1970s.[11] Beginning in the 1960s, whites were also moving to the "Sunbelt" states of the South and Southwest.[12]

A form of Republican majority has since emerged in the South. In the region, the Republican Party has been fairly dominant at the presidential and U.S. Senate level, and less universally successful in races lower down the ticket. Moreover, the realignment has never been and is not to this day complete. Several southern states have remained competitive, and Democrats have even continued to dominate in certain offices, particularly local offices and in some state legislatures and offices below governor.[13] All these factors make the period after the 1960s complicated when it comes to analyzing how partisans may have used election rules and procedures to their advantage.

Despite the complex dynamics at play in the region, some observations can be made. First, immediately after passage of the Voting Rights Act, the most blatantly discriminatory vote suppression practices continued to be utilized primarily by Democrats. The Democrats were still dominant during this period in the South in many elections (though not all); racism combined with the desire to thwart black candidates seems to have trumped the idea that drawing blacks into the electoral process could be a boon for the party. That strategic notion would come later.

Second, with the Voting Rights Act—and federal officials in the South to enforce it—it became increasingly less feasible to prevent African Americans from registering and voting. Indeed, the number of blacks registering and voting surged after passage of the act.[14] As the number of registered African Americans grew, the parties—both of them—turned to changing the structure of elections and redistricting in order to preserve their power.

Third, a realignment of African American voters toward the Democratic Party that began with the New Deal soared during the 1960s, and African Americans have identified as Democrats and voted for Democratic presidential candidates in overwhelming numbers since then.[15] By the time the South turned to the Republican Party at most levels of elected office in the 1980s and 1990s, it was southern Republicans who were most inclined to use election laws to depress the African American and Democratic vote. Not coincidentally, the Democratic Party had fully realized by the early 1970s that its winning ticket—not only in the South—was supported by biracial and later multiracial coalitions.[16] The Republican Party's manipulative use of election laws was an ironic and even perverse revision of tradition. Republicans, so long beaten at the polls in the South because of the exclusion of African American votes, now adopted and refined the very same Democratic Party tactics to secure partisan success at the polls.

The Legal Transformation

The Civil Rights Act of 1964 and the Voting Rights Act of 1965 marked a historic federal intervention into matters of racial and political equality that until that time had been considered a state prerogative. The acts' provisions profoundly shaped and continued to inform electoral strategies not only in the South but across the country. The Civil Rights Act banned discrimination based on "race, color, religion, or national origin" in public establishments that had a connection to interstate commerce or that were supported by the state. Public establishments include hotels, restaurants, gas stations, bars, taverns, and places of entertainment. Title VI of the Civil Rights Act prohibits discrimination in federally funded programs. Title VII of the Civil Rights Act prohibits employment discrimination where the employer is engaged in interstate commerce.

Building on Title I of the Civil Rights Act, which barred the unequal application of voting requirements, the Voting Rights Act with one great sweep outlawed many of the practices that had been used for decades, especially in the South, to disenfranchise blacks. It also ensured that southern states could not evade or backslide from their new obligations, although many would try. Section 2 of the act is a nationwide prohibition against voting practices and procedures—including redistricting plans and at-large election systems, poll worker hiring, and voter registration procedures—that discriminate on the basis of race, color, or membership in a language minority group. It prohibits election practices and procedures that are intended to be racially discriminatory, as well as those that have a racially discriminatory impact. Under Section 5, any changes in election laws or procedures in certain covered jurisdictions, mostly in the South, must be "pre-cleared" by the Department of Justice or by the federal district court in the District of Columbia before taking effect. If the change is found to be "retrogressive" for minorities—that is, if it makes them worse off than they were before the change—the department or court can block the change with an "objection." The act also allows the Department of Justice to send federal observers to certain key locations during elections.[17]

The Southern Political Transformation

Both acts were passed by means of a coalition of northern Republicans and Democrats, and, of course, they became law by virtue of the signature of a Democratic president. Southern Democrats remained staunchly opposed. (In the Senate vote, which was 79–18 in favor of passage, only 4 southern Democrats supported the bill.) This regional alliance had a profound impact on the political attitudes of white southerners toward the parties and changed internal party dynamics as well. Even more important, with these measures, the Democratic Party at the national level became undeniably identified as the party on the side of equal rights for blacks. This new reality altered how southern conservatives saw the party and led many to feel permanently betrayed by the national Democratic Party, and also forced the Democratic Party to change out of strategic necessity. Candidates running on the Democratic ticket would increasingly have to rely on attracting a maximum number of blacks in the South. Over time, this forced the emergence of a new "moderate" breed of southern Democrat.

At the same time that the legal revolutions were in process, and well before the Democratic Party comprehended the changing political landscape in the South, the 1964 presidential campaign of Republican Barry Goldwater advanced the transformation of the South by aligning his message with the perceived interests of white southerners. Richard M. Nixon's "southern strategy" was a further step in the South's change to a majority Republican region, and the election of Republican Ronald Reagan in 1980 completed the region's shift.

Prior to the 1960s, Democrats dominated in the South at the congressional level to an extraordinary degree. In 1950 there were no Republican senators and only two Republican members of the House of Representatives from the South.[18] Even at the presidential level, only twice from 1876 to 1948 did a Republican presidential nominee carry even one southern state. In the 1952 presidential election, the Deep South went solidly for Democrat Adlai Stevenson.[19]

Goldwater, a U.S. senator from Arizona and the Republican nominee for president in 1964, was one of the few Republicans in the Senate who had worked to defeat the Civil Rights Act. His presidential campaign explicitly appealed to the racism of white southern voters, alienating African Americans in the process. During the campaign, Goldwater made it clear that Republicans would stand against civil rights and civil rights legislation, choosing to rely on big white majorities in the South in order to win the election. At the polls, the results were disastrous—a landslide loss to Johnson in which the only states besides Arizona to give their electoral votes to Goldwater that November were the five Deep South states of Alabama, Georgia, Louisiana, Mississippi, and South Carolina (all states in which only a small proportion of African Americans were able to vote). A gleam of political hope for the GOP for the future, however, could be found in the fact that Goldwater carried an estimated 55 percent of southern white voters, and 71 percent of white voters in the Deep South.[20]

Although southern blacks had supported Republicans for one hundred years, including in the presidential election of 1960, that support evaporated in 1964, and southern blacks would continue to vote Democratic for presidential elections in all subsequent years.[21] The new black Democratic vote was even more notable because of the growing number of blacks voting throughout the country. While the Voting Rights Act the following year was the big turning point, beginning in the 1950s the civil rights movement had heightened the political awareness of blacks. As James L. Sundquist has found, the proportion of blacks considering themselves apolitical fell from about 28 percent in the 1950s to 3 percent at the end of the 1960s, and the number who considered themselves strong partisans doubled from 30 percent to 60 percent—most of them Democrats.[22]

Nixon's so-called southern strategy in 1972 furthered the transformation. In the election of 1968, George Wallace had run for president as an American Independent Party candidate on an anti–civil rights platform of maintaining racial segregation. He carried five southern states—Alabama, Arkansas, Georgia, Louisiana, and Mississippi—and clearly sapped political strength from Nixon, who only edged Democratic candidate Hubert Humphrey by fewer than half a million votes. Wallace's success prompted Nixon to adopt a similar anti–civil rights strategy to win these formerly secure Democratic states to the Republican cause. The Nixon campaign in 1972 was designed to exploit racial divisions, and he adopted a stance of federal detachment when it came to active enforcement of civil rights. His opposition to school busing programs for desegregating the schools (mandated by court decisions) became a central theme in the campaign. Nixon's focus on "law and order" and his attack on welfare both had racial undertones. These campaign positions were set on a policy foundation from his first term when he denigrated minority set-aside programs and tried to appoint extremely conservative southern justices to the Supreme Court.[23] In 1972, this approach worked, as Nixon carried every southern state, taking more than two-thirds of the vote in the region and an overwhelming majority of white southerners' votes.[24]

While Nixon's successful effort would not immediately redound to Republicans in 1974 and 1976 because of the Watergate scandal, the effect was real, and it was enduring. By the 1970s, alienation among white conservatives from the Democratic Party and black voters' unwavering support for Democrats made the realignment in the South complete at the level of presidential elections.[25]

Strategies after the Voting Rights Act

The 1960s and 1970s saw a remarkable expansion of voting rights. In addition to passage of the Voting Rights Act of 1965, poll taxes, literacy tests, and voting restrictions on paupers were all banned through legislation and litigation. Residency requirements were limited to thirty days nationwide. The voting age was lowered to eighteen. In 1975, the Voting Rights Act was amended to provide additional protections and greater access for limited English speakers. According to the historian and social policy expert Alexander Keyssar, the total number of new voters added to the electorate was in excess of twenty million.[26] On balance, this period of history was very positive for voter rights, and the reforms instituted all met the standards of the Voter Inclusion Principle.

But the story is not one of sheer democratic progress. During the 1960s and 1970s, seemingly blinded by racism and impelled by the desire to remain in power and keep out competition from anyone—including other Democrats if they were black—Democrats in the South continued to use forms of the party's old discriminatory practices to exclude blacks from the voting process, particularly during primaries. This was of course shortsighted, as a more expansive understanding would have dictated an acknowledgment of the potential of the black vote to give Democrats new advantages against a growing Republican presence; effective partisanship would have counseled the Democrats to solicit and not suppress the African American vote. Hindered by the Democratic leadership's lingering racism and unwillingness to share power, however, the party would grasp this potential only later, after the Republicans had begun to make major advances in the region. By that time, Republicans had borrowed the Democratic playbook, working to exclude blacks in general elections for partisan gain, as will be explored in the next chapters.

The subsequent tug-of-war over electoral procedure took two forms. During this period of transition, both parties used the structure of elections not only to prevent some people from voting, but also to dilute the value of votes cast, especially through at-large elections and redistricting.[27] Although there is no specific agreed-upon definition of vote dilution, in general it is a method of diminishing the political power of a particular group—usually a minority group such as African Americans—without actually blocking access to the ballot. The voting process is arranged so that laws and practices combined with bloc voting by an identifiable group diminish the voting power of another identifiable group to elect a candidate.

As Keyssar has observed, lifting hard barriers to the ballot box moved vote suppression strategies into a new phase, "a prolonged series of conflicts over a related yet distinct issue: the value of each individual's vote. Deterred now from using the voting process as a way to limit voting power, policymakers and others looked rather to the structure of elections to diminish voting power of political opponents." With respect to general elections, "the legal terrain shifted—from the right to vote itself to apportionment, districting, and the structure of representation."[28] Both parties have made use of these tactics, depending on whether it was to their advantage, given the demographics and politics of a jurisdiction.

Despite legal changes on paper, both parties also excluded black voters using variations of well-established forms of vote suppression. Through the 1960s, white Democrats continued to flout the dictates and spirit of the new laws to keep out black competition within the party. Later on, as the Republican Party made gains in the South, Republicans engaged in some outright suppression in order to keep down the black—and Democratic—vote in general elections.

Reports of the United States Commission on Civil Rights (USCCR) issued in the first sixteen years after the Voting Rights Act, along with other contemporary research, provide considerable information on the types of exclusion that continued to be employed against African American voters in the South. In the first years after the passage of the Voting Rights Act, white southern Democrats aimed to keep blacks out of positions of power in the party and to limit their access to Democratic primaries. Maintaining solid blocks of white party leaders was not, per se, something done for partisan advantage. Rather these efforts at suppression were akin to how party leaders protect incumbents from electoral challenges from within the party. Democrats were not yet facing any serious threat from Republicans, but the expansion of the vote to include blacks did threaten the power positions of white southern Democrats, since blacks were now in the position to vote for new black candidates and were increasingly able to do so with success after 1965.[29]

A 1968 USCCR report documents that these intraparty practices

> included exclusion from precinct meetings at which party officials were chosen, omission of the names of registered Negroes from voter lists, failure to provide sufficient voting facilities in areas with heavy Negro registration, harassment of Negro voters by election officials, refusal to assist illiterate Negro voters, provision of erroneous or inadequate instructions to Negro voters, disqualification of Negro ballots on technical grounds, failure to afford Negro voters the same opportunity as white voters to cast absentee ballots, and discriminatory location of polling places. The Commission staff also found instances of racially segregated voting facilities and voter lists in some Southern counties.[30]

Democrats also made attempts in primaries to keep up some aspects of the old but now-banned literacy tests:

> In several counties in Alabama, South Carolina, and Mississippi there have been reports that election officials have refused to provide or allow adequate assistance to illiterate Negro voters. In addition, illiterate voters in some Southern states have been denied the use of aids to enable them to overcome their lack of literacy. In some areas of Mississippi illiterates have been denied the use of sample ballots even though such use is not prohibited by State law. In Virginia officials have rejected write-in ballots cast by illiterates through the use of gummed labels.[31]

These USCCR reports continued to document this type of activity through the 1970s.

Direct Vote Suppression in the 1970s

The USCCR's 1975 report on implementation of the Voting Rights Act ten years on further illuminates how southern states continued to try to suppress minority voting through the 1970s. Many of these practices relate to voter registration. The commission reported, "While formal barriers for the most part no longer exist, the lack of interest and of affirmative attempts to register voters on the part of county registrars become hindrances to participation. These hindrances include restrictive time and location for registration, the inadequate number of minority registration personnel, and purging of the registration rolls and re-registration."[32] The USCCR particularly singled out the practice of purging voter rolls and deleting eligible voters in the process—a practice that would reappear as a partisan weapon in later years.[33] The 1975 report also condemned felon disenfranchisement and noted the difficulty voters who had served their time had getting their voting rights back, another matter that would carry into later years.[34]

The Commission on Civil Rights' report on the eve of the debate over reauthorization of the Voting Rights Act in 1981 underscores how the practices of disenfranchisement of minorities continued in the South throughout the 1970s—still most often in an effort by Democrats to keep out black competition in primaries. The 1981 report documented continuing problems with purging and requiring re-registration. In the mid-1970s the United States attorney general objected under Section 5 of the Voter Rights Act to purging and re-registration laws in Texas and Mississippi.[35] Election administrators moved polling places away from black voters to more distant locations, leading to more Section 5 objections in several states.[36]

Once the Voting Rights Act was implemented and southern states became obliged to submit any changes to election procedures for preclearance by the Department of Justice, the Department of Justice recorded, by means of objections, the types of strategies deployed. The 1981 report lays out the pattern of objections and shows the increased use of vote dilution strategies over vote suppression tactics as the Voting Rights Act took full effect and blatant suppression activities became less effective. By 1981, two-thirds of the Department of Justice's objections to submitted changes in election practices related to dilution of the minority vote, rather than the outright vote denial.[37] The USCCR states that the most prevalent strategy was annexation of white areas to dilute black voting strength; it also found many of the objections were regarding at-large elections and variations of that system, as well as redistricting efforts.[38] Thus we see the shift in tactics given the changing political and electoral conditions on the ground.

The 1981 USCCR report—the last one to be produced for twenty-five years analyzing the effectiveness of the Voting Rights Act—concludes that blacks continued to encounter white resistance to their political participation in virtually every aspect of the elections process. Certainly the system had improved dramatically, but voter exclusion on a wide scale was continuing—and would continue in the years to come. Written in the first year of Reagan's presidency, the report warned of ongoing challenges. While both parties in the 1960s continued to block African Americans from political power—for Democrats via the primaries—the late 1960s marked the beginning of Republican assumption of the vote suppression machinery in presidential elections, which would then move down the ticket over the next two decades and solidify just after this USCCR report was written, with the election of Ronald Reagan to the presidency and the increasing Republican domination of the white South at every level of the federal government.

4

Vote Suppression Goes National — and Republican

The 1950s and 1960s witnessed significant advancements in voting rights. The decade also saw important tactical shifts in vote suppression. The most blatant Jim Crow voting laws disenfranchising African Americans that had persisted into the middle of the twentieth century were largely eradicated by passage of voting rights laws in this period. Yet this progress did not mark the end of efforts to disenfranchise certain groups of voters at the ballot box. The traditional tactic of playing games with voter registration and registration lists persisted. Moreover, new strategies were developed from well-established devices and soon became the preferred weapons for suppressing the vote of political opponents. In the narrow window prior to the passage of the Voting Rights Act of 1965 but after the 1964 Civil Rights Act, political dynamics had already started to shift. Given the strong Democratic tendencies of voters of color as a result of the New Deal and the civil rights movement, and given the backlash against civil rights, operatives in the Republican Party devised a strategy to suppress minority turnout, including now that of Latinos in places they were concentrated,[1] through means that, when employed presumably as intended by the law's authors, were legal: challenging voters' eligibility to vote at the polls.

Challenging Becomes Caging

Challenging a voter's right to vote—when used sparingly and judiciously, by those with specific knowledge of the voter's eligibility—can arguably serve as a legitimate check on ineligible persons voting. The Republicans' use of laws that allow for challenges at the polls, however, skirts the line of voter intimidation and racial discrimination. Sometimes it does more than skirt but crosses over the line. Carried out in an arbitrary and discriminatory manner, these challenges were not employed primarily for the purpose of ensuring the integrity of the vote, but rather as a broad strategy to suppress the vote. As such, these practices clearly violate the voter inclusion principle.

Of course, challenges have been used in various forms for vote suppression throughout American history. For example, interrogating African American voters about their race at the polls in Ohio was permissible under a state law enacted prior to the Civil War that allowed for the posting of challengers at the polls.[2] As we recounted earlier, challenges continued throughout the nineteenth century, especially with respect to immigrants, as voters at the polls who appeared to be of a particular ethnic group would be asked which party they were likely to support or where they lived, as presumably that would be an indication of their immigrant status. If the voter belonged to an ethnic group that tended to support the opposing party, his citizenship would be challenged at the polling place. If he was from a group that generally voted for the party represented by the party agent, that agent would ignore whether he had his papers or not or even encourage his voting regardless of whether he was legally eligible.[3] The problem of indiscriminate challenges persisted into the 1920s throughout the country, particularly in urban areas with large immigrant populations.[4]

The 1960s and the following decades, however, saw vote challenging rise to an unprecedented level and scale, and the current version of this old game had a new wrinkle. Party operatives in many instances sent mass mailings to overwhelmingly minority and Democratic areas, putting anyone whose letter came back as undeliverable on a list of voters to be challenged on Election Day. This practice has become known as "vote caging."

A piece of undeliverable mail is obviously a flawed basis upon which to charge a voter as ineligible. A voter may have moved permanently yet still be in the same voting district and so remain eligible to vote. Returned mail is also occasioned by routine errors and mistakes: voter rolls suffer from typos and other clerical errors; a voter may be temporarily away from her permanent residence; mail may not be properly delivered; mail sent to a listed registration address may be returned as undeliverable because the United States Postal Service does not know that the voter actually lives at the address listed. Multiple-unit dwellings without names on mailboxes, houses or apartments occupied by roommates, families in which a spouse or children have a different family name—all circumstances of this sort can result in the U.S. Postal Service failing to deliver a letter because the addressee is determined to not be in residence. And while these are all common situations for hundreds of thousands of American voters, not a single one of these situations legally disqualifies a registered voter.[5] Indeed, allegations based on vote caging often turn out to be completely illegitimate.[6]

This method of caging, then, marks a more systematic use of the challenge process, which allows party operatives to compile larger lists of individuals and then, by means of this use of errors in postal delivery, to target minority populations. In addition to this important change, the use of caging by Republicans beginning in the 1960s is notable for its geographic scope and centralized direction. In previous eras, vote suppression tactics had been largely local or regional, and they were based on the particular political and racial dynamic of the place. Vote challenging as it emerged in the 1960s was often coordinated from the top and was carried out across the country. These offensives started out on a smaller scale in various states in the late 1950s, and then, in 1962, Arizona was a focus of such activity. Yet it was the presidential election of 1964 that marked the first national effort at partisan vote suppression. It was called Operation Eagle Eye. The approach was simple: to challenge voters, especially voters of color, at the polls throughout the country on a variety of specious pretexts. If the challenge did not work outright—that is, if the voter was not prevented from casting a ballot (provisional ballots were not in widespread use at this time)—the challenge would still slow down the voting process, create long lines at the polls, and likely discourage some voters who could not wait or did not want to go through the hassle they were seeing other voters endure. A Republican memo, obtained by the Democratic National Committee (DNC) in 1964, outlined plans for challenging voters at the polls and described the tactics as including encouraging stalling on lines in Democratic districts, equipping poll watchers with cameras to "frighten off . . . Democratic wrong-doers," enlisting the help of local police sympathetic to the Goldwater campaign, and charging that ineligible Democratic voters were on the registration rolls.[7]

The Lead-up to Operation Eagle Eye

Much of what we know about caging and challenge operations in the 1960 and 1962 elections emerged in the confirmation hearings of the late Supreme Court chief justice William Rehnquist. The role of Rehnquist in the 1964 Republican challenge scheme in Arizona has been reported by others in newspaper articles and in detail by political sociologist Chandler Davidson. As Professor Davidson details regarding events in the early 1960s,

> Political operatives belonging to one party caged voters who were predominantly members of ethnic minority groups likely to vote for the other party. The caging consisted of using do-not-forward letters to identify people who might not be properly registered. Then, on election day, at least some of the partisan operatives—including lawyers—went beyond simply asking election officials to challenge the voters who were on the caging list. In some cases, the operatives attempted to apply literacy tests and were abrasive and threatening. Their intervention sometimes slowed the lines of voters. Moreover, they sometimes broke the election law by arrogating to themselves the roles of challenging the voters' registration and of applying literacy tests when those roles were legally assigned to election officials.[8]

With Rehnquist's death in 2005, however, FBI files from the background investigations for his 1971 confirmation as Supreme Court justice and 1986 confirmation as chief justice were released to the public. These documents provide new details about what has already been reported and underscore the breadth of the operation beyond the alleged efforts of Rehnquist and his cohorts in Arizona.

Some of the documents in the FBI files are redacted, making it difficult in some cases to establish founded assertions of the character of the strategies and who was responsible. The repetitive nature of the stories recorded in the FBI interviews, however, helps to fill in some gaps due to redaction and build an overall account that seems credible.

A 1986 memo from the director of the FBI, William Webster, to the Phoenix and San Diego FBI offices investigating Rehnquist's background provides a historical insight into what was going on in Phoenix during the 1962 election:

> Two white republican voter challengers [one of whom was allegedly Rehnquist] confronted black and minority voters at the Bethune school voting precinct on November 6, 1962. They displayed a card with an excerpt from the constitution and asked blacks and minorities to prove they were literate by reading the excerpt aloud. The activity discouraged the black voters who then did not vote.
>
> As the day progressed, Democratic poll watchers became incensed and telephoned party officials and law enforcement personnel, many of whom arrived at the scene and attempted to dissuade the Republican challengers. Finally, a scuffle ensued, and the Republicans departed.[9]

An FBI interview conducted by the Los Angeles office in August 1986 revealed the impetus behind these vote suppression efforts. The interviewee stated that Rehnquist, who was reportedly the head of a group of Republican lawyers in Arizona, had "'designed a strategy' that would clog the voting polls in heavily minority Democratic precincts by sending an Army of Challengers into these polling places at peak voting periods and thereby intimidate some voters and scare them away from voting or frustrate voters by causing such a time delay that they would give up and leave without voting." The interviewee claimed that this was a strategy designed to help Republicans running for statewide office in close contests.[10]

One of the witnesses in the 1986 hearings and a politician on the scene back in 1962 had a similar assessment. Charles Pine, former chair of the Arizona Democratic Party, said he saw Rehnquist act as an aggressive challenger in 1962. Considering why Rehnquist would organize these "flying squads" to challenge voters in Democratic districts, Pine concluded that if [Rehnquist] could disqualify a substantial number of votes, it conceivably could have an impact upon closely contested statewide races and we had many of them in those years. . . . Highly important offices, and some of these were very closely contested, and 300, 400, 500 votes could make a great difference. . . . And that was the obvious strategy of this. A young attorney told me, who is now a Democrat and was then a young Republican: I was addressed by a member of Rehnquist's group and was told, if we can disqualify enough blacks and enough Mexican Americans, we can elect Paul Fannin Governor in 1962.[11]

An unnamed Phoenix civil rights leader interviewed by the FBI in 1971 had a similar recollection.[12] The file for the full investigation shows Rehnquist to have been associated with vote caging as early as 1962. That association, well documented in the file, did not, however, hamper his confirmation as chief justice, and Rehnquist denied that he had been personally engaged in challenging the credentials of any voter. Rehnquist's assertion was supported by testimony from Vincent Maggiore, then chairman of the Phoenix-area Democratic Party, who stated that he had never heard any negative reports about Rehnquist's Election Day activities.[13]

As interesting as witnesses' retelling of events during these early 1960s elections is the justification for their actions described by those who participated as poll watchers: vague allegations of fraud. An active Arizona Republican who served as a challenger during the 1960 election told FBI officials in 1986 that the "group of attorneys [organized to engage in voter challenges] was established to help combat the growing amount of election frauds that had occurred in previous election years." He went on to explain how the party would know about this supposed fraud: by sending out letters to registered voters in very particular areas and challenging the voting eligibility of anyone whose letter had been returned to them as undeliverable[14]—in short, by vote caging. The supposition among Republican poll watchers appears to have been that if the Democratic Party was not perpetrating fraud by getting illegal voters to the polls, then the Democrats were still benefiting from votes illegally cast. A 1986 FBI interview with a man who had organized a challengers' committee for the 1962 election underlines the partisan motivations. He said that "the Democratic Party was very strong in the early 1960s and Republicans were concerned about challenging 'any and all fraudulent voters' in the 1962 election." In discussing what had happened in the precinct where Rehnquist was alleged to have stopped people to make them read an excerpt from the Constitution in order to vote, he said, "Some of the voters happened to be blacks and other minorities and several of them became discouraged from voting. [REDACTED] suggested that one of the reasons these voters did not vote was because they were aware their illegal status had been discovered by [REDACTED] and other poll watchers."[15]

In his 1971 confirmation hearing, Rehnquist revealed how partisanship coupled with generalized fear of fraud motivated Republican Party operatives. In responding to a question, posed by Democratic senator Birch Bayh, about how the party would send out letters to minorities and then challenge voters whose letters were returned to them, Rehnquist stated openly that they were going after Democrats in areas where—for whatever reason—they believed there might be irregularities:

MR. REHNQUIST. It was not devoted to minority group areas as such; it was devoted again to areas in which heavy Democratic pluralities were voting together, with some reason to believe that tombstones were being voted at the same time. And this was one of the principal means used to try to find letters returned with the addressee unknown and then to challenge the person on the basis of residence if he appeared to vote. I might say that the Democrats made equal use of the same device.

SENATOR BAYH. As I read these newspaper clippings, it does not mention anything about the Democrats doing that. I suppose that does not mean they did it or did not do it, but at least the newspaper reporters did not catch it. If I were a Republican, I would want to keep as many Democrats from voting as I could, I suppose, and vice versa. But this is done in some areas, and I am familiar with this, in those areas that are not just Democratic, but minority groups primarily, whether it is Chicano or black or whatever it might be, where there is more movement back and forth across the street and from one part of the community to another. Can you give me any reason why the NAACP would make this assessment, or did they just have something in for you?

MR. REHNQUIST. I simply cannot speak for them. I know of my own conduct in these matters, and that the letters were mailed out on the basis of mathematical calculations of Democratic votes in precincts together with areas in which there was some reason to believe that there actually were tombstone or absentee voting, and I know from my trips to polling places, as a member of the Lawyers Committee, that some of the precincts certainly had a number of blacks, a number of Chicanos, and many of them were totally white.

The purpose of the scheme was not then to root out fraud, wherever it might come from or be carried out. It was planned to single out particular types of voters for interrogation, many of whom were black or Hispanic and were most certainly suspected Democrats. What he meant by targeting "absentee voting areas" is completely unclear. In any case, 1962 was just a warm-up.

Operation Eagle Eye

The Republicans made no effort to hide their plans to go big with the caging and challenges in 1964. In fact, the party launched an unprecedented nationally organized operation that would exploit existing election laws for partisan advantage. It was not surprising that this effort would arise in a year in which Republican Barry Goldwater ran on an anti–civil rights campaign platform against Lyndon Johnson, who had recently succeeded the assassinated John F. Kennedy as president.

A Democratic National Committee press release from October 27, 1964, explained the Democrats' perception of what was happening that year:

> Under the guise of setting up an apparatus to protect the sanctity of the ballot, the Republicans are actually creating the machinery for a carefully organized campaign to intimidate voters and to frighten members of minority groups from casting their ballots on November 3rd. . . . It is an organized effort to prevent the foreign born, to prevent Negroes, to prevent members of ethnic minorities from casting their votes by frightening and intimidating them at the polling place. . . . Operation Eagle Eye . . . is a program to cut down the vote in predominantly Democratic areas by harassing, frightening, and confusing the voters. . . . The strategy is to help Senator Goldwater by cutting down the vote in large cities in states with many electoral votes.

The press release backs up these charges by discussing a Republican memo outlining planned tactics of challenging voters at the polls, encouraging stalling on lines in Democratic districts, equipping poll watchers with cameras to "frighten off . . . Democratic wrong-doers," enlisting the help of local police sympathetic to the Goldwater campaign, and charging that ineligible Democratic voters are on the registration rolls. Although it is unclear how the DNC obtained this memo, Republicans were not shy about flatly announcing what they planned to do. The national director of Eagle Eye, Charles Barr, told the *New York Times* he expected the operation to challenge or deter from voting 1.25 million voters all over the country, sparing no corner. This led to numerous recriminations in the days leading up to Election Day. As the *Times* put it: "Senator Hubert H. Humphrey of Minnesota, the Democratic Vice-Presidential candidate, denounced the Republican 'Operation Eagle Eye' as an indication that the G.O.P. leadership was determined to 'harass those who are going to vote. . . . It should be called Operation Evil Eye.'"[16]

Throughout the fall of 1964, Republicans sent out 1.8 million pieces of mail to the entire registration list in many of the "suspect" precincts in key cities.[17] Barr was frank in describing the tactic to reporters, who recorded his prediction just before the election that "100,000 poll watchers in 35 cities will take part, and he expects 1.25 million voters to be either successfully challenged or discouraged from going to the polls."[18] The chairman of the GOP, Dean Burch, said that Republicans trained "in the ways of detecting common fraudulent election practices will man the precinct teams." Operatives would make a list of voters to challenge by going door to door checking people's addresses[19]—an even less accurate and certainly more intimidating technique than sending out mailers.

One of the more blatant instances of the GOP using election procedures to disenfranchise Democrats occurred in Minnesota. In the month before the election, reporters uncovered a "kit" prepared for party poll watchers. The materials in the kit explicitly told the poll watcher that he or she was representing the Republican Party, stating baldly, "Your job is partisan. . . . The Republican voters in this state are relying upon you to see to it that the DFL [Democratic Farmer Labor Party] candidates do not receive one more vote in totals in your precinct than those to which they are legally entitled. Let the DFL look out for their own interest." Moreover, poll watchers were further directed, when a question arose at the polls, the challenger should only "(when it's in your party's interest) insist that the law be followed." According to press reports,

> included among poll-watchers' duties in the GOP program are: . . . *Discouraging* election judges in DFL dominated precincts from volunteering assistance to voters. . . . *Watching* for stalling in voting booths in GOP-dominated precincts only. . . . *In DFL precincts*, challenging ballots before they are

deposited if two people enter a voting booth together and vote, particularly in cases where the voters are known not to be Republicans. . . . *Raise a challenge* when certain supposedly improper assistance is given to the voter "and you have good reason to believe these are not Republicans."[20]

While it is unclear what happened at the polls in Minnesota on November 3, 1964, the very existence of such instructions is disturbing enough. We do have evidence, however, that the Republican plan was executed in polling places all across the country. On Election Day, for instance, the *New York Times* reported that "in several areas of the South, Republicans had obtained registration lists in Negro precincts and mailed letters to all on the list. The Republicans said that a number of the letters were returned, indicating the voters were illegally registered. In Atlanta, the Republicans used these letters to challenge 2,000 voters. After a hearing, however, the Fulton Board of Registrars ruled that the letters were not proof of improper registration and rejected the challenges."[21] Similar fates awaited Democratic voters in Miami. The *Miami Herald* reported that "voters by the hundreds, perplexed and downright scared, were snarled yesterday in partisan poll-watching. Over-zealousness and challenges to Negroes dissuaded voters from entering booths, delayed their vote and otherwise disrupted normal procedure." Others who might have been perceived as natural Democratic constituents were also targeted. "Elderly couples, living in Florida in retirement, also were challenged. In Miami, many were so upset that they fled back home without bothering to vote."[22] The polls got so unruly in Miami that a circuit court judge ordered an injunction against the Republicans banning "illegal mass challenging without cause, conducted in such manner as to obstruct the orderly conduct of this election."[23]

Reports of similar activity came in from across the country. In Chicago, according to the *Chicago Daily News*, Eagle Eye had 10,000 challengers in that city alone.[24] The president of the Los Angeles County Young Republicans told the local registrar that his organization was going to assign watchers only to a heavily African American district, where, he claimed, "we have first-hand knowledge of election code violations." In St. George, South Carolina, the NAACP asked the FBI to investigate after finding that every third African American voter was being challenged at the polls; he "added that some white people believed to be supporting the Democratic presidential ticket were also being challenged without cause."[25] In Louisiana, Republicans were not limiting themselves to the efforts of their own volunteers. In that state, the head of the Republican ballot security program instructed workers to "make every effort to obtain the cooperation of the sheriff and local police and law enforcement officers on Election Day. . . . We are advised that all sheriffs in the state of Louisiana, except one, are sympathetic with Sen. Goldwater's election. We should take full advantage of this situation."[26]

There was trouble in the nation's capital, as well. The GOP chairman in Washington, DC, Carl Shipley, announced that he would be putting three poll watchers in each precinct and also hired forty private detectives to monitor the polls. As the *Washington Post* tartly observed, "In a statement which elevated him to a new level of felicity, moreover, Mr. Shipley made it plain that he did not mean to insult the public generally: well-dressed persons will not be challenged, he announced the other day, only 'the kind of a guy you can buy for a buck or a bottle of booze.' " Presumably Mr. Shipley was referring to lower-income voters who he might have also suspected—correctly, according to data—would likely be Democrats. Clearly these were not appropriate standards for whose voting rights should be challenged.

Although Goldwater lost the 1964 election, Operation Eagle Eye was largely successful. The Republican Party had shown that vote suppression could be carried out nationally and the tactics could be employed by volunteers from all over the country. While there is no available information on any massive vote-caging schemes in the elections in the later 1960s and 1970s, the Republican Party used these first organized efforts as a blueprint for elections in the 1980s and 1990s. By that time, they had the operation down to a routine. As Professor Davidson explains, "They focus on minority precincts almost exclusively. There is often only the flimsiest evidence that vote fraud is likely to be perpetrated in such precincts. In addition to encouraging the presence of sometimes intimidating Republican poll watchers or challengers who may slow down voting lines and embarrass potential voters by asking them humiliating questions, these programs have sometimes posted people in official-looking uniforms with badges and side arms who question voters about their citizenship or their registration."[27] Since the 1960s, this playbook has figured prominently in many closely fought elections.

The Republican South and the Reagan Realignment

Unlike Goldwater and Nixon's earlier efforts, Reagan's 1980 campaign was not obviously based on a southern strategy that sought to appeal to southern whites through the rhetoric of race, nor is there research to demonstrate mass caging activity during this presidential election. Much of Reagan's strength among southern whites was due to his messages on cutting taxes, religious values, and building up the military. Nevertheless, his emphasis on keeping the federal government out of people's lives sent a clear message that he was not in favor of imposing a federal civil rights agenda, including busing and affirmative action, on the states. Although he would later change his view, as a political aspirant connected with the Goldwater campaign Reagan had opposed both the Civil Rights Act and the Voting Rights Act, and as governor of California he had refused to criticize George Wallace's advocacy of segregation during his 1968 presidential campaign. Most infamously, Reagan began his 1980 general presidential campaign with a rally in Philadelphia, Mississippi, where civil rights workers had been killed in 1964—a signal to certain white southerners that he had their interests in mind.[28]

The success of Reagan over incumbent president Jimmy Carter in 1980 marked the turning point when, for the first time, more southern whites identified as Republicans than Democrats. Exit polls from 1988 show that, in the eleven southern states, on average 45 percent of southern white voters identified themselves as Republicans, nearly double the average in 1982. Only 34 percent of southern white voters still called themselves Democrats. Based on this evidence, historians of the South, Earl and Merle Black, found that "Reagan's performance in office had allowed the Republicans to displace the Democrats as the new plurality party among southern white voters."[29] The demographic and ideological shifts that began in the 1950s led to a new political landscape. After 1980, southern Republicans started reliably winning congressional contests, whereas previously it was only in presidential elections that Republicans could expect to fare well.

Until 1980, southern congressional seats had been dominated by conservative Democratic officeholders who opposed civil rights and continued to attract white conservative voters.[30] It wasn't just their stance on civil rights that allowed Democrats to hold on to power in the South—they also opposed organized labor and supported low taxes. Perhaps most important, incumbent Democrats were able to exploit all the advantages of years in office and of being part of the majority party in Congress, which allowed them to deliver resources and services to their districts. Over the course of the two decades after passage of the Voting Rights Act, Democrats finally began to realize that it would be easier for white Democrats—especially given the trend of white southerners toward the Republican Party—to win by going after African American votes and building biracial coalitions. As a result, the party began to be politically more moderate, such as by supporting extensions of the Voting Rights Act in the 1970s and taking liberal positions on some issues and a conservative stance on others, such as economic issues. It was through these biracial coalitions of voters that the Democratic Party was able to continue to dominate legislative politics in the South even into the 1980s. As long as 90 to 95 percent of African Americans voted Democratic, Democratic candidates never needed a majority of white votes.[31]

Some officeholders simply abandoned the Democratic Party for the Republicans during this period, including Phil Gramm, Strom Thurmond, Jesse Helms, and Lauch Faircloth. Then there were broader demographic patterns that saw an influx of conservative white northerners to the South, while African Americans continued to migrate out of the South. All these factors came together, and Republicans started to win congressional elections. After Reagan took the presidency, GOP wins came by huge white majorities—a trend that would reach its acme in the 1990s.[32]

Republican Vote Suppression and Democratic Lawsuits

By the 1980s it was fully in the Republican Party's interest to target easily identifiable Democratic-leaning voters throughout the country—primarily African Americans and low-income Americans of all races, since poorer people also tend to vote for Democrats. As a result, caging and challenges continued throughout the country unabated. One of the most documented instances was the "antifraud" initiative that accompanied New Jersey's 1981 gubernatorial contest between Republican Thomas Kean and Democrat James Florio. The national Republican Party formed a National Ballot Security Force that mailed 200,000 letters to registered Democrats in predominantly minority neighborhoods in New Jersey. In part because the Republican operatives used outdated lists, 45,000 letters were returned as undeliverable, and these were brought forward as bases for challenging the voting rights of people on the registration list.[33] The party also dispatched off-duty police officers in official-looking garb to heavily minority districts, posted signs that warned that polls were being patrolled by security force members and offered a $1,000 reward to anyone giving information on election law violators.[34] As usual, Republicans justified these measures by raising the specter of fraud. The head of the state Republican Party, Philip Kaltenbacher, pronounced, "Anyone opposed to ballot security obviously must be supportive of election fraud."[35]

In 1981 the Democratic National Committee and the New Jersey Democratic Party sued their Republican counterparts, alleging violations of the Fourteenth and Fifteenth amendments, as well as provisions of the Voting Rights Act, and in 1982 the Republican committees were forced into a consent decree that barred them from engaging in such activities. In a consent decree, a court-ordered settlement, the court orders an injunction against the defendant and continues to oversee the case to ensure the injunction is followed. If the defendant does not follow the order, other penalties are available to the judge. The key provisions of this consent decree were:

2. The RNC and RSC . . . agree that they will in the future, in all states and territories of the United States: . . .

(e) refrain from undertaking any ballot security activities in polling places or election districts where the racial or ethnic composition of such districts is a factor in the decision to conduct, or the actual conduct of, such activities there and where a purpose or significant effect of such activities is to deter qualified voters from voting; and the conduct of such activities disproportionately in or directed toward districts that have a substantial proportion of racial or ethnic populations shall be considered relevant evidence of the existence of such a factor and purpose; . . .

3. The party committees agree that they shall, as a first resort, use established statutory procedures for challenging unqualified voters.[36]

Unfortunately, this consent decree and the attendant spotlight on their campaign activities did not stop Republicans from continuing to engage in vote challenges and caging. These deliberately discriminatory practices continued to occur over coming decades, leading the Democratic Party to return to the same court for relief under the consent decree later on.

The next occasion of note was 1986. In Louisiana, Republicans sent mailings to 350,000 voters in districts that had voted heavily for the Democratic presidential candidate in 1984, and 30,000 came back, mostly from black voters. The RNC then used the returned letters to demand that elections officials purge the voters from the rolls.[37] Once again, the Democrats filed a lawsuit under the 1981 consent decree. During the litigation, a memo from Kris Wolfe, the Republican Party's Midwest director, to its southern political director Lanny Griffith emerged that read, "I know this race is really important to you. I would guess that this program will eliminate at least 60–80,000 folks from the rolls. . . . If it's a close race . . . which I'm assuming it is, this could keep the black vote down considerably."[38] The court ultimately issued a restraining order against the Republican Party. The judge characterized the caging activities as "an insidious scheme by the Republican Party to remove blacks from the voting rolls. . . . The only reasonable conclusion is that they initiated this purge with the specific intent of disenfranchising blacks and their right to vote."[39] Unfortunately, Louisiana was only the tip of the iceberg, as vote suppression through caging and challenge was now firmly established as a centralized, national strategy for partisan gain.

In 1986, the GOP actually hired an outside company to manage its ballot security program.[40] That outfit claimed it had found voter fraud in Indiana, Pennsylvania, Missouri, New Jersey, and Louisiana—although fraud was never reported or verified in any of these states. The DNC accused the RNC of ramping up the ballot security program to disenfranchise mostly minority voters in Georgia, California, Michigan, and elsewhere.[41] In these states, the Republicans used their faulty lists to plan vote challenges at the polls, and then turned the names over to the FBI for investigation.[42] In Houston, Republicans planned to put partisan poll watchers solely in inner-city precincts, the so-called minority precincts. In denying any racial basis for the choice of locations, the county Republican chairman explained, "If you plot those on a map, they are all in the inner city, and that's where the Democratic vote is going to be 90 to 95 percent straight ticket. That's where the abuses are going to happen. They are not going to happen in [the predominantly white areas of] west Harris County, in Clear Lake City or Kingwood."[43]

The chief counsel of the Republican Party readily admitted that they had spent a "substantial" amount of money on ballot security programs throughout the country because, he said, "We don't think dead people should be allowed to vote. They've been voting for a long time and we think they vote for Democrats most of the time."[44] That message, of course—echoed throughout the ranks of Republicans that year—came from the top. The chair of the Republican Party, Frank Fahrenkopf, had called voter fraud a "national plague." And he saw no problem with efforts to check the voting eligibility of minority voters. He insisted that "he did not think a voter being called by an FBI agent about their voting eligibility would be intimidating."[45]

The lawsuit forcing a halt to these activities, based on violations of the New Jersey–based 1981 agreement, was formally settled on July 23, 1987.[46] Even this second consent decree did not stop operatives in the Republican Party from launching effort after effort to abuse election procedures for partisan gain, all in the name of preventing fraud. Yet these two consent decrees provided the foundation for the Democratic Party and others to return to court repeatedly to try to put a stop to this form of vote suppression.

For example, the year of 1990 in North Carolina rivaled 1981 in New Jersey for the breadth and audacity of Republican efforts. The senatorial election, with Senator Jesse Helms defending his seat against African American Democrat Harvey Gantt, was already racially charged when Republicans announced their latest ballot security program. In that atmosphere, the Republican Party proceeded to send out 150,000 postcards in Democratic, nearly exclusively African American, areas. The postcards warned recipients that "When you enter the voting enclosure, you will be asked to state your name, residence and period of residence in that precinct. . . . It is a federal crime, punishable by up to five years in jail, to knowingly give false information about your name, residence, or period of residence to an election official." The postcards went on to intentionally misinform voters of their voting rights by claiming that if a voter had moved within thirty days of the election, he or she could not vote.[47]

Even the Republicans had trouble defending this tactic. According to the *Washington Post*, Jack Hawke, the chairman of the state GOP, "contended the postcards were sent to voters who had recently moved, but he acknowledged that an indeterminate number were sent to voters—many of them black—who had not moved in years."[48]

The Democrats filed suit again on the day before the election, but the judge held that he could not find a violation of the consent decrees because they applied only to the national Republican Party, not a state party. The Department of Justice investigated and found that black voters constituted 97 percent of the voters targeted.[49] The department filed suit, charging the Republicans had intimidated voters in violation of the Civil Rights Act and Voting Rights Act. The Republicans and the Helms campaign were forced into yet another consent decree in 1992 that enjoined them from intimidating voters or engaging in any ballot security program "directed at qualified voters in which the racial minority status of some or all of the voters is one of the factors in the decision to target those voters." From 1992 to 1996, the state Republican Party was required by the DOJ to obtain court approval before implementing any other ballot security programs.[50]

Despite the lawsuit and accompanying publicity, the Republicans went ahead and made the usual trouble—there were complaints throughout Election Day that Republicans were challenging and intimidating voters.[51] Similar enterprises would continue in various states and municipalities throughout the 1990s and 2000s.

Caging and the Harm to Voter Inclusion

Challenges to certain groups of voters for partisan purposes was an idea hatched in the nineteenth century, reintroduced in the 1950s, and perfected in the 1960s. In the 1980s and the early 1990s, the tactic was deployed expansively throughout the United States. The evidence that the Republican Party has systematically used it as a plan of action to swing voting margins has only grown in recent years. When more blatant forms of vote exclusion—such as the poll tax (barred by the Twenty-fourth Amendment to the Constitution in 1964 and with respect to the states held unconstitutional by the U.S. Supreme Court in 1966)[52] and literacy tests (suspended by the Voting Rights Act in 1965)—were barred by law and could no longer be used, there was pressure from within the Republican Party to find another tactic at a more sophisticated level, possibly within the technical outer limits of the law but clearly designed to disenfranchise. Even after the Republican National Party was forced into a consent decree in the early 1980s barring it from engaging in these types of activities, vote challenges, facilitated by caging, continued to be an important weapon at the polls.

Partisan caging and challenging cannot be accepted by a healthy democracy. These tactics may distort election results and have the potential to skew the makeup of the electorate. That we continue to allow these abuses to go on so frequently—that the laws still make these strategies possible, if not fully permissible—sends the wrong message, especially to targeted communities, about the United States' democratic values.

Because just elections demand equal respect for all citizens, caging and challenges when used in this way flatly fail the test. The arbitrary, racially targeted manner of these vote-challenge operations flouts their own rationale as a measure intended to prevent fraud and denies the equal standing of citizens; the flimsy evidence upon which the challenges rest makes them patently disrespectful. Republican participants might say it is their right to question eligibility as a necessary function of the democratic system. But they do not do it in a way that helps to increase the fairness of elections or legitimize them. They carry out these practices in ways that stretch and sometimes break the law, attempting to suppress the participation of certain segments of society. This violates the principle of equal access to the election process. These partisan programs also fail the test of balancing liberties where a conflict might exist. Even if we accept the right to challenge another voter's eligibility—which, when done by a partisan rather than an informed and trained election worker, for example, is dubious—plainly the way in which the Republicans have carried out these challenges for decades is much more detrimental to the process than beneficial.

Most important, having one's right to vote challenged unfairly at the polls, without a strong basis for suspicion or evidence of ineligibility and often due solely to the color of one's skin, harms a voter's sense of citizenship and democratic pride individually and undermines the value of and our collective interest in an equal and just democracy.

5

THE BATTLE OVER MOTOR VOTER

At the same time that caging was being used to disenfranchise voters in the 1980s and into the '90s, another skirmish was being fought on a different battlefield, one that would ultimately push in the other direction, that of greater voter inclusion: passage of the National Voter Registration Act (NVRA), called the "motor voter" law.

The enactment of NVRA was the culmination of years of fighting to make the registration system easier to navigate and access. The research had been clear for years that the obstacle of voter registration was a huge factor in this country's low rate of voting.[1] Yet it was not until the 1980s that the problem began to be addressed seriously. Indeed, the United States was then (and remains so today) one of the few democracies in the world to make it the responsibility of the individual voter that he or she get on the registration list. Elsewhere, it is the responsibility of the government.[2] In this sense, the NVRA was a modest, incremental step toward full voter inclusion. And yet it was controversial.

The National Voter Registration Act was passed in 1993 and opened up the voter registration process in a number of ways, including by requiring registration services at departments of motor vehicles (DMVs) and public assistance agencies, allowing voters to register by mail, and requiring state elections officials to supply voter registration drives with voter registration forms. The law also has a number of provisions regarding the maintenance of voter registration lists. States may remove names from the voter registration list only in the following circumstances: (1) at the voter's request; (2) when the voter has been convicted of a felony or judged mentally incompetent as provided for by state law; and (3) through a program to remove voters who are ineligible because of death or change of residence. Furthermore, states may not remove a voter from the registration list as a consequence of moving unless (1) the voter confirms in writing that the voter has moved outside the registrar's jurisdiction, or (2) the voter has failed to respond to "a postage prepaid, pre-addressed return card sent by forwardable mail" and has not voted in two consecutive federal elections following the date of the notice.[3] These new provisions regarding the maintenance of voting lists, which are national in scope, are important changes that increase the integrity of the voting rolls and prevent partisan tampering.

The contribution of NVRA to voter inclusion and voter participation is clear. NVRA has been responsible for literally tens of millions of new voter registrations,[4] and as private legal actions against states for failure to implement the law have increased, and been successful, those numbers have continued to rise.[5] Research studies fairly universally show that NVRA has had a significant impact on registration rates, and government statistics demonstrate a tremendous rise in registration (by nearly 30 percent) as a result of better implementation of the law at the state level. Unfortunately, there is a relative dearth of research on the impact of the NVRA on voting, and much of the information that does exist may suffer from significant limitations. Nonetheless, the available research suggests that, at a very minimum, there has been a modest impact on actual voter turnout rates.[6] Moreover, the potential of NVRA is far from being realized.

Registering to vote at DMVs and by mail is largely taken for granted now, but the battle over NVRA's enactment was long, contentious, and partisan. President George H. W. Bush vetoed motor voter when it came to his desk in 1992, calling it "an open invitation to fraud and corruption."[7] Many other Republicans fought against it. In 1993, passage of the law was almost entirely on a party-line basis, with Democrats voting for it and Republicans against. Republicans were widely believed to be against the bill because of their perception (ultimately wrong) that the law favored Democrats. Most of them did not say that outright, but claimed it would lead to "fraud."

The NVRA debate and litigation are a case study of one party fighting, on the supposed basis of combating election fraud, a reform that was predicted to and has, to some extent, increased participation in the political process. The argument of fraud was at best incorrect and at worst completely false, as there has never been any evidence that NVRA has in fact led to an increase in fraud at the polls.[8] Therefore, the account of the passage of NVRA is not an example of a party using existing election law to suppress the votes of the opponent, but rather of an effort by a party to block a reform that would open up access to the process and potentially increase the number of Americans participating in elections. The dynamic is not unlike battles from the past over voter registration. It is comparable to the contests between Democrats and Republicans at the turn of the twentieth century over broadening access to voter registration and making registration easier, versus making it more restrictive, for instance by requiring the voter to frequently appear in person, or imposing voter registration rules only in urban areas.

Just as it was wrong to try to block measures to ease the registration process more than a century ago, it was wrong in a democracy to do so some twenty years ago. Measures that increase voter participation, assuming no strong competing reasons not to undertake them, are legitimate even if—as was claimed by some Republicans, albeit somewhat inaccurately—they only benefit one side. Therefore, within our voter inclusion paradigm, passage of the NVRA was not only legitimate but beneficial to American democracy.

Barriers to Registration before NVRA

Even though there was an increase in registration in the South after passage of the Voting Rights Act, from 1964 to 1980 overall voting went down 8 percent. Part of this decrease is attributable to the efforts of local politicians—of both parties—who continued to resist expansion of the franchise even as the national parties saw it as in their interest to expand the voting rolls.[9] For example, local officials for both Democratic and Republican parties blocked making voter registration part of federal poverty programs in the 1960s. They simply did not want to risk including any new voters in the shaping of the electorate.[10] Even as formal barriers began to diminish in the 1970s and 1980s, informal, local rules served to restrict the opportunities to register. For example, in-person registration was still ordinarily required; there would be only one registration office in an entire county, with limited hours; and there would be no such offices in minority neighborhoods.[11]

In the early 1980s, however, the concept of third-party voter registration drives—voter registration sign-ups conducted by local civic organizations—began to take shape. This led to a unique moment in the story of party tactics with respect to voter mobilization—the political Right, fearing the power of these third parties to register likely Democratic voters, began at first to work to register and mobilize their own voters rather than try to suppress the activities of the other side. The Republican Party began to undertake a targeted registration program aimed at signing up likely Republican voters as the political Left attempted to mobilize voters by registering them at public service agencies.[12] In this case, partisan politics led to a push for voter inclusion and the registration of more eligible voters. This type of response was politically ethical and smart. It also fit the model of the voter inclusion principle—mobilization rather than suppression tactics are legitimate, even if they are aimed only at one party's constituencies.

In what may have been an unfortunate miscalculation on the side of the progressive institutions and community, this healthy competition came to an abrupt, albeit temporary, halt with the Republican landslide election of 1984. Ronald Reagan's resounding defeat of Walter Mondale, in which Mondale carried only his home state of Minnesota and the District of Columbia, took the air out of progressive mobilization efforts.[13]

Despite the setbacks of the 1984 election, in which Democrats not only lost the presidential race but also lost sixteen seats in the House of Representatives (while also remaining a minority in Senate with the gain of but one seat), the movement toward making voter registration easier—especially for poor people—based on grassroots work and organizing that had begun a few years earlier, continued to take root and intermittently flower at the state and municipal level. The key mechanism of voter inclusion was gubernatorial executive orders allowing voter registration at departments of motor vehicles and government agencies in six states.[14] Nonetheless, as late as the mid-1980s, voters had to report to a central office in order to register in sixteen states, while eleven more states had procedures for appointing people to be deputy registrars but rarely actually appointed anyone.[15] Local officials, again of both parties, continued to enforce other types of arcane rules to make registration difficult, as part of their incumbent protection programs.[16]

The Fight in Congress

In the late 1980s and early 1990s at the national level Democrats came around to be very supportive of the concepts behind what ultimately became the National Voter Registration Act. Almost all the votes along the way to passage of the bill were along party lines. However, as we will see, through the agreement of a few reform-minded Republicans and the election of Bill Clinton as president, supporters of NVRA ultimately won the battle if not the war of actually getting the provisions implemented.

In creating the NVRA, Congress, with a Democratic majority in both the House and Senate, was spurred on by the fact that in 1992 there were almost 70 million people who did not vote in part because they were not registered.[17] Moreover, there was by then much evidence indicating that a disproportionate number of these nonvoters were lower-income and less-educated Americans and that this situation was worsening.[18] The income gap in the United States was also becoming a voting gap. Congress was thoroughly aware that reforming voter registration laws would not be a solution to this problem, but efforts to facilitate voter registration would at least lay the groundwork; more Americans would be in a position where they at least could opt to vote if they chose to or were persuaded to do so.[19]

NVRA was not the result of just one fight in Congress. Indeed there were several contests, in both the House and the Senate, in the late 1980s and early 1990s. During the 1990 debate, senators tried to appease Republicans who "portrayed the recipients of benefits as 'weak minded and susceptible to intimidation' and argued that public assistance agency workers would coerce recipients to register as a condition of getting benefits because they were 'survivors of the New Deal who were trying to put socialism in this country,' " by requiring beneficiaries be provided a special statement before registration that advised them of their right to complain if they had their registration interfered with or coerced.[20] This did not moderate Republican opposition, and each attempt to bring some variant of motor voter forward was defeated in party-line votes. In 1992, the Democrats did manage to get a filibuster-proof majority in the Senate, and the bill had the support of the House. However, it was vetoed by President George H. W. Bush.

During the House debate over rules for voting for the bill in 1992, Republican representative David Dreier of California called NVRA the "National Voter Fraud Act," saying the bill "provides de facto voting rights to nonresidents; it provides cover to corrupt officials that pad the voter rolls with deceased and nonexistent individuals; and it usurps States' rights to administer their constitutional authority to regulate their elections process."[21] In debate over the bill itself, Representative Robert Livingston, a Louisiana Republican, said the bill "requires the States to implement mail registration, with registration at welfare and unemployment offices, and encourages states to adopt election day registration. All in a costly Federal mandate with no funding to help the States comply with big brother's wishes. This is not a serious bill. The Democrats have done a great job of loading this turkey up with every fraud-inducing provision possible to gain a certain veto." And Representative Ronald Packard, a California Republican, stated, "As a reasonable person would conclude, this bill invites voter fraud. The agencies which administer social services to illegal immigrants are given the power to register them to vote. Furthermore, it only asks them to promise they are citizens, under penalty of perjury. This distorts the objective of democracy by allowing those who are not legal citizens to participate in a process they have no business participating in."[22]

Representative Spencer Bachus, an Alabama Republican, "warned that the NVRA would register 'millions of welfare recipients, illegal aliens, and taxpayer funded entitlement recipients,"[23] lumping all these different groups into one heap of illegitimate voters in language very reminiscent of that observed at the turn of the century. The minority report of the Senate Rules and Administration Committee on the NVRA was replete with charges of likely fraud.[24]

The Republicans' partisanship was especially apparent with respect to the provision requiring that public assistance agencies provide voter registration forms. People who used such agencies tended to be part of a Democratic-leaning demographic—poorer and disproportionately minority citizens, who also were disproportionately unregistered and disenfranchised and most in need of easier voter registration. A number of Republican members of Congress supported the bill when it did not include this mandate. As soon as this provision was added, the Republicans did an about-face and fought the bill.[25]

With Clinton's election to the executive office, however, Democrats controlled both the Congress and the presidency, and the measure finally passed in 1993 and was signed into law. The law in its final form stated that Congress was moved to take this action because it found that "discriminatory and unfair registration laws and procedures can have a direct and damaging effect on voter participation in elections for Federal office and disproportionately harm voter participation by various groups, including racial minorities."[26] That broad and democratic rationale for the legislation did not assuage Republican senators and representatives. Indeed, on the first day of the next congressional session, Republicans introduced six bills to block or hinder the implementation of NVRA. Two bills would have repealed the act entirely (H.R. 370 and S. 218); two would have made compliance by the states voluntary (H.R. 236 and H.R. 60); and two bills would have delayed implementation of the act until federal funds were appropriated to fund it (S. 91 and H.R. 736).[27]

The Fight over Implementation in the States

Even after passage, the fight at the federal level carried over into the states. Seven states refused to implement the law and fought the NVRA in the courts.[28] All those states had Republican governors.[29] As a result of these efforts, the U.S. Department of Justice was forced to sue California, Illinois, and Pennsylvania in January 1995 for noncompliance. The issue of voter fraud was raised as part of each state challenge to the act; however, none of the courts found evidence to support such claims.[30] Every court that considered the issue found the law to be constitutional, including two courts of appeal and six district courts. The Supreme Court refused to hear an appeal by California.[31]

Although Michigan passed implementing legislation, Governor John Engler, a Republican, issued an executive order declaring that the state would not comply until it received more federal funds to implement it, a major complaint of all the states challenging the act. Michigan residents and voting rights groups sued for enforcement, and the U.S. Department of Justice joined them. The state claimed that the act was unconstitutional because it exceeded the power of Congress to regulate elections and argued that it was a directive to the states without financing. A federal appeals court found that this was a misreading of the Constitution.[32]

In 1994, the South Carolina legislature passed legislation implementing NVRA, and the State Election Commission was ready to put it into motion without additional funding. However, the outgoing Republican governor, Carroll Campbell Jr., vetoed the legislation, and, with the support of the new Republican governor, David Beasley, the state attorney general, Charlie Condon, sued the United States government, challenging the NVRA's constitutionality on the grounds that the law infringed on the rights of the state of South Carolina. (The partisan and prejudicial motives for opposition were evident; the Republican chairman of the South Carolina Election Commission, Rusty DePass, said his party opposed the measure because "we all know who's on welfare. . . . We all know who those people vote for.")[33] A federal judge rejected Beasley's arguments against NVRA and ordered that the state implement it. The judge in the case noted that the arguments that the law tramples on states' rights was the same argument used to fight the Voting Rights Act in 1965. The judge rebuffed the argument that the act was unconstitutional because of the Tenth Amendment, as that does not apply when the federal government is ensuring civil rights.[34]

Recourse to arguments regarding voter fraud as a means to block implementation also proved unsuccessful for Republican partisans. When NVRA passed, Illinois governor Jim Edgar's spokesperson called it "an invitation to election fraud,"[35] and the state refused to implement the law. However, Judge Richard Posner of the Seventh Circuit, by most estimations a very conservative judge, criticized Republicans on the voter fraud claim, writing in his opinion, "The federal law contains a number of safeguards against vote fraud, and it is entirely conjectural that they are inferior to the protections that Illinois law offers."[36] Posner rejected Illinois's refusal to implement the new law, and when Edgar lost his appeal in the Seventh Circuit, the *Washington Post* editorialized that

> since almost all of the objections to this law seem to be coming from Republicans, it is of interest that the ruling declaring it constitutional comes not from judges famed for "liberal activism." Rather, it is a unanimous decision by a three-judge court, two of whose members—Chief Justice Richard Posner and Circuit Judge Frank Easterbrook—are respected by conservatives as two of the most thoughtful jurists in the country. We hope it persuades Republican governors to drop their suits and obey the law.[37]

The hopes of the *Washington Post* were misplaced. In Virginia, Secretary of State James S. Gilmore and Governor George Allen, both Republicans, argued that the law would lead to an increase in fraud.[38] Governor Allen challenged the law as unconstitutional and lost.[39] Not a single legal challenge to NVRA was upheld in the courts.

Finally, echoing rhetoric from a darker era, in Arkansas, when the House there initially refused to pass implementing legislation, one Republican legislator stated, "It's about time to say 'I'm sorry but the state of Arkansas is going to stand its ground.' We're going to stand tall. We're going to take back states' rights."[40]

The Reality of NVRA

As one reporter described in the year after NVRA was implemented, "For all the rumblings, hardly anyone's predictions have turned out to be exactly right. No single political party has seized control, crooks haven't marred elections, costs haven't gone through the roof, and lines at Motor-voter registration sites haven't grown to enormous lengths."[41] Not only did it not enable fraud or create bureaucratic headaches, NVRA was, in fact, an immediate and clear success. In the first three months after implementation, the mechanisms established by NVRA allowed for the registration of 2 million voters.[42] In the first year, 11 millions citizens registered or updated their voting address. Of the more than 11 million voters who enrolled or updated their registrations in 1995, 5.5 million registered in driver's license agencies, 1.3 million registered in public assistance agencies, and 4.2 million registered by mail.[43] According to the report of the Federal Election Commission (FEC) in 1997,[44]

> States reported a total of 142,995,856 registered voters nationwide for 1996, amounting to 72.77 % of the Voting Age Population (VAP). This is the highest percentage of voter registration since reliable records were first available in 1960. . . .
>
> In summary, the report finds that voter registration in States covered by the NVRA rose in 1996 by 1.82 percentage points—or some 3,390,000 people—over 1992, the previous comparable election. It should be noted, however, that the NVRA was in effect for only 22 months or less in the covered States.

Georgia alone added more than half a million new voters in that first year.[45] The FEC further reported that all the problems that Republicans charged would afflict the system just did not occur.[46]

In the face of such evidence—not just a net increase in voter registration but also an absence of accompanying fraud—one can only conclude that Republicans tried to block the NVRA largely because they believed it would increase the number of Democrats on the voting rolls. (Even as some Republican challenges were being brought forward in the states, early statistical evidence was demonstrating the success of the law.) They wanted to prevent any Democratic gains, even if it meant keeping voter registration procedures more difficult and thus more of a barrier to participation for all voters (including Republicans). In states like Illinois, Michigan, South Carolina, and Virginia, partisan strategy trumped democratic principles.

Yet, in the period immediately after the implementation of the act, a funny thing happened: more Republicans than Democrats registered to vote through NVRA. In jurisdictions around the country, elections administrators reported that more Republicans were taking advantage of the law's provisions, particularly the ability to register while at the DMV. For example, in the year after NVRA was implemented, more Republicans than Democrats registered to vote in Florida. Throughout the South, as well as in northern states such as Pennsylvania, the law led to dramatic registration gains for the Republican Party. The reason behind all this was apparent—far more people were registering through the motor-voter provision than were registering through the agency-based provision of the law. A *Wall Street Journal* report found that new voters registering at DMVs outnumbered those registering at public assistance agencies by a margin of 4 to 1.[47] Several academic studies have taken a broader look at what, if any, the partisan impacts of NVRA are. The general consensus is that the impact is marginal on all sides mostly because nonvoters tend to be less partisan overall.[48]

Moreover, even as Republicans were crying fraud during the debate over mail registration, there was already evidence that this just was not a persuasive point. According to the Senate Rules and Administration Committee Report regarding the bill,

> A study by the Congressional Research Service of States having mail registration procedures in 1984, found that "voter registration officials in all eighteen States for which data are available reported they have had little or no more fraud with post card registration. Several said they have had no more fraud with post card registration than with in-person registration." In fact, Governor Barbara Roberts of Oregon testified that her State instituted mail registration in 1975, and that despite the fact that Oregon does not have a notarization or witness requirement, Oregon has not experienced any cases of fraud or fraudulent voting with mail registration. Governor Roberts stated that there was "Literally no abuse of the system."[49]

In passing NVRA, Congress was well aware of the alarms being raised about its increasing the potential for fraud and sought to address any concern. Even if the charges were overstated by Republicans, the law established safeguards against voter fraud. The bill mandated that the voter in many instances must sign an attestation of eligibility in person when registering at a DMV, providing more scrutiny than in the average registration transaction. NVRA also made it a federal crime to knowingly put false information on the registration form, including information regarding age and citizenship. Agency-based employees were clearly prohibited from influencing an applicant's registration. Finally, the law established national standard procedures for keeping the election rolls up-to-date and accurate while not unfairly or wrongly purging any eligible voter from the list.

The claim that NVRA would lead to noncitizens registering and voting en masse was not realized either. The fears about voter fraud through mail registration and civic voter registration drives were also unfounded. While there were cases of persons filling in registration cards with phony names, most often when the persons were working for an organization and being paid according to the number of completed cards they submitted, these cases were easily discovered and dealt with by election administrators and, frequently, the employing organizations themselves. Most important, such instances, it is agreed, did not lead to actual fraud at the polling place. A report to the U.S. Election Assistance Commission found that experts and studies agree that this is the case.[50] There are almost no known cases in which someone filled out a registration form in someone else's name in order to impersonate and vote for him at the polls.[51]

All the claims about the new list maintenance provisions swinging the door open to illegal voting proved unfounded as well. The NVRA in fact tightened the process for taking people off the rolls in many states. It allowed for the creation of "inactive lists," which gathered the names of people who failed to respond to the address notification mailing. Such voters were completely eliminated from the registration list if they failed to vote in two consecutive federal elections, a period that could be as little as two and a half years. In half of the fifty states, this provision in the law actually shortened the length of time a voter could be on an inactive list and resulted in a mandate to eight states that had not been routinely purging voter registration lists of inactive persons.[52] Those cases in which bloated registration lists were in fact used to cast illegal votes were almost entirely through absentee ballot fraud, one of the few areas in which there is some amount of actual fraud.[53] In general, purging people wrongfully from the list has been a much bigger problem than too many inactive people being left on the rolls.

Continuing Problems

Abuse of the voter registration lists, though of course going back decades, reemerged to widespread public attention after the 2000 election when it was revealed that thousands of voters in Florida were wrongfully identified as ex-felons, tossed off the registration list, and denied the right to vote. This was due to the malfeasance or misfeasance of the Republican secretary of state, Katherine Harris.

There were also problems with implementation. As noted above, registration at DMVs proved highly successful and, studies show, a net gain for the Republican Party. However, from the beginning, implementation of registration practices through public assistance agencies was troubled. Only one million people were registered through the agencies in the first nine months of implementation, although scholars estimated three to four times that number could have been. The reasons varied by state. In some places agency workers were not instructed on the law; in others the state would not provide adequate numbers of forms; and in states like New York, budgets for implementation of the program were cut.[54]

This provision of the law continued to be neglected and unenforced. Section 7 of NVRA "requires states to offer voter registration opportunities at all offices that provide public assistance and all offices that provide state-funded programs primarily engaged in providing services to persons with disabilities." This section was added by Congress specifically to address the problem of low registration rates among marginalized communities, and was meant as a complement to the motor voter and mail registration provisions. The act reads:

> The agency-based registration program is designed to reach out to those sectors of the population which are not likely to have driver's licenses or other identification cards issued by a motor vehicle agency. . . . A Department of Transportation study noted that almost 50 percent of those persons who do not have a driver's license have annual incomes of less that $10,000. As a result, motor-voter registration programs may not adequately reach low income citizens and minorities. Active public and private agency–based voter registration programs available through such public agencies as State public assistance offices, State unemployment offices, or programs primarily engaged in providing services to persons with disabilities, as well as at private offices and locations in areas of low registration, are more likely to reach these eligible citizens, who are likely to have contact with a number of these agencies.[55]

Neither registration at the DMV nor mail registration was deemed sufficient to address the problem of registering people in poor and minority communities: "While mail registration procedures make registration convenient, in communities where resources are limited, it has been demonstrated to be ineffective in registering those who have historically been left out of the registration process. Thus, in some instances, mail registration is inferior to agency-based registration."[56] Considered as a whole, the agency-based portion of the voter inclusion effort was critical to the over-all success of NVRA. It was not an extraneous element but, effectively, the third leg that balanced and supported the total voter inclusion effort.

Yet it has been obvious for some time now that many state-based gov-ernment agencies simply have not complied with this provision, and that the number of people registering to vote through such agencies has been low as a result.[57] Nationally, voter registration applications processed through public assistance agencies declined 59.64 percent in 2003–4, com-pared with 1995–96.[58] Compared with 1995–96, in 2005–6 there was an 80 percent nationwide decrease in voter registrations from public assis-tance agencies. Nine states decreased the number of agency-based reg-istrations by 90 percent or more. In a sign of how rapidly this situation continued to deteriorate, states only registered half as many voters in public assistance agencies in 2005–6 as they did as recently as 2003–4.[59] At the same time, applications processed through other sources, such as departments of motor vehicles and mail, rose by 22.43 percent during the same period. The numbers were even worse in certain states. Eleven states saw declines of over 80 percent.[60] At the same time, 29 percent of Ameri-cans remained unregistered in 2008. Only 63.7 percent of Americans with household incomes below $20,000 a year were registered to vote, leaving over 34 percent still unregistered.[61]

Beginning in about 2008, states—through their chief state elections officials and public agencies—were forced to take remedial measures in response to the pressure of advocacy groups and, sometimes, litigation brought by voting rights groups such as Demos, the Lawyers Commit-tee for Civil Rights, and Project Vote.[62] As a result, more states started implementing the Section 7 provision much more vigorously, with impres-sive results. Ohio's public assistance agencies, for instance, reported over 84,000 voter registration applications completed at its offices in just the first five months after a settlement agreement with the nonpartisan democracy organization Demos and its partner organizations, an average of almost 17,000 registrations per month. In the two years preceding the settlement, Ohio's public assistance agencies reported an average of only 1,775 regis-trations per month. In Missouri, 235,774 low-income citizens applied for voter registration at the state's agencies in a little under two years, follow-ing a successful court action to improve compliance—an increase of almost 1,600 percent. In North Carolina, there has been a sixfold increase over the state's previous performance since working with organizations to comply more effectively with the NVRA. The number of voter registration applications from Virginia's public assistance agencies increased fivefold.[63]

The whole concept behind the National Voter Registration Act was to make it easier for all Americans to take the requisite step of registering to vote. Through Section 7, the law intended to make registration accessible to poor people, who were and continue to be underrepresented on the voter registration rolls. Yet many Republicans fought hard at the federal and state levels to block this measure, making it a hard-line partisan battle. As had been customary for more than a hundred years, the alleged justification for opposition to a measure that would allow more citizens to partake in the system was the potential for fraud. The reality was and is that the NVRA has been an enormously useful tool in registering more citizens to vote and that it did not and has not caused an increase in fraud. Moreover, with increasing dedication to enforcement of the Section 7 public agency provisions of the NVRA, both by the U.S. Department of Justice and voting rights groups, there is the potential to bring millions of more Americans into the political system. Under our voter inclusion framework, this is an inherent good, whether it is more beneficial to one party over another or not.

6

THE ELECTION OF 2000 AND ITS FALLOUT

The presidential election of 2000 was a national drama the likes of which no one alive had ever seen. A race too close to call on election night was still not decided when voters woke up the next morning, as the narrow margin in Florida triggered a recount of that state's votes. Al Gore's lead in the national popular vote meant nothing if Florida's electoral votes were given to George Bush. With the presidency hanging in the balance, the nation watched as the recount drama spun out for more than a month, including involvement of the U.S. Supreme Court.[1] In the end, Bush was deemed to be the victor in Florida, and was thus declared the next president.

During the recount of the votes in Florida, the whole country was given a view into what really went on behind the scenes in the voting system. While people in previous eras had been well aware of obvious disenfranchisement measures aimed at particular communities, the public of the twenty-first century had little idea of how dysfunctional and under–resourced our decentralized system of election administration was, and how easily the system could be manipulated to partisan advantage. As a nation we learned that the vote manipulation practices that originated over one hundred years ago were still with us in force, albeit sometimes cloaked in more subtle forms. Reporters, political scientists, and legal experts have since chronicled the efforts to manipulate that Florida vote, including, of course, the famous punch-card ballots, the felon purge, the butterfly ballot, and the multiple legal maneuverings of the two parties. These rampant irregularities, and their apparent effect on the outcome of the election, sparked national outrage.

A large portion of the population believed (and still believes) that the election was "stolen," first through the vote suppression and denial that occurred during the voting process, and then through the ruling of the Supreme Court that halted the vote recount. Much of the attention focused on the failure of punch-card ballot machines to accurately record votes, the butterfly ballot that led some voters to mistakenly vote for Pat Buchanan, and the argument that machine failure disproportionately took place in communities of color. There was also outrage at the use of a list of persons with felony convictions who were not allowed to vote, a list that turned out to be dramatically in error. When there were problems with the voter registration list, in many instances the voter simply was turned away from the polls and given no opportunity to even cast a provisional ballot. Many Americans felt the election system had completely broken down, that many American citizens who were perfectly eligible to vote had been disenfranchised, and that as a result the wrong candidate won the election.

It is also telling to note that, while widespread claims of voter disenfranchisement were made (and frequently substantiated), even during the heat of the recount, when the outcome was uncertain, very few claims of voter fraud arose. In fact, there were no known cases of voter impersonation at the polls in the 2000 election in Florida or anywhere else.[2] When efforts to subvert the election process were discovered, what seemed to be at work were mostly efforts to disenfranchise eligible voters.

The Help America Vote Act

In the debate in Congress over how to respond to the problems evident in the 2000 election, there was much disagreement over what the biggest problems were, and even greater disagreement on what the solutions should be. One part of the debate was instigated by the revelation—a surprise to many in the public—of just how different systems of voting were, depending on what state or even locality a voter happened to live in. This was most obvious in the range of voting machines used throughout the country and how each voting machine system recorded votes with a varying level of accuracy. As a result, there was much discussion about whether a new law should mandate that states act so as to make this extremely disparate system more uniform or whether the federal government should simply provide financial incentives for reform. In addition, many Republicans believed voter fraud was a major problem and ought to be a priority when determining the legislative response—even though there was no evidence to suggest that voter fraud was the primary cause of any of the breakdowns that occurred in 2000. Democrats, on the other hand, felt the biggest revelation of the 2000 election was the number of voters who were disenfranchised through faulty machines, inaccurate purging of voter rolls, sloppy registration lists, and poorly trained poll workers. As a result of this divergence in view, drafting the legislation was problematic, as each side tried to insert language suiting its goals.

Perhaps the most controversial issue debated as legislators cobbled together a voting bill involved the proposition of requiring voters to present identification at the polls. Many Republicans, with Senator Kit Bond of Missouri championing the cause, wanted all voters to have to show identification when voting. Proponents of this provision argued that if someone needed to show identification to buy alcohol, take an airplane, or even rent a video, he or she ought to have to show ID to vote. Civil rights advocates and many Democrats adamantly opposed such a requirement, saying it would disenfranchise many voters, making voting more difficult for Latinos, African Americans, the elderly, and the disabled, as members of such groups are less likely to have the various documents required under the provision.[3] A compromise was struck, and the final bill required that only people who were registering for the first time in a given jurisdiction and who registered to vote by mail were required to present identification when registering, and, if they failed to do so, present identification when voting. Moreover, the identification required did not need to be a photo ID, but could be something from among a list of alternative identifying documents. However, the bill did provide that this was a minimum standard and that states had the latitude to go beyond it if they chose to do so.

After much back and forth, Congress's solution to the election fiasco of 2000, the Help America Vote Act (HAVA),[4] was signed into law on October 29, 2002. In addition to the new voter identification provision, the act attempted to improve our election system in two ways: first, by requiring the states to implement certain voting reforms, especially with respect to the voting machines used, the registration system, and the employment of provisional ballots for voters who showed up at the polls but did not appear on the voter list; and second, by providing the states with ample cash to accomplish those reforms.

Since punch-card ballot machines became the focal point in the media and the popular consciousness of the 2000 fiasco, the law provided a special pool of financing for replacement of them in those states still using them. The law established the Election Assistance Commission, which was to be responsible for the distribution of the funding, conducting studies, and generally administering the program. In total, the Help America Vote Act authorized $3.9 billion to be distributed to the states over three fiscal years.

Most of these changes encouraged by HAVA appeared on the surface to be reasonable, and moderately positive. At the same time, however, the law left out reforms that would have addressed many major problems revealed by the 2000 election. Nonetheless, the infusion of federal resources, state centralization of the voter registration list, and the requirement that states provide provisional ballots to those who do not appear on voter registration lists appeared to create the opportunity for more voters to cast a ballot, and have that ballot count. And, in many instances, these reforms have in fact been employed to improve the accuracy of the voter list, and to enfranchise people who were subject to administrative errors in the registration process by providing them with provisional ballots. The first-ever federal provision of money for the election system was also extremely important; as a result, today we are using more-accurate voting machines, and in some places we are assisted by better-trained poll workers. In some states, however, many of the act's provisions have been turned on their head and used as means to disenfranchise voters. This is hardly what many hoped would emerge in the aftermath of the 2000 election. It is certainly evidence of the way in which electoral reform can be manipulated to partisan advantage.

The Particular Problem of Voter ID

As predicted by some, the narrow version of an ID requirement that was included in HAVA became very problematic in that it led to a subsequent flood of more-stringent voter identification requirements enacted at the state level. Attempts through state legislation to require voters to produce a government-issued photo identification at the polls in order to cast a ballot is certainly a means of manipulating the voting system. Requirements for ID suppress voter turnout among certain groups of people who are likely to vote Democratic. Those votes are suppressed with almost zero evidence of a countervailing need to do so, as the claims regarding voter fraud are unsubstantiated at best and instances of political gamesmanship at worst. It is highly ironic that one of the more lasting legacies of the response to the 2000 election debacle—which galvanized our attention on the importance that all legitimate votes be counted and all eligible voters be allowed to vote—is a measure that is designed to turn people away from the polls and ensure they are not able to cast a ballot that will be counted.

By drastically exaggerating the extent of polling-place fraud that occurs, Republicans have managed to pass bills in a majority of states that add identification requirements to what HAVA mandated as a minimum and have successfully passed laws in Indiana, Georgia, Kansas, Wisconsin, Texas, Tennessee, Alabama, Pennsylvania, and South Carolina that require government-issued photo identification from every single voter. In every one of these states, the legislative votes have been almost entirely along partisan lines, with Republicans voting for the restrictions and Democrats voting against. The partisan motives behind these laws is not well hidden. In dissenting from the Seventh Circuit Court of Appeals decision to uphold Indiana's draconian identification bill, Judge Terrence T. Evans wrote, "Let's not beat around the bush: The Indiana voter photo ID law is a not-too-thinly-veiled attempt to discourage election-day turnout by certain folks believed to skew Democratic."[5] As former Texas Republican Party political director Royal Masset told the *Houston Chronicle* in 2007, while he didn't agree there was widespread voter fraud, "an article of religious faith" among Republicans, as he put it, was that an ID law "could cause enough of a drop-off in legitimate Democratic voting to add 3 percent to the Republican vote."[6]

It's not hard to understand why voter fraud at the polling place is in reality so rare. In-person polling place fraud simply makes no sense. Just to change one vote, a would-be perpetrator would have to know in advance who on the registration list is not going to show up so that he can come in and say he is that person. If the person is caught, he receives five years in prison and a $10,000 fine. If he is not a citizen, he is deported. All this effort would need to be made in order to swing a single vote. Someone who really wanted to have an impact on the election outcome would be much better advised to engage in absentee ballot fraud or buying votes, forms of vote fraud that actually do take place.[7]

The facts of the legislative campaigns across the nation for ID requirements bear out Judge Evans's assessment. How voter identification was passed in Georgia in 2005 is particularly illustrative. The debate over the law—which required every voter to present a government-issued photo identification at the polls—was highly acrimonious and completely partisan. Indeed there was a Democratic walkout in both chambers during the debate. Democrats, particularly African American legislators, compared the bill to poll taxes and literacy tests.[8]

The radically partisan character of the legislative debate was not a surprise, given the genesis of the bill. The lead Senate sponsor of the bill, Cecil Staton, was inspired to propose this legislation by the right-wing blogger Erik Erickson. Erickson, known for his contributions to the website RedState.com, wrote in August 2005, "After months of handwringing over what to do over voter fraud, we came up with a suggestion as a first step: require photo identification at the polls. It's simple and it's commonsense. So, we suggested the idea down in Georgia. Senator Cecil P. Staton, Jr. picked up the ball. Despite personal attacks on his integrity, [the] Senator submitted S.B. 84 to require the use of government issued photo id to vote at polling locations."[9] In an earlier post, Erickson responded to complaints about the requirement by the Senate minority leader, Robert Brown, a Democrat, by stating "We all now have to have identification to get into a lot of federal buildings. So, why should it be easier to vote—a right we certainly don't want abused. . . . Full disclosure: I helped write one of the first drafts of the Voter ID bill."[10]

Comments about the bill by its sponsor in the lower chamber are also illuminating as to the intent behind it. The Department of Justice's review of the bill revealed this interesting tidbit:

Rep. [Sue] Burmeister said that if there are fewer black voters because of this bill, it will only be because there is less opportunity for fraud. She said that when black voters in her black precincts are not paid to vote, they do not go to the polls. . . . Rep. Burmeister also explained the exemption of absentee ballots from the identification requirement. She does not support this but accepted this into the final version because the absentee voting process creates a paper trail, which will prevent vote fraud, and will ensure that rural voters can vote even if they cannot make it to a DDS office.[11]

After the bill's passage, the *Augusta Chronicle* reported that Burmeister dismissed complaints that minorities would be facing similar restrictions on voting that were used to deter blacks from the polls in past generations and that she went on to state that if a person could secure proper ID so as to buy cigarettes, then that same person could make sure to have proper ID to vote. The *Chronicle* quoted her as saying, "I will make the contention that minorities, especially the poor community, smoke more and the elderly smoke more than your other classes" by way of suggesting that they had to have some form of ID. She did not make the distinction between buying cigarettes, which is not a right under the Constitution, and voting, which is a right.[12]

There was no meaningful public discussion of the merits of the bill or any potential disparate impacts of the voter ID law. According to the Department of Justice review, "Susan Lacetti Meyers, Chief Policy Advisor to the Georgia House of Representatives, who worked with Rep. Burmeister in developing the legislation, told us that the Legislature did not conduct any statistical analysis of the effect of the photo ID requirement on minority voters."[13] A member of the State and Local Governmental Operations Committee, which was responsible for first reviewing the bill, wrote the following:

At no time during any of these hearings did the bill's proponents cite even one example of voter fraud that would have been prevented by HB 244. After hearing almost no meaningful testimony, the committee passed the bill along partisan lines, with every Republican supporting it and every Democrat opposing it. . . . Second, in the same bill, Republicans expanded the potential for election fraud by stripping away restrictions related to absentee ballots. Notably, cases related to absentee ballots constitute the largest number of verifiable cases of fraud in Georgia, including the Dodge County vote-buying case that was erroneously claimed as justification for this bill.[14]

The legislative history and Department of Justice review allow us to see inside the voter ID lawmaking process, and the partisan motivations that are behind these efforts.

Including Georgia, ten states currently require government-issued photo identification in order to vote, and it is likely that more will pass such restrictions either legislatively or by ballot initiative in 2012. The laws in Wisconsin and Texas are particularly restrictive, as they do not even allow for student identification from a public university to be used. Since the passage of the Help America Vote Act, the issue of voter identification has become the most controversial and divisive issue in election reform, particularly in states that have pressed for the most stringent requirements.

Other states are much less restrictive than those referred to above. The way the HAVA provision was crafted, states are allowed much leeway in formulating their specific requirements. Some simply ask voters to sign affidavits—under penalty of perjury—if they do not have photo ID, and let them cast regular (nonprovisional) ballots. Other states that do require identification usually do not require photo identification but instead accept a wide range of both photo and nonphoto ID, including a voter registration certificate, utility bills, a paycheck, a personal check, a student ID, or a Medicaid or Medicare card. The remainder of the states follow the HAVA ID rule that simply requires that voters who register to vote for the first time in a jurisdiction supply some form of ID—and it could be one of very many forms of ID—or their driver's license number or the last four digits of their social security number. At the polls, most of these states require that the voter establish his of her identity by signing a poll book, and the poll worker then compares the signature with the one on file.

The laws that require government-issued photo identification—most commonly a driver's license or a non-driver's identification that is issued by the department of motor vehicles—pose the greatest threat to voting rights. For now, the Supreme Court has held such laws constitutional.[15] Yet to many observers, these new voter ID laws are just a more subtle reincarnation of one of the oldest partisan and racist voting manipulations in our history: the poll tax (which is unconstitutional). In states that have enacted ID laws, if one does not already have a current driver's license or one of another small number of government documents with a photo that has the same name on it as the one on the voter registration form, the requirement will be a serious impediment to a voter. If the voter comes to the polls without the right kind of ID—or at least right as far as a particular poll worker is concerned—he cannot vote by regular ballot that day. In most of these states he must instead vote a provisional ballot, and the only way the ballot will be counted is if the voter returns to election offices with the necessary ID within a certain circumscribed number of days. There is no doubt that such a requirement serves as an effective bar to the franchise, and, again, the requirement is described as a remedy to a problem that does not exist: rampant voter fraud.

The potential for strict ID laws to skew election outcomes is huge. About 11 percent of Americans do not have a driver's license or non-driver's government ID. Voters without such documentation are far more likely to be among these demographics: African Americans, immigrants, the poor, people with disabilities, and senior citizens. Academic study after study has shown this connection between demographics and ID possession.[16] A national survey by the Brennan Center found that Americans earning less than $35,000 were twice as likely to lack ID as Americans who earned more than that, and that African Americans are more than three times as likely as whites not to have ID. Indeed, the survey found that one-fourth of African Americans do not have a government-issued photo ID.[17]

Most of the states have policies in place by which they are obligated to provide free identification (including picture IDs) to the indigent who request it. However, the process by which one can claim such free identification is not simple, free, or quick. First, a person will be required to find his or her way to a department of motor vehicles, which may be many miles and even hours away and have limited hours.[18] Once there, he or she will need to present other evidence of identity, most commonly a birth certificate. If a person does not have a birth certificate handy, then he or she will have to navigate the system in order to obtain a birth certificate or other similar documentation. A voter might have to pay up to $45 for a birth certificate, $97 for a passport, or over $200 for naturalization papers (all of which can be used to gain a photo ID issued by the state).[19] Many identifying documents cannot be issued immediately, so potential voters must allow for processing and shipping, which may take from several weeks to an entire year. Finally, people who may have gotten married or for some other reason have a different name on the birth certificate and voter registration may face additional challenges. Looked at from this perspective, the requirement of photo ID in order to cast a ballot certainly places barriers between a person and the voting booth. Because some of those barriers are financial, the comparison to the poll tax is legitimate.

Proponents justify ID laws by saying they are necessary to prevent fraud. As has been repeated throughout, vote fraud that is addressed by voter identification laws is practically nonexistent. The chances of someone committing polling place fraud—the only kind of fraud an ID would address—are less than the chances of getting hit by lightning. Also of note, not one case of election fraud brought by the U.S. Department of Justice over the last several years was of the type that would have been addressed by voter identification. This was the case even in an environment in which assistant U.S. attorneys were under enormous pressure to pursue these types of cases.[20] It is especially telling that in every one of the federal cases regarding voter ID, the states defending such rules have not come up with one case of voter fraud that would have been prevented by the new voter identification laws. Justice John Paul Stevens essentially admitted this in the Supreme Court opinion in *Crawford v. Marion County [Indiana] Election Board*. He could find two examples of fraud to support the state's— and his—justification for the law: the Boss Tweed regime in New York in the nineteenth century and a single case of possible impersonation fraud in the Washington state gubernatorial election of 2004—neither case in Indiana, of course.[21]

Advocates now seem to have beaten a tactical retreat and are claiming we need to have voter ID laws because voters perceive this type of fraud to be a problem, and we cannot allow their confidence in the system to wane. The Supreme Court bought into this argument too, notwithstanding the fact that studies show that belief in the existence of fraud has zero impact on voting behavior.[22] Moreover, it is very convenient that the people making this new argument are the very ones that hit people over the head with the false idea that it *was* a problem, leading them to this misperception. Even as the rationale for the voter ID requirements change, the laws remain on the books in various states, upheld by the Supreme Court, and they effectively suppress the vote among classes of citizens that are deemed to be likely Democratic voters.

Indeed, voter identification laws, since 2000, have been the weapon of choice for Republicans seeking to manipulate the electorate in order to have a better chance of winning elections. The pace of passage of these laws increased exponentially in 2011 with newly elected Republican majorities and supermajorities in a number of state legislatures, and newly elected Republican governors.

Manipulated Yet Again in 2004

While many Americans regard the 2000 election as a fiasco, far fewer realize that, in terms of voting irregularities, the 2004 election may have been even worse. The purported margin of victory—with George W. Bush defeating John Kerry by three million votes—led many to believe that the process went relatively smoothly. However, repeatedly that year a number of partisan election officials and party leaders usurped the process and manipulated the Help America Vote Act in ways that disenfranchised voters.[23]

The many forms of nefarious manipulation of the 2004 election have been reported on extensively by journalists, lawyers, advocates, and academics.[24] Perhaps the most notable aspect of the 2004 election was the resurrection of the time-tested vote caging and challenge schemes on a national scale. Comparisons to Operation Eagle Eye are certainly apropos.

In Ohio, for example, prior to Election Day, GOP officials challenged more than 35,000 new registrants solely on the grounds that postcards mailed to them were returned as undeliverable. The challenge list targeted predominantly minority, urban, and Democratic districts.[25] Challenged registrants were required, just days before the election, to attend a hearing and to prove their eligibility to a judge. This practice went on in some areas until the courts put a stop to it on the eve of the election.[26]

In conjunction with this effective caging strategy, the Ohio GOP announced that it would hire people to go to the polls on Election Day to challenge the right to vote of preselected registrants. The plan set off a rush of last-minute lawsuits and conflicting rulings and appeals across various jurisdictions. The result of this chaotic litigation was great uncertainty about what would happen on Election Day. While the district court judges said that the challenges were unconstitutional—one saying that they were meant to intimidate black voters—a federal appeals court ultimately ruled the challenges lawful. It was estimated that "in Ohio, all of the precincts in about a dozen counties that contain 91 percent of the state's black population—including urban areas like Cleveland, Cincinnati,

Dayton, Toledo, and Akron" were targeted by Republican challengers.[27] In response to the appeals court ruling, the Ohio Democrats made plans to post their own people at the polling sites to challenge the challengers.

In other battleground states, Republican officials pursued similar plans—caging voters, filing challenges, and deploying challengers. In Florida, the GOP developed a database of thousands of voters it wanted to challenge on Election Day. And in Wisconsin, the state Republicans "used the U.S. Postal Service software to scrutinize the addresses of over 300,000 registered voters"—but only in heavily Democratic Milwaukee. The party challenged 5,600 Milwaukee voters. After the Milwaukee city attorney reviewed the list, he found that many of the alleged nonexistent addresses actually did exist.[28] While party officials claimed that this new level of scrutiny was needed to thwart possible fraud, at least one Republican strategist was more candid after Election Day, telling the *New York Times* that the challenges were "a big head fake," a way to distract Democrats from getting out the vote at the crucial last hours.[29]

According to elections experts, in 2004 upward of 500,000 individuals across the country had their eligibility "probed" via matching their registrations against databases, and 74,000 voters were challenged on Election Day.[30] Reports subsequently emerged that documented a much wider effort. Surveying forty-three pages of e-mails between Republic Party operatives, reporters found that they contained

> blueprints for a massive effort undertaken by RNC operatives in 2004, to challenge the eligibility of voters expected to support Democratic presidential candidate John Kerry in states such as Nevada, New Mexico, Florida, and Pennsylvania. One email, dated September 30, 2004, and sent to a dozen or so staffers on the Bush-Cheney campaign and the RNC, under the subject line "voter reg fraud strategy conference call," describes how campaign staffers planned to challenge the veracity of votes in a handful of battleground states in the event of a Democratic victory. Furthermore, the emails show the Bush-Cheney campaign and RNC staffers compiled voter-challenge lists that targeted probable Democratic voters in at least five states: New Mexico, Ohio, Florida, Nevada and Pennsylvania.[31]

As was true in 1964, when Operation Eagle Eye was in full force in Arizona, the challenging strategies were not ad hoc local efforts but national plans connected with the RNC.

Many tactics beyond caging and challenges were used during the 2004 election. There was widespread manipulation of registration requirements, from the ridiculous—such as the Ohio secretary of state's requirement that all registration forms be submitted on paper that was of certain paper stock, eliminating the possibility of printing the form off the Board of Elections website—to the sublime, such as Arizona's passage of a requirement that all voters provide proof of citizenship in order to register to vote. The Arizona law led to tens of thousands of Americans having their voter registration forms rejected, in many instances likely leading to disenfranchisement. Also rampant were deceptive practices that meant to misinform a voter rather than challenge him or her at the polls, and as is usually the case, the perpetrators were never discovered. Just as one example, in Milwaukee, a flyer purportedly from the "Milwaukee Black Voters League" was distributed in African American neighborhoods. It read, in part:

SOME WARNINGS FOR ELECTION TIME

IF YOU'VE ALREADY VOTED IN ANY ELECTION THIS YEAR YOU CAN'T VOTE IN THE PRESIDENTIAL ELECTION.

IF YOU [OR ANYBODY IN YOUR FAMILY] HAVE EVER BEEN FOUND GUILTY OF ANYTHING, EVEN A TRAFFIC VIOLATION, YOU CAN'T VOTE IN THE PRESIDENTIAL ELECTION.

... IF YOU VIOLATE ANY OF THESE LAWS YOU CAN GET TEN YEARS IN PRISON AND YOUR CHILDREN WILL BE TAKEN AWAY FROM YOU.

On numerous occasions poll workers demanded identification from voters where it was not required, most notably on Native American reservations in South Dakota. Before, during, and after Election Day 2004 there were also suspicious voting machine malfunctions. For example, in North Carolina a machine failed to record 4,500 votes, and in Ohio a computer error gave President Bush an additional 3,900 votes in a jurisdiction with 800 voters.[32] These sporadic but still prevalent irregularities and deceptive efforts, when considered in conjunction with coordinated RNC activity in battleground states, shows the general election of 2004 to have been riddled with problems, and thousands of voters were actively kept from casting a ballot.

In many states, what seemed like the positive HAVA reform of requiring a voter who did not appear on the voter registration list to be given a provisional ballot—designed to ensure no voter would go to the polls without casting a ballot—was completely twisted by partisan election officials. The flaw of HAVA was that it required voters be given a provisional ballot, but did not instruct states as to how or when these ballots were to be counted. As a result, many partisans turned them into "placebo ballots" by narrowly construing which provisional ballots should be counted and which should be just thrown away without any further involvement from the voter. Most notably, many elections officials mandated that if a provisional ballot was cast in the wrong precinct—even if it was in the right county—it should be simply tossed aside. Thousands of voters were disenfranchised this way.

Did HAVA Fail?

Acts of vote manipulation that took place widely in 2004 clearly violate the voter inclusion principle: they decreased the amount of participation without any reasonable democratic justification for doing so. Efforts at voter suppression are, we know, nothing new in American electoral politics. But what was new in the early 2000s was the growing realization of how the manipulation of the vote for partisan gain was built into the election system.

In the aftermath of the 2000 election and, particularly, the debacle in Florida, most people already realized what were the major problems with our voting system: flawed voting machines (especially prevalent in communities of color), unclear rules about recounts, inaccurate felon disenfranchisement lists and problems matching the names on those lists with registration rolls, people showing up to vote that did not appear on the registration list, and bad ballot design. HAVA was an attempt to address some of these problems, and, on balance, the legislation did make improvements. However, HAVA was itself liable to manipulation and partisan strategies, and Republican officials turned this effort at electoral reform against itself. So, the question arises: Was HAVA a failure?[33]

A principal flaw in HAVA was that it attempted to address the issue of voter fraud, and hence voter identification, as part of the overall package of reforms—an issue that was not a major concern during the election. As Charles Stewart has observed: "It seems indisputable . . . that voter fraud was the least systematically documented problem that HAVA eventually addressed. Alongside careful, if preliminary, attempts to quantify the number of lost votes due to machine malfunctions, polling place problems and registration snafus, the best evidence of a comparable-sized problem with voter fraud consisted of a few anecdotes, most of which dissolved as cases of *fraud* upon close examination."[34]

Even if the anecdotes of fraud were true, they were primarily about voter registration fraud, a separate problem. Stewart also makes the astute point that "in retrospect, it is striking that the provisions of HAVA that have ultimately caused the most controversy were prompted by issues that did not arise at all in Florida, and only were introduced in the congressional process through the side door."[35]

Perhaps as a result of the political process through which the bill was written, HAVA failed to provide sufficient clarity in certain of its provisions that were meant to address other concerns. For example, by failing to require explicitly that provisional ballots cast within a county be counted for those races in which the voter was eligible to vote, HAVA did voters a disservice. Election officials who wished to manipulate the vote count installed rules that disenfranchised eligible voters who cast provisional ballots.

Another striking failure of HAVA is that the legislation completely ignored the issue of felon disenfranchisement. This was an enormous issue in Florida and during the recount. The list of felons who were barred from voting was fatally flawed, and the highly restrictive rules in Florida around regaining one's voting rights after committing a felony and serving one's time became a major focus of attention. Yet language on felon disenfranchisement appears nowhere in the law. The law also makes no prescriptions for ballot design, even though the "butterfly ballot" was such a point of controversy in the Florida election. It further failed to address the very serious issue of partisan election officials running the system. In the case of Florida in 2000, legal authority regarding the election rested with the Republican secretary of state of Florida, Katherine Harris. In this particular case, she made a series of controversial decisions throughout the process. But the larger point is that it is an invitation to election abuse to have a partisan officer overseeing what should be a fair election. The incentives and opportunities to manipulate the vote are too numerous. The opportunities on the part of party operatives to tamper with the vote are only multiplied by the fact that, in the decentralized American system, tremendous discretion over how to conduct an election is left to the states and localities. HAVA did little to better organize this patchwork and often unequal system of elections.

HAVA has not been a complete failure, however. Among the positive reforms and outcomes were getting rid of punch-card ballot machines and requiring machines that notify voters of overvotes—both changes that led to fewer spoiled ballots in subsequent elections; requiring that voting machines be accessible to persons with disabilities; requiring that voters not found on the registration list be given a provisional ballot; requiring a statewide voter registration database, which makes the system more accurate and effective when used and managed properly by election officials; funding for voter education and poll-worker training; and, perhaps most important, for the first time, providing federal funding for elections. While there have been some other positive developments in our voting system since the enactment of HAVA—including making voter registration easier, especially through same-day registration, and improvements in the system for military and overseas voters—the prevailing theme has not been one of progress. Rather than heralding an era of real reform to our voting system, the 2000 election and the manipulation of HAVA and other procedures since then have ushered in another era of voter disenfranchisement. It did not have to be so, and if the voter inclusion principle had been applied, it would not have been so. But the dictates of partisan manipulation of voting reform for political purposes had, in many instances, won out over democracy again.

7

A Slight Upswing

The 2008 presidential election was a bit of a reprieve from the dramatic and widespread election manipulation that took place in 2000 and 2004. Slightly improved turnout across the whole voting population, and much increased turnout among traditionally disenfranchised voters, gave advocates of voter inclusion, in the parlance of the year, hope.

Most notable was the experience of North Carolina. For the first time in the state's electoral history, North Carolina implemented a combination of in-person early voting and the ability to register and vote at the polling place during this early voting period. With the outreach the Obama campaign and civic organizations to make best use of these new tools, the achievement was phenomenal. Indeed, North Carolina had the largest increase in voter turnout in the country. Some 236,700 people became new voters through same-day registration, and 39 percent of those were African American. More than 5 percent of the 4.2 million North Carolina voters in the 2008 election registered when they went to vote. Some 691,000 African Americans voted during the early voting period—51 percent of the

1.32 million black registered voters in North Carolina.[1] This provides us with an example of how, under the principle of voter inclusion, same-day registration and, to a somewhat lesser extent, early in-person voting provide a mechanism for using an election rule to increase turnout for one's side in an entirely legitimate way.

The prevailing tone of the 2008 election season, particularly on the part of the Democratic Party and the campaign of Barack Obama, was one of expansion, inclusion, and engagement. Certainly, partisanship motivated the Democrats who were active in get-out-the-vote campaigns, and newly registered young and African American voters were, on balance, more likely to support Obama than John McCain, the Republican candidate. However, partisanship was employed to expand the registered electorate and not limit it or suppress it—and the playing field was open to both parties to take maximum advantage of reforms such as same-day registration to increase support, as the Obama campaign did.

2008 Overall

There was no catastrophic meltdown in the election, but there was plenty of attempted partisan gamesmanship of the system. The fact that problems on Election Day were not as pervasive as they might have been can be attributed to experience gained by voting rights advocates, election administrators and lawyers, and the courts over eight contentious electoral years in which they all engaged in microscopic but necessary scrutiny of the registration and voting process. Many of the fights over registration and ballots that had previously played out after the election were waged well before the polls opened. More often than not, and in contrast from the previous two presidential election cycles, litigation resulted in court opinions that supported the rights of voters. Much of this litigation regarded partisan wrangling over the registration process. Many organizations spent the months (and even years) prior to the election working with election administrators and elected officials to iron out the problems ahead of time. Organizations and election administrators also took substantial initiatives to educate voters and to recruit and train poll workers. For their part, voting rights groups strived to ensure that elections officials had a proper understanding and interpretation of election laws and were prepared to follow them and implement them in a uniform, nondiscriminatory fashion. In many respects, the increased scrutiny, funding, and education created an environment that was conducive to full democratic participation.

Despite these developments, thousands and thousands of voters faced unacceptable and unnecessary barriers to voting at the polling booth in 2008. Some issues arose because of a lack of preparedness, but some seemed due to attempts by the Republican Party to use election laws for partisan advantage by suppressing the vote.

Allegations were made against Democrats as well in 2008, particularly during the primaries. For example, a group loosely tied to Hillary Clinton's campaign, Women's Voices Women's Vote, was accused of making robo-calls to residents in predominantly African American communities in North Carolina telling them a voter registration packet was on the way—after the registration deadline had passed and many of these voters had already registered. It made it seem as if they might not be registered.[2] The Clinton campaign also seemingly tried to deter students who attended college in Iowa from participating in the caucuses if they were from out of state, by saying the caucuses were "a process for Iowans" and that the Iowa primary "needs to be all about Iowa and people who live here, people who pay taxes here."[3] Obama's popularity with younger people and his campaign's focus on getting students to participate in Iowa was well known. During the general election, Democratic secretary of state Jennifer Brunner was also accused by Republicans of acting in a partisan manner when she failed to report details of voters whose information did not match that in other government databases, and indeed sued her for her refusal to do so. Claiming she was trying to allow ineligible voters to vote, they wanted the names of those who had non-matches so that they could challenge their eligibility. Although there was unfortunate lack of clarity by the secretary about what the process would be that year, the reality is that rejecting citizens for non-matches would have actually disenfranchised many legitimate voters and not likely resulted in ineligible voters voting, as will be described in depth below. Republicans also tried to tie the Obama campaign and the Democratic Party to the controversy surrounding voter registration by the community organizing group ACORN, in which it was accused of submitting false registration forms. However, no connection was ever demonstrated, and many of the allegations against the group proved overblown.

Overall, however, as has been the case over the last five decades, it was Republicans who predominantly engaged in vote suppression tactics through manipulation of the laws and procedures.

Registration Issues

The rules and procedures for voter registration were the cause of the most controversy in 2008. Indeed, in the wake of HAVA, by 2008 registration had become the battleground of partisan contention. Caging and challenges, the weapons of partisan choice from the 1960s until 2000, were less prevalent. In cases where caging and challenging were attempted in 2008, the vigilance of voting rights groups and the effective use of litigation foiled efforts at suppression. As a case in point, early on in the fall election season it was reported that Republican officials were planning on using lists of people whose homes had been foreclosed as a basis for mounting challenges to their right to vote at the polls. In Michigan, this led to the Democratic Party suing for an injunction prohibiting challenges on the basis of being in foreclosure.[4] The Republic National Committee ultimately was forced to enter into a joint statement that bound both parties not to challenge voters solely on the basis that a voter's home was in foreclosure.[5] In Ohio and other states, election administrators sent out directives and statements that foreclosure was not a legitimate basis for a challenge.[6] Prior to the election, the Montana Republican Party challenged the eligibility of 6,000 registered voters in six counties—all Democratic strongholds. A lawsuit by the state Democratic Party forced the Republicans to shut the operation down.

When it came to using voter registration rolls for partisan advantage, however, the story was a bit different. In 2008, numerous voters registered to vote but were not on the registration lists when they came to vote, and they had to cast provisional ballots,[7] which, given the irregular handling of such ballots in various jurisdictions, were not always counted. Across the country in the weeks leading up to the election, there were overblown charges against ACORN, a group that registers thousands of people in poor and minority communities, and other voter registration organizations regarding voter registration fraud. This led to Republican demands for and then litigation seeking the names and other information of all voters who had been registered by ACORN, as was the case in Pennsylvania, seemingly so they could be investigated and/or challenged.[8]

The root of the problem was the lack of clarity in the Help America Vote Act around the actual details of implementing the new registration rules. HAVA required states to create statewide voter registration databases that would allow for registration rolls to be matched with information from a state's Department of Motor Vehicles or the federal Social Security Administration. The legislation did not, however, explain what was to be done with the resulting information regarding quality of the match. Republicans at the state level saw an opening to manipulate the new rule for partisan advantage. They demanded in the weeks before the election that the strictest matching standards possible be used for a voter to remain on the rolls, which would have excluded a great many voters from the registration list. In some instances, Republican secretaries of state also illegally purged existing voters from the rolls in violation of the National Voter Registration Act's prohibition on such removal within ninety days of an election except under limited circumstances.[9] This was not new: the issue of overly broad purging of the registration rolls has come up throughout the second half of the twentieth century.

In 2008, some of the biggest controversies around voter registration rules took place in Florida, Georgia, Ohio, and Colorado.

Florida

Florida, with its "exact match" or so-called "no match no vote" rule, was again the focal point of the electoral debate. Republican secretary of state Kurt Browning, in the month before the registration deadline, mandated that if the state could not validate the voter's data by comparing it with other statewide databases or the database the Social Security Administration maintains, the registration would be regarded as a "non-match." Once declared a non-match, after further perfunctory review the voter's registration could be rejected. The standard put forward by Browning was an exact match between data. Compounding the matter, the secretary of state insisted that a non-match could not be rectified by a voter coming in with supporting identification when he or she voted. Instead, the voter had to take the extra steps of presenting documentation prior to the election or casting a provisional ballot and returning with identification after the election. But supporting evidence that would clarify identity and allow a person to vote a regular ballot on Election Day was not to be allowed, although that process would have been much easier for voters to comply with.

There are many reasons such data might not match—reasons that say nothing about the voter's eligibility or identity. Beginning with simple typographical errors and including names with unusual spellings, surnames with hyphens, and the inclusion or exclusion of middle names and initials—the opportunities for inexact matches across databases are numerous. This is particularly likely for Latino voters (who may or may not use their mother's maiden name). Errors are more likely to be made with regard to voters with hard-to-spell or unusual names, often immigrants and African Americans. Relying on the Social Security Administration database for verification is particularly problematic. SSA's database has been found to have up to a 29 percent error rate when used for voter verification.[10] Browning's rigorous enforcement of the nonmatch rule led to over 22,000 voters having their voter registration initially blocked in the state. By Election Day, some 10,000 of these voters had yet to take the extra (and unnecessary) step of resubmitting an ID. As a result, their ability to vote was in jeopardy. Rejected voters statewide were disproportionately minorities. Slightly more than 27 percent were listed as Hispanic, and 26.8 percent of those rejected were black. Rejected registered voters were four times as likely to be Democrats as Republicans.[11]

On Election Day in Florida, the exclusionary impacts of the secretary's actions were ameliorated because of work that had gone on prior to the election. The nonpartisan organization Common Cause had been able to obtain lists of voters whose registrations were affected and personally contact many of them in order to inform them of the need to bring supporting identifying material to the municipal elections office prior to the election. Moreover, the county registrars had somewhat of a mass rebellion against the policy when many of them opted to allow voters to solve the problem with supporting identification when they arrived at the polls.[12] At least during early voting, some country registrars allowed registered voters on the non-match list to prove their identities and cast a ballot.[13]

Georgia

In 2008, the secretary of state of Georgia, Karen Handel, started instituting a "citizenship check" or verification of not only new registration forms but also of voters already on the registration rolls. The procedures flagged certain voters as noncitizens based on records from the Georgia Department of Driver Services (DDS). The records, however, contained out-of-date citizenship information because DDS fails to update them to reflect the thousands of Georgia residents who become U.S. citizens each year. Since the errors were made due to out-of-date records on citizenship, it was clear that this practice was going to impact naturalized Americans more than others. Those who were flagged were denied the right to vote unless they presented written evidence of citizenship.[14]

In October 2008, a coalition of voting rights groups filed a lawsuit challenging the voting procedures after a number of U.S. citizens had been incorrectly flagged as noncitizens.[15] A federal court ruled before the election that mismatched voters who had not proved their citizenship to a local board of elections prior to Election Day had to be allowed to cast a challenged ballot, which meant it wouldn't automatically be counted. The voters had to be informed of the steps they had to take in order to have their ballots counted under state law, the ruling said. It was expected that voters would have to attend a hearing in which they would have to prove their citizenship after Election Day. After the election the Department of Justice interposed objections to the new law under the department's Section 5 authority to pre-clear or not clear changes in voting laws in certain covered states if the change would negatively impact minority voters. The department found that the Georgia secretary of state was seeking to implement a "flawed system [which] frequently subjects a disproportionate number of African American, Asian, and/or Hispanic voters to additional, and more importantly, erroneous burdens on the right to register to vote. These burdens are real, are substantial and are retrogressive for minority voters."[16] Not surprisingly, many voters were disenfranchised as a result of this exclusionary move. According to the *Atlanta Constitution Journal*, about 5,000 had their eligibility contested. In Gwinnett County alone, 300 people used the paper "challenge" ballot because the state questioned their citizenship status. Of those, 192 returned to the county elections office to bring documents proving they were citizens; 108 voters did not return.

In Cobb County, 227 people cast challenge ballots on Election Day. Of those, 161 returned to furnish their documents.[17] Georgia election administrators themselves said the problem was not that any of these voters were actually not citizens. In fact, according to DeKalb's election administrator,

> When the Georgia secretary of state gave DeKalb an updated list of voters who were not thought to be citizens last fall, there were more than 700 names. Many of those, though, were flagged incorrectly, from something as simple as transposed numbers on their driver's licenses or because they had common names. . . . Some of those red-flagged had even been registered for 25 years and were able to bring in their old voter ID cards, which showed their place of birth. None of the Election Day voters in DeKalb whose ballots were challenged tried to pass muster with false documents, which would have indicated an attempt at fraud. Instead, no one showed up Friday afternoon at the DeKalb election office training room to bring the right documents. The 39 bright pink envelopes, showing they were challenged, will end up being tossed.[18]

As one columnist pointed out, "the fact that so many *did* provide documentation only served to bolster the contention of voting-rights groups that the process for flagging voters had been badly flawed. That claim was further strengthened by the fact that the system now seems to have flagged not only naturalized citizens like [the plaintiff in the lawsuit], but also U.S. born voters whose citizenship has never been in question,"[19] demonstrating that an evident desire to seem tough on supposed noncitizen voting ended up ensnaring voters of all kinds in a scheme that might have disenfranchised American voters of all political persuasions.

After extensive litigation and a minor change to the pool of people who would be subjected to the citizenship check, in late 2010 the Department of Justice very suddenly approved the practice, apparently making the private litigation filed before the election "moot."[20] This meant that Georgia could go forward with a program the department had previously found resulted in wrongful burdens on minority voters.

Ohio

After the 2004 election, when Ohio had been the focal point of electoral controversy, strides had been made in state election law under the leadership of a new secretary of state to avoid major problems. And while problems were often avoided, there were certainly unjust efforts to suppress the vote. In October 2008, for instance, the Republican Party filed a lawsuit seeking to force the secretary to verify with the Social Security Administration database and the DMV the voter registration information of everyone who had registered since January 1, flag non-matches, and require marked voters to vote by provisional ballot. Of the 665,000 people who had registered since January 1, over 200,000 had some discrepancy between their registration forms and information on other databases. As can be expected, most of these discrepancies had nothing to do with the eligibility of the voter to cast a ballot. The case moved through the appellate courts until it came to the U.S. Supreme Court, which decided against the GOP suit, though not on the merits of the case but rather on the basis of standing.[21]

Colorado

There were two registration problems in Colorado in 2008. First, the Republican secretary of state, Michael Coffman, insisted upon an extremely narrow registration rule that disqualified voter registration applications if the applicant failed to check an irrelevant box on the Colorado registration form. Voters who provided their Social Security number rather than their driver's license had to check a box that stated, "I do not have a Colorado driver's license or Department of Revenue Identification Number." Thousands of voters had their registration blocked for failure to check that single box. This of course had the potential to disproportionately impact voters without driver's licenses, who also tended to be disproportionately urban, of color, and lower income.

In addition, voting rights groups sued the secretary of state for purging thousands of voters from the registration rolls in clear violation of the National Voter Registration Act's restrictions on systematic purging of registration rolls within ninety days of an election. The secretary's claim was that the purged voters were ineligible or duplicates, but that did not permit him to ignore the NVRA's prohibition on voter purging right before an election, a protection against potential abuse of the system in the heat of campaigns. A federal court forced the secretary to agree to allow the voters he had improperly purged to vote by a provisional ballot that would be presumed by election offices to be legitimate unless proven otherwise.

In a remarkable move, even after the court's order, the secretary of state resumed purging voters from the books, in violation of the law. The parties went back to court, leading the judge, in an emergency hearing just days before the general election, to angrily order Coffman to stop doing so.[22]

Tinkering with voter registration rules to suppress voting is of course nothing new. That the means for doing so were more subtle than the nineteenth-century methods (such as requiring only urban voters to register) does not mean voter exclusion did not nonetheless occur.

The voter inclusion analysis is not as straightforward in some of these cases. Accurate voter registration lists are important for a fair election. However, the means of accomplishing this, for example through an "exact match," were not effective for achieving this end and served to throw eligible citizens off the rolls unjustly more than anything. That the tactics tended to exclude voters of color disproportionately made them all the more suspect. Maintaining the accuracy of the voter registration list while ensuring voter inclusion can be achieved by following existing laws such as the NVRA, using methods that actually work by including some flexibility in the data comparison process, as many successful states do, and ensuring the maximum possible amounts of transparency and notice to voters. This type of registration list maintenance regime would be in accordance with the voter inclusion framework.

Long Lines

While Americans were proud of the historic turnout in some places and among certain groups on Election Day, the amount of time some citizens had to wait in order to vote was not just an unfortunate consequence of increased voter participation.[23] The delay at many polling places could have denied many voters their right to cast a ballot. While in many precincts voting took only a matter of minutes, in Detroit and St. Louis some voters had to wait in line for five hours.[24] In the St. Louis area the longest wait was six hours. While the commitment of so many to wait no matter how long it took was inspiring, some voters inevitably could not wait that long—they worked for hourly wages, could not get that much time off, or had child care responsibilities. And once again the distribution of resources, in terms of staffing and voting machines, was random at best and possibly discriminatory at worst. This problem was widely predicted by voting rights advocates, who warned that states did not have enough voting machines for the expected turnout and had no plans in place for ensuring that the machines available were allocated strategically and fairly. Some advocates came to refer to this situation as a "time tax," suggesting a connection to poll taxes once used to block the poor and working class from the ballot.

After the election, a team of researchers published a report on the performance of the election. They found that African American respondents to their survey reported waiting on long lines far more often than whites or Hispanics. Some 27 percent of African Americans reported long waits, compared with 11 percent of whites and 13 percent of Hispanics.[25] The report found that 20 percent of African Americans waited more than half an hour to vote, compared with 14 percent of whites and 15 percent of Hispanics.[26] This disparity in the efficiency of polling stations in predominantly black and white neighborhoods had been found in 2004 as well. An assessment by academics of voting in Ohio, done for the Democratic National Committee, found that "scarcity of voting machines caused long lines that deterred many people from voting. Three percent of voters who went to the polls left their polling places and did not return due to the long lines. . . . Statewide, African American voters reported waiting an average of 52 minutes before voting while white voters reported waiting an average of 18 minutes. Overall, 20 percent of white Ohio voters reported waiting more than twenty minutes, while 44 percent of African American voters reported doing so."[27] So the problem was hardly new. But the record turnout of voters in 2008, particularly African Americans, brought this disparity into high relief.

Were long lines simply the result of inadequate numbers of machines? Was any of this by design of partisan election administrators, given the data on the disparity in length of lines in majority African American as compared with majority white voting districts? The data are insufficient to say. But officials knew going into the election that there was going to be much higher turnout in certain states than in the past, yet in many places, especially swing states where turnout would be highest, there were simply not enough voting machines provided to handle the capacity.

An indication that Republicans may see some advantage in long lines, at least in retrospect, is the more recent attempts by Republican legislators to reduce early voting in several states. As the *New York Times* observed, "Early voting, which enables people to skip long lines . . . has been increasingly popular over the last 15 years. It skyrocketed to a third of the vote in 2008, rising particularly in the South. And that, of course, is why Republican lawmakers in the South are trying desperately to cut it back. . . . Republican lawmakers . . . have taken a good look at voting patterns, realized that early voting might have played a role in Mr. Obama's 2008 victory, and now want to reduce that possibility in 2012."[28]

Students

In the 2008 primaries the number of voters under thirty nearly doubled from the comparable election of 2000, to 6.5 million. Young people, polling indicated, were also overwhelmingly in favor of Democrats and Barak Obama in particular. In October a *USA Today* / MTV / Gallup Poll of registered voters eighteen to twenty-nine years old showed Democrat Obama leading Republican John McCain by 61 percent to 32 percent, "the most lopsided contest within an age group in any presidential election in modern times."[29] While the expected historic turnout by young people was tremendously exciting, it also meant that youth, and more particularly students, who are easily identifiable, also became a target for vote suppression.

Students had been blocked from voting many times before. Suppressing the student vote has been most common in jurisdictions where the college campus population was more liberal than the surrounding community. As in the past, in 2008 partisan election administrators themselves were the ones most often making registration and voting difficult for students, usually in the guise of questioning students' right to register and vote from the school they attend. Under a 1979 Supreme Court ruling, students do have the right to register and vote from their campus address, and any residency requirements must be applied to students in the same manner as all other citizens.[30]

Allowing students to vote in the community they currently call home is, under the voter inclusion principle, something those who are concerned with advancing our democracy should consider legitimate and encourage, and is a voting rule that either party can seek to take advantage of by mobilizing the youth vote.

It is well established that young people vote at far lower rates than any other age population. Despite the excitement at the time, according to the U.S. Census, only 58.5 percent of would-be eligible voters age eighteen to twenty-four and 66.4 percent age twenty-five to thirty-four were registered to vote in 2008, the lowest rates of registration among all age groups.[31] The reasons for this may be multifaceted, but it is clearly in the common good to address this problem and have more of our younger citizens engaged and participating, and having their interests heeded and respected by those in power. It is important not just for the election at hand, but for the future. Studies have shown that if a habit of voting is established early on, it tends to extend throughout a lifetime.[32] Attempts to discourage youth voting are, on the other hand, not legitimate. There is no evidence that allowing students to vote from their schools has created problems, and it is entirely within the rights of students to feel that the community they are invested in is the one they are living in. They live there for several years, pay taxes, and contribute to the economy and, in many cases, the civic life of the community.

Virginia, for instance, has a long history of erecting barriers to student voting and in 2008 was the scene of the most egregious examples of attempts to suppress the student vote. Early in the fall, the registrar in Montgomery, Virginia, home of Virginia Tech University, warned students that if they registered to vote there that would jeopardize their scholarships, financial aid, car and health insurance, and status as a dependent on their parents' taxes.[33] These assertions were all false. Several students withdrew their registration applications as a result, however, and while no claims were made regarding partisan motivations, votes were suppressed. Another local registrar, in Radford, Virginia, home to Radford University, simply automatically denied, in violation of the law, all registration applications from students who listed a dormitory as their address.[34] There was a similar situation in El Paso County, Colorado. A county clerk in Colorado Springs sent a letter to students at Colorado College, a relatively progressive bastion in an otherwise conservative jurisdiction, telling them that they could not vote at school if their parents claimed them as dependents on their federal tax returns.[35] This claim was also completely untrue.

Students were also targeted by deceptive practices. A flyer was disseminated on the campus of Drexel University in Philadelphia warning that undercover officers would be waiting at the polls, looking to arrest voters

with outstanding warrants or parking violations.[36] On Election Day someone managed to hack into the computer system at George Mason University in Virginia and send out an e-mail to the entire student body that
appeared to be from the school's provost telling them that Election Day
had been moved to Wednesday, November 5.[37] In all these cases, voting
rights organizations promptly intervened and ensured that students were
not denied the right to register and not deceived. This preelection work
included legal letters and exposing the problem through the media.

Latinos Grow as a Target

Since 2000, voter turnout among Latinos has been steadily rising, and
while Latinos have for some time been more likely to vote for Democrats,
the Obama campaign led some to observe that Latinos might be in the process of becoming a bulwark of the Democratic electorate. However, the
electoral pattern since the middle of the 1990s has been complex. In 1996,
Bill Clinton garnered 77.7 percent of the Latino vote. George W. Bush had
been relatively popular among Latinos in his home state of Texas, and Latinos were somewhat more supportive of his candidacy than they were of
other Republican candidates. In 2004, John Kerry was able to capture only
59.5 percent of the Latino vote, an 18.2 percentage-point swing in only
eight years. The Obama campaign swung that shift back fairly dramatically. About one in eleven Latinos (8.9 percent) changed their votes—68.4
percent of Hispanics voted for Barack Obama.[38] The combination of increased turnout and voting for Democrats has, in turn, made Latinos increasingly a focus for vote suppression schemes. However, the fact that the
political allegiances of Latino voters are very much in flux suggests that
these strategies, in addition to being unlawful and unjust, are politically
risky.

The charge that noncitizens are illegally voting has been made in many
elections across the history of the United States. As the Latino community
has grown in the United States in the last decade and increasingly flexed its
political muscle, these charges have escalated dramatically, as has use of political rhetoric attacking immigrants and specifically Latinos for political
gain. These overheated allegations are then used to justify the enactment
of disenfranchising policies that deter Latinos from going to the polls.

The targeting of Latino voters escalated in the 2010 midterm elections, as the claims about noncitizen voting became even more exaggerated and malicious, and outside groups and candidates used anti-immigrant rhetoric for political gain. This rhetoric was not only used to curry favor with some white voters, but also presumably was meant to add to an already oppressive climate of fear for Latinos that might deter them from participating. Candidates, particularly in Nevada and Louisiana, aired ugly anti-immigrant campaign ads that portrayed Latinos as menacing predators. The Republican group Latinos for Reform ran an ad in Nevada saying "Don't vote this November. This is the only way to send them a clear message. You can no longer take us for granted." This advertising spot was supposed to run in several more states before the controversy around it forced the group to pull it off the air.[39] Jesse Kelly, a Republican candidate for the U.S. House from Arizona, cited "rumors" to wrongfully accuse opponents of busing Mexicans over the border to vote.[40] Also in Arizona, an anti-immigrant group sent an e-mail to over one million members that repeatedly said, "Stop Illegals from Stealing the Election!" It said thousands of illegal immigrants were working to turn out voters who were sympathetic to them. "Our grassroots army of VOTER FRAUD PREVENTION VOLUNTEERS will stand vigilant across the nation. We will be the first and strongest line of defense to ensure that only legal citizens vote on November 2nd, but to do this, we need your help today!"[41]

When it was announced that the Department of Justice would be sending people to watch the elections in Arizona, William Gheen, executive director of Americans for Legal Immigration, said "They're sending them out because the Obama administration is doing everything it can to make sure as many illegal aliens [as possible] vote in 2010."[42] The truth is that voting by noncitizens is exceedingly rare, and where it does take place it is usually because the individual has been advised incorrectly by a poorly informed voter registration drive worker that he or she can vote.[43]

This fearmongering and launching of unfounded charges backfired on Republicans in 2010. The Latino share of the electorate rose in comparison to 2006 and 2008, especially in places where the anti-immigrant rhetoric was the worst, such as Nevada, Colorado, and Arizona. In many midterm elections, for state and national office in these states, Latino votes made the margin of difference.[44]

Nonetheless, we can expect vote suppression tactics and claims of noncitizen voting to compel citizen activists to challenge and harass Latinos at the polls, and to promote more laws requiring voter identification at the polls and documentary proof of citizenship in order to vote.[45] While these measures ostensibly seek to secure the vote for citizens, the effect will be that naturalized and Latino voters will be discouraged and in some cases blocked from registering and going to the polls. Naturalized citizens are less likely to have driver's licenses and other forms of identifying documentation.[46] Latinos are 6 percent less likely than whites to have a driver's license or other government-issued photo ID. Latinos as a group are more likely to be poor and lack the resources necessary to obtain identification if they do not already have it.[47]

2008 and Beyond

Shifting demographics and the imperfect reforms instituted by HAVA mean that the principle of voter inclusion will continue to be tested in new ways and on various fronts. The increasing political power of the Latino population has effectively opened up a new front of vote suppression in electoral contests. As we have seen before, partisanship and prejudice often travel together. However, the key thing from the standpoint of election strategy is whether a demographic is identifiable and leans toward one party. After Obama's victory in 2008, although a few Republicans argue the party should continue courting the Latino vote, some Republican operatives are more likely to see Latino votes as ones to suppress and not ones to encourage.

Not only are the use of election laws and policies to deter Latino voting contrary to the voter inclusion principle, but so surely are political rhetoric and imagery designed to make certain voters reluctant to participate because they may confront hostility at the polls or unfounded allegations and challenges. Indeed, as we saw in 2010, the political climate has become more viciously anti-immigrant and anti-Latino. We can thus expect that securing Latino participation in elections will be a challenge to the voter inclusion principle in the years to come.

More broadly, the electoral system remains liable to manipulation. The election results of 2008 were not close, and the fights over the rules governing the voting were less intense, less widespread, and quickly forgotten by most. This raises the danger of complacency on the part of American voters who would like to think that the irregularities and injustices of 2000 and 2004 are now just part of history. This complacency presents some degree of risk for the future, given that the interpretations of the registration laws, especially under the Help America Vote Act, remain up for grabs and could easily continue to be manipulated to disenfranchise eligible voters, as they were in 2008. Unacceptably long lines—and a paucity of any requirements regarding allocation of voting machines—persist and continue to threaten to disproportionately affect certain groups of voters more than others. Complaints about the election process were muted in the afterglow of a historic election outcome, but the rules were nonetheless used for partisan purposes once again.

8

Effects on Election Outcomes

All this evidence of partisan manipulation of election law for the purpose of winning elections raises the question: Did the manipulation work? Did candidates win elections as a result of the partisan disenfranchisement of some segment of the electorate? In many instances it is difficult if not impossible to say. So many variables are at play in the electoral process. It is never clear how many people do not vote as a result of a barrier. And if failure to vote was due to a barrier, it is not easy to determine which barrier it was. Moreover, we never know how many voters, deterred by the restrictions in place, never even bother to try to vote at all. And even if we could obtain such information, we could not know with absolute certainty how they would have voted.

Nonetheless, some educated assessments can and have been made. First, the disenfranchising laws enacted in the late nineteenth century had a direct effect on the fates of the Republican and Democratic parties and their candidates. The widespread use of poll taxes, literacy tests, and outright intimidation at the polls skewed voting results by means of the exclusion of African Americans from the ballot in the South and ethnic immigrants in the North. In contemporary times, the one unjust legal barrier that has demonstrably impacted elections is the persistence of laws that disenfranchise persons with felony convictions. While there is some evidence that more modern tactics such as caging and voter identification laws have had an impact on election outcomes in recent contests, there is insufficient information to come to any definite conclusions on those. Looking at the historical variation in the effect of vote suppression underlines how the American voting system has, overall, become more open, fair, and secure. Compared with a century ago, elections are much cleaner and the voting population more numerous as a percentage of the overall population. Across this process, however, abuses have persisted.

Election outcomes are, of course, only one and, I would argue, not the most important measure of the damaging effects of vote manipulation and suppression. When an eligible voter is turned away or his or her vote is discounted, that individual's engagement in the system and exercise of a fundamental right is lost. Disaffection and reluctance to participate in the future are possible results of vote suppression, no matter the consequence for a given election. The voter inclusion principle is founded on our core democratic intuitions about government being representative of the people and each person having the right to be represented. Every effort at vote suppression harms democracy, and it harms democratic citizenship.

Early Disenfranchisement Schemes

Disenfranchisement laws enacted in the late 1800s and early 1900s had a direct impact on election outcomes. J. Morgan Kousser's seminal study on the issue of the impact of these laws on African American participation and on partisan outcomes demonstrates the difference such laws made.[1] He makes these assessments based on the historically sound assumption that most African Americans would have voted Republican in the South had they been allowed to vote. Moreover, we can observe the extraordinary transformation in the electorate that took place after most of the so-called Jim Crow laws were eliminated by the passage of the Voting Rights Act of 1965 to extrapolate the impact the previous disenfranchisement had on the process. The growth of African American electoral participation and its impact, then, are indicators of the negative effect of restrictive Jim Crow laws.

Overall, the effect of the passage of disenfranchising laws meant to exclude African American—that is, Republican—votes near the end of the nineteenth century had the effect of keeping black voter registration and voting astoundingly low throughout the South. For example, in Alabama only 1.3 percent of blacks were registered. In Louisiana, it was 1.1 percent. In South Carolina, 3.8 percent of black Americans were registered to vote.[2] This was accomplished in large part through the introduction of the secret ballot, poll taxes, various types of literacy tests, and stringent registration procedures.

Although the secret ballot is today a mainstay of our democratic process, secret-ballot laws were enacted primarily in order to prevent the illiterate and uneducated—mostly poor whites and blacks—from voting, in order to maintain partisan advantage. The states of Arkansas, Alabama, and Louisiana were all without poll taxes or registration laws, but in the 1890s they enacted secret-ballot laws. After these laws were passed, black voter turnout in Alabama fell only 15 percent, but in Arkansas it fell from 71 percent to 38 percent between 1890 and 1892. In Louisiana the turnout of black voters plummeted from 69 percent in the April 1896 gubernatorial election to 24 percent in the November presidential election, when one would expect voter turnout to rise. White voter turnout also declined, but only by 8–12 points.[3] It was clear at the time to all involved that a primary purpose behind this was to maintain Democratic dominance in these states.

One piece of persuasive evidence of the dramatic impact of poll tax laws on black voter participation is the difference between turnout in Georgia, a state with a poll tax, and Florida, a state without a poll tax measure, during the 1880s. In the presidential election of 1880, black turnout in Georgia was 39 percent; in Florida it was 88 percent; in 1884 it was 38 percent in Georgia and 86 percent in Florida; and in 1888, black voter turnout was 19 percent in Georgia and 64 percent in Florida.[4] It is clear that the laws passed during this era had the impact Democrats desired. Given the dramatic numbers involved, it is impossible to imagine that the outcomes of elections would not have been different if African Americans, and to some extent poor whites, had been able to vote.

Another device used at the turn of the century but not previously discussed here is the eight-box law. This procedure required voters to deposit ballots in eight separate boxes, depending on the contested office; the hitch was that voters would need to be able to read the labels on the different boxes to vote correctly. A ballot in the wrong box was disqualified.[5] The eight-box law, as a *New York Times* article from 1895 explained, "practically operates as an educational qualification, and as a result, wipes out effectually the ignorant negro majority."[6] The scheme worked. In South Carolina, the eight-box law cut the Republican vote by two-thirds, and it cut the black vote and overall turnout by half.[7]

The cumulative impact of these discriminatory disenfranchisement laws on the electorate can be seen starkly in two states: Florida and Tennessee. Florida was not among the early states to adopt the disenfranchising laws that were being enacted throughout the South. But when it started to become solidly Democratic in the 1890s the state adopted such measures as registration, the poll tax, the eight-box law, and the secret ballot, and effectively disabled the opposition. As Kousser pointed out, "Three of every four adult males voted in 1888, before the major amendments in the Sunshine State's electoral statutes; in the next statewide contest four years later, only one-third voted. In the 1888 presidential race the Democratic ticket prevailed by a 3–2 margin; in 1892 by better than 5–1."[8] Turnout in Florida in 1890 plunged below 50 percent for the first time in twenty years,[9] and the disenfranchisement measures virtually eliminated the Republican Party.[10]

Like their fellows in Florida, Tennessee Democrats in the 1880s began passing election laws meant to perpetuate their dominance. First, they required voters in towns or districts that cast five hundred or more votes in the 1888 election to register at least twenty days before the election. They also passed a secret-ballot law. The Democratic newspaper in the state did not hide the intent behind the secret-ballot law: As Kousser reports, " 'The Democratic Party represents nine-tenths of the intelligence and property of the state and a measure for its protection is therefore for the best interests of the state. Certainly the [secret-ballot law] is for the benefit of the Democratic Party.' "[11]

After expressions of concern from some in the party from white rural areas, the Democrats agreed the secret ballot would apply only to the state's four largest cities. In 1890, when turnout fell by about one-third in the state, it fell by two-thirds in these urban areas, and the Republicans lagged far behind the Democrats in the cities, such as Nashville and

Memphis. "The Democratic margin over the GOP in congressional races throughout the state amounted to only 2.3 percent in 1888, but it jumped to 18.4 percent in 1890, to 26.2 percent in 1892, and never fell below 10 percent thereafter."[12]

After the first election under the new legal regime, including the registration law, the secret ballot, and a poll tax, newspapers across the state touted the laws as having been the linchpin for Democratic success, and testified to the suppressive effect they had on black turnout. As Kousser reports, the *Memphis Daily Appeal* declared that " 'The vote has been cut down woefully and wonderfully to be sure, but the ratio of Democratic majorities has been raised at least four-fold. . . . The enemy is completely annihilated.' Furthermore, the Tennessee populists charged that the poll tax disenfranchised 50,000 voters, while the Republicans estimated that the new statutes cost them between thirty and forty thousand votes."[13] The numbers bear these observations out. Before passage of the new laws in 1888, voter turnout was 78 percent in Tennessee. In 1890, after the laws went into effect, turnout fell to 50 percent. The Republican Party thereafter collapsed in the state.[14] Similar trends and results could be charted across the South.

Removing Voting Restrictions through the Voting Rights Act

Three-quarters of a century after the vigorous institution of Jim Crow laws, legislative electoral reform would change the political makeup of the electorate, removing many voting restrictions with the Voting Rights Act of 1965. In the same way that exclusion of African Americans had strong partisan impacts in the earlier part of the twentieth century, the sudden infusion of increasing numbers of African American voters after the passage of the act not only confirms the impacts from the earlier era, but again shifted election outcomes. While no broad analysis on this has been done, a few clear examples were pointed out at the time. Moreover, the changes in the number of registered voters were so dramatic during a time when African Americans were quickly becoming solidly Democratic, it is hard to imagine there was not an effect on some elections. Another measure of the impact of the Voting Rights Act is the number of black candidates elected to office after 1965. It is evident that these candidates would never have won without the overwhelming support of a newly enfranchised African American electorate.

According to reports of the United States Commission on Civil Rights, just between 1965 and May 1967, 566,767 new black voters registered to vote in the South.[15] In Mississippi, black registration rose from 6.7 percent to 59.8 percent;[16] in Alabama, from 19.3 to 51.6 percent; in Georgia, from 27.4 percent to 52.6 percent; in Louisiana, from 31.6 percent to 58.9 percent; and in South Carolina, from 37.3 percent to 51.2 percent.[17] The demographic of eligible voters had shifted significantly in a short amount of time.

At the same time, there was a significant rise in the number of blacks voting, and, it was reported, the outcomes of some races were altered by that change. The USCCR report of 1968 states, "A survey by the Voter Education Project found that in 1966, the growing Black vote was a major determining factor in who won and lost elections across the South. In fact, the Black vote actually supplied the winning margin for a U.S. Senator in South Carolina."[18] Although the survey did not identify the senator, it is safe to assume it refers to the special election that Democrat Ernest Hollings won in a squeaker, with a margin of fewer than 11,000 votes out of 436,000. The USCCR further reported that, according to the Voter Education Project, "at least one Governor, in Arkansas" was elected on the basis of new black voting strength. In 1966, the Democratic Party lost the governorship for the first time in the modern era to the Republican candidate, Winthrop Rockefeller, who was a pro–civil rights Republican, "a racial liberal who developed a coalition of progressive Democrats disenchanted with the conservative Faubus machine, newly enfranchised African Americans, and traditional Republicans to gain the office and reelection in 1968 over Faubus protégés."[19] The Voter Education Project survey also reported that two congressional elections swung on the new black vote, though it did not identify who the candidates were.[20]

During this period, black officials, who obviously would never have won office without the Voting Rights Act's elimination of voting restrictions and the resulting increase in the number of black voters, came into public office at the state and municipal levels in considerable numbers. "After the 1966 elections, the number of local Black officeholders and legislators in the 11 Southern States was 159; after the 1967 elections the number exceeded 200—more than twice as many as were serving when the Voting Rights Act of 1965 was passed."[21]

By 1972, more than one million new black voters were registered in the seven southern states.[22] The percentage of blacks registered in these seven states rose from 29 percent in 1964 to 56 percent in 1972.[23] Alabama increased by 197,320 new black registrants, Georgia by 282,337, Louisiana by 190,006, Mississippi by 239,940, North Carolina by 40,427, South Carolina by 67,850, and Virginia by 130,741, for a total of 1,148,621 new black registrants.[24] This increase led to much higher rates of black voter turnout in the presidential election of 1968. In 1968, while national turnout dropped slightly, turnout increased in all seven southern states covered by Section 5 of the Voting Rights Act.[25] Correspondingly, by April 1974, the number of black elected officials in the South had again increased dramatically, to 963, including one member of Congress and thirty-six state legislators, again presumably owing to the unprecedented power of new black voters.[26] This number then more than doubled in the next six years: in July 1980, a total of 2,042 blacks held public office in the southern states covered by the Voting Rights Act's provisions.[27]

By 1989, black officeholding in Alabama was almost commensurate with the black population.[28] One can only conclude that the number of black elected officials was directly tied to the influence of the new black voters—in other words, the removal of racially and partisan-motivated election laws changed who was elected to office.

Felon Disenfranchisement

Over 5 million Americans are barred from voting today because they have been convicted of a felony at some point. About a million of those citizens are still serving time in prison; the other 4 million are living and working in our communities. About 1.4 million African American men, or 13 percent of all adult black men in the United States, are disenfranchised in this way—a rate seven times the national average.[29] In Florida and Alabama, the rate of imprisonment in 2004 was over 30 percent; that same year, due to felony convictions, in Mississippi, Iowa, New Mexico, Wyoming, and Virginia, 20 to 25 percent of black adult males were disenfranchised. That compares with a national disenfranchisement rate of 2.4 percent for the overall adult population.[30]

When we talk about "felons" we are not for the most part talking about murderers or robbers. Many of these people are convicted of nonviolent crimes; three out of every five felony convictions do not even lead to jail time.[31] They can include acts like passing a bad check. In one moment of irony, when Senator Ted Stevens of Alaska was convicted of failing to report gifts on his ethics forms, he could run for re-election but could not have voted for himself upon sentencing.[32]

The huge number of people with felony convictions has everything to do with the change in approach to criminal law in the 1980s and 1990s that increased the number of crimes considered felonies. And even though crime rates dropped in the 1990s, the national prison population grew at an unusually high rate because of the so-called war on drugs that increased penalties for drug crimes. These new sentencing rules for drug offenses also had a disproportionate effect on minority communities, particularly African Americans. African Americans are convicted of drug crimes at a much higher rate than white Americans, despite the fact that white Americans report higher rates of drug use. The disparities in the criminal justice system for African Americans and whites can be seen throughout the process from arrest, conviction, sentencing, and incarceration.[33]

While the tide has been slowly shifting away from the harshest types of bans on voting for people with felony convictions—lifetime bans and policies that make it virtually impossible to regain voting rights—it is clear that in recent history Republicans have been the major force in keeping felon disenfranchisement laws intact. In 2002, an amendment was offered in the Senate as part of the bill that ultimately was the Help America Vote Act. It simply stated,

> The right of an individual who is a citizen of the United States to vote in any election for Federal office shall not be denied or abridged because that individual has been convicted of a criminal offense unless, at the time of the election, such individual—
>
> (1) is serving a felony sentence in a correctional institution or facility; or
>
> (2) is on parole or probation for a felony offense.[34]

The vote on this measure represents the only full roll-call vote of the Senate on this issue. It was overwhelmingly defeated, with just three Republican senators supporting it.[35] Perhaps more telling, *no* other bill restoring voting rights for ex-felons[36] in the House or the Senate—and there have been many—has ever been sponsored or cosponsored by a single Republican. In recent years, the picture at the state level has been mixed, with a few Republican governors making modest measures to relax felon disenfranchisement laws.[37] But, by and large, it has been Republicans who have seen it as in their interest to keep Americans who have been convicted of a felony out of the voting process.[38]

There is substantial statistical research demonstrating that the maintenance of felony disenfranchisement laws has had an actual impact on election outcomes. Jeff Manza and Christopher Uggen have been the leaders of the research in this field. They have undertaken studies that consider the social and demographic characteristics of felons, including age, race, gender, education, income, and marital status, and then extrapolate from that data whether they would have voted and, if so, which party they would have been more likely to vote for. (Though a few critics have taken issue with using solely socio-demographic data to determine whether and how ex-felons might vote, the work has been mostly praised and cited widely.)[39] Manza and Uggen found that turnout rates among ex-felons between 1972 and 2000 would have been low—about 35 percent in a presidential election. They further reported that 73 percent of ex-felons would have voted for Democratic candidates. As a result, the results of the research startlingly demonstrate that since 1972, the outcomes of numerous Senate races would have been different, as would the 2000 presidential election.[40]

For example, the Democratic candidate for the U.S. Senate would likely have prevailed in Texas in 1978, when Republican John Tower ran and won in a close campaign. He edged out Democratic congressman Robert Krueger 1,151,376 (50.3 percent of two-party vote) to 1,139,149 (49.7 percent of two-party vote). Tower's plurality over Krueger was 12,227 votes.[41] In Kentucky the results would have been reversed in the 1984 U.S. Senate race. That year, Republican Mitch McConnell ran against incumbent Democratic senator Walter Huddleston. McConnell won by four-tenths of a percentage point.[42] This was the case again in 1998—Jim Bunning got 569,817 votes in Kentucky, while Democrat Scotty Baesler got 563,051 votes. The results of Florida's Senate races in 1998 and 2004, and Georgia in 1992, would also have been upturned. In Georgia in 1992, it was the large number of *nonincarcerated* felony probationers and parolees that likely cost the Democrats the election.[43]

Moreover, had disenfranchised felons been permitted to vote in the 2000 presidential election, Al Gore would have won Florida and thus the election, according to Manza and Uggen:

> There are more disenfranchised felons in Florida than in any other state (approximately 827,000 in 2000). Had they participated at our estimated rate of Florida turnout (27.2 percent) and national Democratic preference (68.9 percent), Gore would have carried the state by more than 80,000 votes. But even if we make drastically more conservative assumptions, Gore would still win. For example, if we halved the estimated turnout rate and consider only the impact of *ex*-felons to vote, Gore's margin of victory would still have exceeded 30,000 votes, more than enough to overwhelm Bush's narrow victory margin (and to reverse the outcome in the Electoral College. The outcome of the 2000 presidential race thus hinged on the narrower question of *ex*-felon disenfranchisement rather than on the broader question of voting restrictions on felons currently under supervision.[44]

These researchers also apply their methodology to gubernatorial races and find it is possible that four races would have resulted in the losing candidate winning the election had ex-felons been enfranchised: gubernatorial elections in Alabama in 1994 and 2002, the New Jersey gubernatorial election in 1981, and the gubernatorial election of 1978 in Texas.[45]

New Election Laws and Recent Elections

After the 2000 election, many asserted that the election was stolen from Al Gore, and many Americans still believe that to be the case. Whether it was the suspiciously confusing ballot designs, the high number of "spoiled ballots" in African American districts, the counting of military ballots, or the Supreme Court's stunning and sudden intervention to end the recount and grant George Bush the presidency, perhaps millions of Democrats believed and some continue to believe that Al Gore was the true winner of the 2000 election, and the fact that he lost was the direct result of actions taken by Republican elected officials and election administrators in Florida. Some news analyses after the election demonstrating that if Gore had asked for a recount of the whole state he would have gained enough ballots to win only added fuel to the fire. That Gore won the nationwide popular vote by a substantial margin made the outcome especially frustrating for his supporters.

It is clear that innumerable voters were disenfranchised in the 2000 election. It is also most likely that enough of those who were wrongly disenfranchised would have voted for Gore to tip the election. By that measure, it is not unreasonable to believe that Gore should have won an election he lost by 537 votes in Florida.

Activities both before and after the election on the part of some Republicans were highly suspicious, yet it is hard to point to any particular clearly partisan tactic that tipped the difference. It is difficult to know what were simple mistakes and what were deliberate acts of manipulation. For example, do we know for a fact that inferior machines were purposely placed in jurisdictions likely to vote Democratic? It may well be that poor ballot design and punch-card ballot machines, along with varying methods for counting and not counting those votes by elections officials, cost Gore the election. But it is hard to say that this was done in a deliberate effort to deny Gore voters their vote. We know that minorities and language minority voters were thwarted at all sorts of turns in their legitimate attempts to vote, and more so than white voters. Yet it is impossible to prove this was done in a coordinated partisan effort.

The one area that is a possible exception is how the officials in the governor's administration and elections officials treated the felon voting list and the subsequent purging of legitimate voters from the registration rolls. This is, again, a tactic Republicans have used repeatedly over the last several decades, and it was employed in Florida in 2000. While the impact of the *legal* disenfranchisement of people with felony convictions in Florida played a demonstrable role in the outcome of the presidential election in 2000—just in that state, 620,000 ex-felons were excluded from participating[46]—much attention was additionally paid to the issue of the extraordinarily flawed felon disenfranchisement lists that elections officials used to strike voters from the registration lists. According to the USCCR investigation and report on the 2000 election, there is ample evidence that thousands of voters were improperly placed on the ineligible list. For example, the supervisor of elections office for Miami-Dade County received two felon disenfranchisement lists—one in June 1999, and another in January 2000. Of the 5,762 persons on the June 1999 list, 327 successfully appealed and, therefore, remained on the voter rolls. Yet the USCCR reported that

Another 485 names were later identified as persons who either had their rights restored or who should not have been on the list. Thus at least 14.1 percent of the persons whose names appeared on the Miami-Dade County list appeared on the list in error. Similarly, 13.3 percent of the names on the January 2000 list were eligible to vote. In other words, almost one out of every seven people on this list were there in error and risked being disenfranchised.[47]

According to the USCCR, African Americans were more likely to be on the Miami-Dade list. In fact, African Americans represented the majority of persons—over 65 percent—on both the June 1999 and the January 2000 lists.

Making the Florida process especially controversial was the state's contracting out of the creation of the felon disenfranchisement list to a for-profit private corporation and, even more so, the instructions the company was given for matching voters' names with those on the felon list. The company, DBT Online, was told by the state in 1999 not to provide a list of exact name matches, as had been originally planned. Rather, the state decided to require only a 90 percent name match, which produced "false positives," or partial matches of the data. Moreover, the Division of Elections required that DBT Online perform "nickname matches" for first names and to "make it go both ways." Thus, the name Deborah Ann would also match the name Ann Deborah. At a meeting in early 1999, the supervisors of elections expressed a preference for exact matches on the list as opposed to a "fairly broad and encompassing" collection of names. DBT Online advised the Division of Elections that it could produce a list with exact matches. Despite this, the Division of Elections nevertheless opted to cast a wide net for the exclusion lists.[48] In 2000, the year of the election, the state actually reduced the standard even further, to require only an 80 percent match.[49]

According to the company, DBT Online, it advised the Division of Elections of the likelihood that a significant number of false positives existed and made recommendations to reduce those numbers. A representative from the company, George Bruder, asserted that DBT Online "specifically suggested to state officials that narrow criteria be used in creating the lists, which would lower the false-positive rate, and therefore, minimize errors in the number of names matched. . . . He [Bruder] testified that the company recommended, for example, that it develop criteria requiring an exact match on the first and middle names."[50] Moreover, he "insisted that 'the state dictated to us that they wanted to go broader, and we did it in the fashion that they requested.' "[51] This resulted in a far higher number of voters being identified as felons in confusion with someone else. What is more, the state asked the company to include in its lists felons disenfranchised in other states.[52] "Emmett Mitchell, former assistant general counsel for the Division of Elections, instructed DBT Online that felons from states with no executive board of clemency must apply for clemency in Florida to have their voting rights reinstated." This is an obvious misinterpretation of the law. Two Florida courts of appeal have ruled that if an individual enters Florida with his or her civil rights, then through the full faith and credit clause of the U.S. Constitution, he or she need not apply for clemency upon arriving in Florida.[53]

This inclusion of people who had moved to Florida alone might have had a profound impact on the election. The number of people in Florida in 2000 who moved to the state with a prior felony conviction was in the range of 50,000–100,000. About 80 percent of ex-felons had come into the state with their voting rights restored, which the state of Florida was supposed to recognize.[54]

There were some who believed at the time that the state's taking the unprecedented step of contracting out the registration list to a private firm and taking approaches such as using a matching standard more likely to produce false matches and wrongly including ex-felons from other states was purposeful and partisanly motivated.[55]

After the election, the *Palm Beach Post* conducted a computer analysis that found at least 1,100 eligible voters wrongly purged from the rolls because of the problems with the felon lists. As the *Post* put it, "With Bush winning Florida and the presidency by a scant 537 votes over Democrat Al Gore, these voters—some wrongly identified as felons, and many more wrongly turned away based on felony convictions in other states—could have swayed the election had they been allowed to vote." The paper calculated it this way: at least 108 nonfelon voters were included on the list, and in many of those cases they were on the felon list even though they did not share the same name, birth date, gender, or race with the person on it. The *Post* found, in fact, that 1,300 voters were initially matched with a felon even though they were obviously and self-evidently not of the same race or gender. Another nearly 1,000 voters were people with felonies in other states who should have had their voting rights respected by the state but did not. Even knowing those mismatches had occurred ahead of time, the state did nothing to revise its procedures. The paper also found that the state database included dozens of people who had their crimes reduced to misdemeanors and thus did not fall within Florida's felon disenfranchisement law. Blacks made up 44 percent of those removed from the voter registration list but constituted only 11 percent of Florida voters.[56]

Meanwhile, even ex-felons in Florida who wanted to vote and were probably eligible to vote if they could have successfully gotten through the clemency process faced backlogs in the Office of Executive Clemency of six months to a year. At the time of the election, there were 187,000 former felons in the state who had completed parole but not received clemency. Even if only a small percentage of them could have gotten through the process in time and voted, it might well have been enough to turn the election.[57]

The USCCR concludes in its report that the "Florida legislature's decision to privatize its list maintenance procedures without establishing effective clear guidance for these private efforts from the highest levels, coupled with the absence of uniform and reliable verification procedures, resulted in countless eligible voters being deprived of their right to vote."[58]

While the outcry was not as loud in 2004, probably mostly because George Bush won the national popular vote, there were many people who believed that partisan manipulation of election laws and procedures in the swing state of Ohio by the Republican Party and the Republican secretary of state Kenneth Blackwell "stole" the state electoral votes for George Bush, who won by fewer than 120,000 votes in that state.[59] It is difficult to demonstrate that the fairly obviously deliberately partisan actions they took were sufficient to swing enough votes to alter the outcome of the election. But the case has been made by some. And again, because the motives behind the official activity that took place are sufficiently suspect, and the numbers of votes affected are disputed, the argument has never gotten very far. But there is a reasonable argument.

Some of the partisan maneuvers of the Republican Party and Kenneth Blackwell were outlined in the previous chapter on the 2004 election. Whether Republican Party operatives were able to get the numbers to tip the balance is less clear. Certainly some researchers and commentators tried to make the case. The matter was also taken up at the federal level when the House Judiciary Committee Democratic staff under the leadership of Representative John Conyers undertook an investigation of the Ohio election. Their 2005 report states:

> We have found numerous, serious election irregularities in the Ohio presidential election, which resulted in a significant disenfranchisement of voters. Cumulatively, these irregularities, which affected hundreds of thousands of votes and voters in Ohio, raise grave doubts regarding whether it can be said the Ohio electors selected on December 13, 2004, were chosen in a manner that conforms to Ohio law, let alone federal requirements and constitutional standards. . . . We find that there were massive and unprecedented voter irregularities and anomalies in Ohio. In many cases these irregularities were caused by intentional misconduct and illegal behavior, much of it involving Secretary of State J. Kenneth Blackwell, the co-chair of the Bush-Cheney campaign in Ohio.[60]

The report goes through the various tactics Blackwell and the GOP undertook during the pre–Election Day period and subsequently, such as the requirement that registration forms be of a particular paper stock to be valid; actions taken to have voters purged from the rolls; caging; suspicious and possibly intentional misallocation of voting machines in the state leading to longer lines in Democratic jurisdictions; challenges at the polling place; restrictions that Blackwell, by directive, placed on counting of provisional ballots; irregularities in how the voting machines operated, such that intentional tampering cannot be discounted; and a variety of suspicious activities that took place around the vote counting and the recount throughout the state. It is clear throughout the report that many of these disenfranchising activities disproportionately impacted minority voters.

The House Judiciary Committee further observed that it is possible that machine misallocation may have led to hundreds of thousands of votes not being cast because of long waits and that machine shortages were overwhelmingly concentrated in urban, minority, and Democratic jurisdictions. Blackwell's order that provisional ballots cast in the wrong precinct be discarded might have resulted in the disenfranchisement of tens of thousands of voters. The committee report also says that Republican challenges at the polls "could easily have reduced minority turnout by tens of thousands of voters, if not more."[61]

Robert F. Kennedy Jr., in a well-known article in *Rolling Stone* magazine,[62] attempted to go through all the various machinations that took place in 2004 and attach specific numbers of votes to them to come up with a number of flipped votes that would have easily upended the election outcome. Again, there is no question that thousands of legitimate voters were wrongfully disenfranchised in Ohio and elsewhere, often because of partisan tricks. Whether these instances of disenfranchisement changed the election is more difficult to determine. If one took into account the cumulative impact of all these wrongs, then it is reasonable to conclude that John Kerry would have won Ohio if the vote had not been manipulated. But again, it is impossible to prove the numbers add up, and in some instances—though perhaps not all—it is impossible to say that the disenfranchisement was the result of a partisan Republican scheme. Indeed, a report of the investigation launched by the Democratic National Committee, led by academic experts and other consultants in 2005, underscores that the egregious disenfranchisement that took place in the state of Ohio was nonetheless not sufficient to have changed the election outcome.

Unequal Impacts

While the evidence of whether wins or losses resulted from exclusion of voters is unclear, what is abundantly clear in every instance is that certain groups are excluded more than others. While the DNC report concludes that it is impossible to definitively say disenfranchisement swung the 2004 election result, the report describes numerous instances of shameful vote suppression that disproportionately impacted minority, and thus likely Democratic, voters. For example, the study concludes that "three percent of voters who went to the polls left their polling places and did not return due to the long lines" and that this affected minority voters much more than white voters in the state, with African Americans having to wait on line to vote an average of fifty-two minutes, while whites had to wait an average of eighteen minutes.[63] Blacks were also much more likely than white voters to have their registration status challenged at the polls—4 percent of black voters who were in fact registered reported being challenged, while only 1 percent of whites were.[64] With respect to the machines, the number of ballots spoiled was higher in precincts that voted for Kerry.[65]

As investigations of the 2000 and 2004 elections demonstrate, in terms of the manipulation of modern-day election law, it is difficult to discern how many people were disenfranchised by a particular tactic, how they voted or would have voted, and whether those lost votes would have turned the election. For example, while caging and challenges at the polling place clearly took place in 2004 and for many years prior to that, and those efforts were targeted at Democrats and minorities, no one has been able to come up with any real numbers as to how many people were affected, and it is probably impossible to do so.

The same is true in the case of voter identification laws. Numerous analyses have been done on the impact of voter identification laws, and while all of them concede that a certain number of voters will be disenfranchised by strict requirements, the estimates vary widely, from as low as 1.2 percent to as high as 10 percent.[66] And in examining individual elections since the laws were passed, there has been no agreement on impact on turnout or outcomes. These ambiguous conclusions come as no surprise. There are so many factors that go into whether someone will vote and do so effectively or not—successful voter registration, the poll workers who deal with the voter, the usability of the machines and ballots, the closeness of the race, and the weather, to name a few—that it is effectively impossible to tease out any one and say that it was the proximate cause for the failure to vote or the suppression of one's vote. In an analysis of the voter ID research to date, for example, political scientists Robert S. Erikson and Lorraine C. Minnite conclude that current research tools have not been able to accurately capture the impact of voter ID rules on turnout.[67] Perhaps given a series of elections over many years, such estimates of disenfranchisement will become more accurate.

Nonetheless, numerous studies have demonstrated that groups that are traditionally more likely to vote for Democrats are disproportionately impacted by such laws. Indeed, it is safe to say that to the extent there has been disenfranchisement as a result of these voter ID laws—and even the laws' supporters admit to some—it has suppressed Democratic votes. A recent study hypothesizes that strict voter ID laws "could have an important impact on elections in states with a high number of immigrant voters, or states with demographics that are disproportionately affected by more stringent voting laws."[68] Exit polls from the November 2006 elections in California, New Mexico, and Washington state showed that majority

Democratic constituencies such as minorities and immigrants were significantly less likely to have access to basic identification documents than the white population, as were those with lower levels of education and income.

As the preceding analysis indicates, the evidence is virtually indisputable that, beginning in the late nineteenth century, partisan manipulation of election law, combined with outright voter intimidation, harassment, and violence, altered election outcomes in favor of Democrats in the South prior to the passage of the Voting Rights Act in 1965. Similarly, the electoral impact of the lifting of voting restrictions after the passage of the Voting Rights Act confirmed the effect that the barriers had during that time. There is also substantial reason to believe that more-recent elections have been severely affected by politicized decision-making, particularly when considering felon disenfranchisement laws.

Yet it must be emphasized that while the question of whether or not partisan manipulation of election law "worked" is important to assess as a political matter, it is not, as a matter of democracy, the foremost question. It is not the winner or loser of an election, or even the number of votes suppressed, that we should be solely focused on. As has been discussed throughout, it is the fact that anyone is disenfranchised wrongfully that should concern us, especially if it occurs through political machinations. For those who are targeted, and possibly for the electorate at large, partisan vote suppression is likely to increase cynicism, distrust, and disdain for the political system and politicians, whether the outcome is changed or not. It is also the case that denial of individual votes, especially when it is the poor and communities of color that are more likely to be disenfranchised, allows elected officials to pay less attention to the issues of concern to those groups—and often they do just that.

9

How to Increase Participation

The voter inclusion principle argues that vote suppression for partisan gain is virtually never legitimate, but increasing participation through legal and legislative maneuvers is legitimate and ethical, even if it is to the disproportionate benefit of one side. Until now, I have discussed the ways in which the political parties have relentlessly violated this principle. Here I explore how they can embrace it. It is a formula for improving our democracy. Perhaps in some instances, it is also a recipe for winning elections.

The parties and candidates can play a primary role in strengthening our democracy by increasing inclusion in a number of ways throughout the electoral process. My recommendations for partisan action will follow the trajectory of that process, from voter registration through vote counting. The voter inclusion principle does not require that parties set aside partisanship or not seek electoral advantage. The principle does, however, require that parties do so by expanding the electorate.

Registration Reform

Studies showing varying effects on actual turnout notwithstanding, there are without question critical disparities in who is and is not registered to vote in this country. As a necessary initial step to participation, we must recognize that this imbalance is not sustainable. Both parties have political reasons to want to see registration reform work, and in pushing for these ideas, they will improve democracy in the process.

As has been discussed, the National Voter Registration Act provision regarding public assistance agencies has been neglected. Democrats particularly have reason to believe that it would be useful to fight for more rigorous adherence to that provision. Democrats, who are somewhat more mobile than Republicans, should also be concerned about the failure of states to enforce NVRA rules that require election officials to allow a voter who has moved within the county to reregister on Election Day. At the same time, there is reason to believe that the DMV provision of NVRA, which is also not operating at full power, disproportionately is of use to Republicans.

It is obvious that people who make use of public benefit agencies tend to be lower income, are more likely to be a minority, and more likely to lean Democratic. In 2004 the lowest-income Americans voted for John Kerry over George Bush by a margin of 2 to 1;[1] in 2008 Obama trounced McCain among these voters by a 3-to-1 margin.[2] Moreover, research has found NVRA to be most beneficial for people who move more frequently,[3] who are more likely to be Democrats. While, as stated, registration may not necessarily translate into turnout, it is a necessary prerequisite that must be met. Thus, it makes sense politically for Democrats to push hard for enforcement of this already existing election law. But it also makes sense ethically and for democracy's sake because it potentially expands the franchise among the voters who are now most marginalized politically and socially.

Democrats should not stop at a litigation or lobbying strategy for enforcement of the act, however. As elucidated, for election reforms such as NVRA to work, parties need to intercede and *make* them work. Hence, it is incumbent upon Democrats, both politically and for democracy, to engage in major public education about the opportunities to register to vote at public agencies, and to teach people about their right to be afforded those opportunities while interacting with public assistance programs.

But it makes sense for Republicans to urge effective compliance with NVRA, too. As noted, more Republicans than Democrats seem to register through contact with DMVs. As was described, when NVRA first passed, more Republicans were taking advantage of the law's provisions because far more people were registering through the motor-voter provision than were registering through the agency-based provision of the law. More so than the rest of the NVRA provisions, registering through a DMV is also more likely to indicate turnout. Research finds the motor voter provision increases turnout by 4.7 percent.[4]

It has become clear that DMVs are not doing a great job of following the policies and procedures of NVRA. There have been several reports over the years of voters registering at DMV offices only to find themselves absent from the registration list come Election Day because the form somehow never made it from the DMV to election administrators and onto the rolls, angering and disenfranchising many voters.[5] According to a memo to the Department of Justice from Demos and other election reform organizations, in 2008 "press reports and calls coming into the 1–866-OURVOTE Election Protection hotline indicated many instances of problems with voter registration at motor vehicle departments. Specifically, in states across the country, citizens registering to vote at motor vehicle departments are not appearing on states' voter rolls, suggesting that motor vehicle departments are failing to transmit completed voter registration applications to the appropriate elections officials, in violation of Sections 5 and 8(a)(1)(A) of the NVRA." The memo goes on to cite numerous incidents in which voters who registered through the DMV went to the polling place only to find their names not on the list.[6] In Maryland, it was found after the 2008 and 2010 elections that 25 percent of citizens who registered to vote through the DMV did not make it onto the voter registration list.[7]

Therefore it makes complete sense for the Republican Party to want to do more to ensure that the DMV provisions of the law are enforced and possibly strengthened. At the same time, this would be good for democracy, because voters would not be disenfranchised due to administrative foul-ups.

The NVRA also provides for mail-in registration that allows organizations to more easily conduct registration drives. Under our current system, third-party registration groups are necessary to fill the void left by the government in its failure to proactively ensure Americans are registered to vote. Laws should not be enacted that unnecessarily suppress these groups' efforts.

There is no question that these groups are responsible for the registration and potential participation of millions of voters. In 2004, at least ten million new registrations were submitted by larger voter registration groups alone, over 20 percent of the total number of registrations.[8] Nonpartisan liberal-leaning groups have registered huge numbers of poor and minority voters whom no one else would have reached out to. Right-leaning groups have effectively targeted churchgoers.[9] Several groups focus their voter registration drives at young people.

A few groups have had serious problems with their volunteer registration procedures,[10] but overall the good these groups do in terms of boosting participation far outweighs any rare difficulties they may cause. Moreover, taking steps like ensuring that groups train their workers properly, requiring groups to make best efforts to adhere to the same turnaround time that agencies must under NVRA—ten days—and banning the paying of workers by the number of registration forms they return are effective ways to overcome many of the problems that have occurred, and strike an appropriate balance under the voter inclusion principle.[11] Accordingly, the principle dictates that third-party registration groups be allowed to operate, albeit within certain reasonable constraints.

No nonpartisan group, as all these organizations are, is legally permitted to target only members of one party or another or to refuse to register someone based on their party preference. Yet Republicans, instead of offering reasonable solutions to address problems with the system, have taken steps to make it harder for these groups to do their jobs. As a result, such measures do not represent ways of protecting other strong countervailing democratic values.

Perhaps some Republicans believe (and they may be right) that there are more voter registration organizations that target Democratic-leaning constituencies. Unfortunately, the Republican response to this has been to seek to diminish the abilities of these groups to bring new voters into the system. But wouldn't a more appropriate response, from the point of view of promoting democracy, be to encourage the creation of third-party organizations that might also bolster registration among groups seen as likely to vote for Republicans?

We should not rely on advance registration through these methods alone. Election Day registration (EDR) is a vital reform that ought to be pursued throughout the country. Allowing voters to register at the same time they go to vote is the one structural change for which there is consistent evidence that it improves turnout dramatically. Numerous studies conducted on EDR have repeatedly demonstrated a significant positive impact on voter turnout,[12] and the data say that there is no significant partisan advantage inherent in EDR, despite the resistance to it from many Republicans.[13]

EDR simplifies the registration process by allowing voters to register to vote on Election Day when they arrive at the polls. It is currently offered by Maine, Idaho, Minnesota, New Hampshire, Wisconsin, Montana, Iowa, the District of Columbia, and Wyoming, and for the first time in 2008 during early voting in North Carolina. North Dakota does not require registration at all.

In the 2000 and 2004 elections, turnout in states with EDR was 8 to 15 percentage points higher than in states that did not offer EDR, and overall, in the 2004 election, voter turnout was 13.8 percentage points higher in states that offer EDR (73.8 percent turned out) than in states that do not (60.2 percent turned out). Of the five states with the highest turnouts in 2004, four offered EDR.[14] The pattern repeated itself in 2006 when the average turnout in EDR states was 48.7 percent, compared with 38.2 percent in states without EDR.[15] The trend continued in 2008. As always, the states with the highest turnout in the country were EDR states: Iowa (69.2 percent), Maine (73 percent), Minnesota (77.9 percent), New Hampshire (71.9 percent), and Wisconsin (72.2 percent).[16]

Election Day registration is a reform where greater attention by the parties in particular could do much to increase its already measurable benefits. It is a tool that with more party activity could raise voter participation rates even higher than it already does. It is therefore something that the parties should not only get behind, but which they also have an ethical obligation to promote to its maximum potential for the good of democracy.

The Democratic Party has particular reason to push EDR. The United States is a highly mobile society, with tens of millions of people moving every year. In 2005, forty million Americans moved. Latinos, the unemployed, and renters, who tend to be lower in income, had the highest rates of moving. Younger citizens are also more mobile than the rest of the population.[17] In the 2008 presidential election, 21 percent of potential voters between the ages of eighteen and twenty-nine did not register because, they reported, they did not meet the registration deadlines in their states.[18] At the same time, in 2008, on average, 59 percent of young Americans in EDR states voted—compared with 50 percent of their peers who did not live in EDR states.[19] In recent elections, young people have been voting disproportionately for Democrats.[20]

Both parties can easily use Election Day registration to their advantages while doing the positive work of increasing turnout at the same time. The parties already have lists of who is registered to vote. If they can obtain other membership lists from various organizations that include their likely loyalists and compare them to the voter registration lists, they can very specifically target voters who are their natural constituents but are not registered in the final days leading up to and on the day of the election.

Moreover, with EDR, parties and candidates are forced to speak to all potential voters—not just already registered, known, and likely voters. Although this may be what makes current politicians reluctant to adopt EDR—elected officials of all stripes would prefer to know well in advance who is in the electorate—from the perspective of a healthy democracy it is one of its most attractive features. In EDR states, parties are more likely to see it in their interest to go beyond the usual suspects in their mobilization strategies, including targeting younger people, who are more mobile, may only start paying attention to the campaigns after traditional registration deadlines have passed, and are less familiar with registration rules. The Democratic Party should mobilize some who fall outside the profile of a consistent voter in EDR states in the last days leading up to the election, especially minority, younger, poorer, and less-educated voters. While according to a cold political calculus this would be a relatively worthless exercise in most states that have voter registration deadlines of up to thirty days ahead of time, it would likely be quite a sensible shift of resources in the closing days of the election in EDR states. The strategy could be one of throwing all mobilization efforts into turning out registered likely voters in the early days of the campaign while shifting at least some of the attention to a greater swath of the nonregistered voters in the late days. Republicans too could employ such a strategy among their natural but unregistered constituents.

As the parties can use EDR so effectively to increase turnout among those who should be their voters, they should be pressing hard for passage of EDR laws in other states and at the federal level. If EDR was national policy, the rate of voter registration in this country would rise by an estimated 5.7 percent, representing hundreds of thousands of voters.[21]

Eventually this country should be moving in the direction of automatic, permanent registration, otherwise known as universal registration. The idea that the federal government should assume complete responsibility for registering citizens to vote, as is the practice of most other democracies of the world, has started to catch on not only among voting rights advocates, but also with a wide range of election administrators and policymakers. However, getting there is likely to be a fairly slow process on any large scale.

In the interim, we should make the system of registration as easy to navigate as possible for all the people, including those with the least resources, while still maintaining the integrity of the voting system. A number of reform proposals exist that move in this direction, to the benefit of American democracy and political interests.

One way that has been suggested to start the process going is ensuring that all high school graduates are registered to vote. The organization Fairvote has proposed making voter registration a requirement for graduation, mandating registration to register for classes at colleges and universities, or making voter registration a community service requirement. Fairvote and others have further recommended that the registration age be lowered to sixteen so that schools can engage all students—including those that may not graduate—in the process of learning about the election system. These students still would not be able to vote, but when they turned eighteen they would automatically receive a notice of eligibility and a booklet of information about the voting process.[22] Several states have already enacted such programs.[23]

It is also important that the thorny issue of college students voting from their college campuses be sorted out in a way that maximizes student participation. As noted in the discussion of the 2008 election, a variety of efforts have been made to suppress student voting, and this may well worsen in the years to come. Given the current trend of young people and especially students toward support of Democrats, that party should make every effort to get these clarifying rules passed and enforced. Students must be given the option of voting from their campus address. By law, if students consider their college to be their primary residence, they are entitled to register from their campus address. Students do not have to know where they are going to be living after graduation in order to consider the campus their residence; they just have to have no present intention to go back to their parents' house. The preponderance of case law has overturned laws that place the burden on the students to prove that school is their primary residence.[24]

As has also been discussed, strict voter ID laws are also very problematic for students. Very often students do not have picture ID, such as a driver's license, with their current address on it, and in restrictive ID states, college IDs are not legally sufficient to vote. All states should allow students to use a current student ID as identification for voting, and must allow for students with out-of-state driver's licenses to use them for voting.

Anyone who cares about improving the low rates of participation among students ought to insist on these measures. From a political perspective, it makes sense for both parties to champion student voting rights in their efforts to secure majorities in the future. Studies indicate that "party identification develops in early adulthood," after which point a person's party identification generally remains consistent for the rest of his or her life.[25]

Taking steps to improve youth participation in the 1980s and much of the 1990s would have been to the distinct advantage of the Republicans. In 1986, Norman Ornstein wrote that the party that secures the youth vote is the party in power in the next generation. Republicans had a strong hold on the youth vote in the 1980s, when Ornstein was writing, and by the 1990s the Republicans held power in Congress, a grip that has only recently begun to loosen.[26] However, polls now show current young voters are leaning Democratic—the youth vote went for Obama by a staggering 2-to-1 margin.[27] This could easily flip again. The point is, increasing the pool of young registrants gives both parties easily targeted new voters that they can direct their messages at and hope to attract to the party for the long term.

Newly naturalized citizens are another group that could be targeted in a campaign toward universal registration. This should be appealing to both parties, who each have natural constituencies among different immigrant groups and should both be competing for the Latino and Asian votes in particular.

Numerous organizations have urged that registration forms be made available at naturalization ceremonies.[28] Thanks to registration groups such as the League of Women Voters, there sometimes are volunteers at the ceremonies to provide the new citizens with registration forms and information about their new voting rights. The parties sometimes conduct drives outside the ceremonies as well.

Nonetheless, it should undoubtedly be a government responsibility to provide voter registration services at all naturalization ceremonies. The United States Citizenship and Immigrant Services office (within the Department of Homeland Security), the entity responsible for naturalization ceremonies, should be designated as a voter registration agency under the NVRA. This would mean distributing voter registration materials and voting information, assisting voters with those forms, collecting them, and sending them to the appropriate election official in the jurisdiction at the time a new citizen is sworn in at all naturalization ceremonies.[29] This would seem rather unobjectionable, and yet it has proved difficult to bring about within the halls of the citizenship agency and the U.S. Capitol.

Naturalization rates among immigrants are rising steadily in general, to about 650,000 a year.[30] And as might be expected, a large proportion of those who are naturalizing or are likely to naturalize over the next few years are Latinos, a group increasingly likely to vote for Democrats. Indeed, in the 2006 congressional elections, Latinos voted for Democrats 69 percent to 30 percent.[31] In the 2008 election it was 67 percent for Obama and 31 percent for McCain. The Republicans should also support the measure. They are seeking to regain their share of the Latino vote, other immigrant constituencies may well lean in the Republican direction, and there is evidence that many new Americans have undefined or weak party preferences and are open to the overtures of both parties.[32]

The Campaign Period

One of the most troubling aspects of recent elections has been the proliferation of "deceptive practices" leading up to the election. Deceptive practices are efforts that seek to mislead voters about the voting process in such a way as to prevent them from voting, such as by providing blatant misinformation about where or when to vote. In 2007, then Senator Barack

Obama introduced legislation that would criminalize deceptive practices; when such practices were discovered, officials would be required to immediately take action to ensure that the deception was publicized and, working with community groups and others, make sure the correct information was disseminated to the affected community. In December 2011, senators Charles Schumer (D-NY) and Ben Cardin (D-Md) introduced a similar bill, the Deceptive Practices and Voter Intimidation Prevention Act of 2011.[33]

A law such as this, whether enacted at the federal or state level, might provide a boost to turnout. First, voters would be less likely to be led astray and end up not being able to vote or not having their vote counted. In addition, voters generally would have more confidence in going to the polls because they could feel assured that the information they received about the process was likely accurate. Indeed, it is possible that a campaign to disseminate corrective information might even boost turnout in itself, since voters would become aware of the deception that had been directed at them and become all the more motivated to defy it.

Passage of such laws is also clearly in the parochial interest of the Democrats. Deceptive practices are almost always squarely targeted at Democratic constituencies, such as African American voters, and occasionally directly attributable to Republican campaigns.[34] Therefore, the increase in turnout resulting from such measures would redound to the Democrats.

By championing such measures, though, Democrats would also be giving a huge boost to the integrity of elections. Moreover, the perniciousness of such blatant disinformation campaigns is such an affront to any concept of just elections that measures to combat them should be supported vigorously by members of both parties. Such practices violate the voter inclusion principle in every imaginable way. They squarely take aim at voting rights and are designed purely as a vote suppression mechanism.

Besides increasing communication in order to debunk deceptive information, we need to do a better job of informing Americans about the voting process. Dennis F. Thompson speaks directly to voter education in his discussion of just elections, saying "If we know that some modest improvements in voter education could decrease the frequency of voter error and failed to take steps to implement them, we are in effect denying less experienced voters the opportunity to cast a ballot. Equal respect demands more than that."[35]

Democrats would be wise to back reforms that promote increased voter education about the electoral process and how to vote, because the party's demographic base is likely to be somewhat less educated and lower income and thus less likely to have the resources necessary to seek out this kind of information. For new voters and voters who have been historically marginalized, the voting system can seem daunting. For these voters, being prepared before entering the polling booth can give them the confidence to turn out. Indeed, an earlier version of the Help America Vote Act required that states mail, no later than ten days before a federal election, a sample ballot, information on poll hours, and a notification of voters' rights. A sizable number of the members of the National Commission on Federal Election Reform of 2001 recommended that every jurisdiction be required to provide every voter, in advance of the election, a sample ballot and basic information about voting procedures.[36]

Sending a sample ballot and polling place information before the election can have an impact on turnout. Research has demonstrated that sending a sample ballot raises turnout by 2 percent. Among the least educated voters, sending a sample ballot leads to a 6.2 percent increase in participation. Sending polling place information raises turnout by 2.5 percent overall, and 7.4 percent among the least educated.[37] Other studies have shown these reforms to be particularly effective in turning out younger voters.[38]

Both parties would also potentially be helped by requiring, through FCC licensing, that television and radio networks provide a certain limited amount of free air time not only for candidates or campaign messages, but for messages about how to vote. Since 1934, broadcasters have been obligated to serve the public interest in exchange for free access to the public airwaves, and with the transition to digital television, there is now a unique opportunity to see this obligation put to work.[39]

Achieving this might best be done by adapting a 2002 proposal.[40] Paul Taylor and Norman Ornstein suggested a system in which the two major political parties would be provided block grants of broadcast vouchers to use as they saw fit, including passing the time on to candidates. Minor parties would be eligible for smaller blocks of time. In a voter inclusion version of this system, parties would receive block grants to air a certain number of ads on any broadcast outlet regarding how to vote and make sure your vote counts. Parties could then strategically use this information to try to target it to voters they think are more likely to be friendly. For example, the Democrats might see it as advantageous to use their free air time on ethnic media, Republicans on Christian evangelical stations.

Free air time has long been touted as a means toward increased participation.[41] There is evidence to suggest that armed with more knowledge, more people will participate. Studies conducted in other countries show a strong correlation between level of knowledge and participation. Indeed, some observers believe that lack of knowledge about politics and the political system is the defining reason behind low participation in the United States.[42] Therefore, even partisan-driven voter education efforts through the airwaves and otherwise are socially and politically beneficial in that they are likely to boost political engagement.

Voting before Election Day

There is just cause to support the continuation of and improvement upon limited in-person early voting. While extreme early voting, such as for several weeks before Election Day, goes against the grain of the voter inclusion principle, early voting over the course of a couple of weeks would be an ethical and democratic good under certain circumstances, which, to some extent, it is incumbent upon the parties to create. The Democrats demonstrated in the 2008 election that early voting could be used to the party's advantage while also creating this good.

Thirty-two states have some form of in-person early voting, and for most of these states this is a new development of within the last six years. The number of Americans casting their votes early has been rising steadily over the last few years, to almost one-third of voters in 2008. The trend is likely to continue in that direction.

Up to the 2008 election, generally speaking, the preponderance of the evidence told us that early voting does not increase turnout, but merely provides another means of voting for people who would have voted anyway. Even still, there were arguments for some amount of early voting in an age in which working people are overtaxed as it is. Not being able to conveniently get to the polls on a certain day within certain hours is understandable. Election administrators also tend to favor it because it eases the burdens and workload of Election Day itself.

More important, the 2008 election demonstrated what research had previously indicated: the turnout picture starts to change once the parties swing into action. Republicans traditionally have had a built-in advantage when it comes to early voting, making it a measure they too should support: data demonstrate that early voters more often are Republicans, which given the demographic profile of core Republican voters is not surprising.[43] But for the Democrats, 2008 showed that some extra effort can make this reform one that works for their party, too, and for the cause of increased voter participation.

Important research has found that while early voting, in the absence of party activism, does not lead to new voters participating, when early voting is "exploited" by the parties, it does lead to a significant increase in participation. As the authors of the research note, "early voting is not self-actuating"; it requires a push from the party apparatus.[44]

This was already seen to some degree in 2004 when the parties provided buses to audience members at rallies to actually go to poll sites; but it really took off in 2008. Almost one-third of voters voted early in the 2008 election, many of them proactively mobilized to do so by Democrat Barack Obama's presidential campaign.[45] Indeed, the margins Obama racked up during early voting were key to his success.[46]

Republicans are certainly just as capable of using early voting to increase participation among the party faithful, as their vaunted turnout machine demonstrated in past elections, making early voting a reform they should support. Democrats and Republicans should push for longer and more varied hours for early voting, and longer poll opening hours on Election Day as well. If early voting's utility is supposed to be a convenience, it actually needs to be convenient for working people. This means early morning, evening, and weekend hours. The research cited above indicates that this too would result in a further boost in voting rates.[47] While data are mixed, longer poll hours may boost participation on Election Day as well.[48]

The question arises that if some early in-person voting is a good thing, why limit it to only a couple of weeks? There are several reasons why extending the number of early voting days beyond this point is not, on balance, justified. First, asking that the parties and campaigns invest in serious mobilization for a couple of weeks is one thing; asking that this activity go on for several weeks is quite another. Parties and campaigns simply are not likely to be able to sustain such activity over such a long period, resulting in diminishing returns on the reform; simply from a financial perspective, it would be too great a strain. Research shows that, especially when campaigns are not able to access information about who is voting early, early voting does increase campaign costs substantially.[49] In an era of ever-escalating campaign costs and the concomitant need for the candidates, the parties, and their supporters to continuously raise increasing amounts of money, this is not a desirable outcome.

There is also the very serious concern about early voters voting on the basis of what turns out to be obsolete or wrong information. Significant information can emerge or a noteworthy event take place toward the end of the campaigns that might influence voter choices. A voter might even be effectively disenfranchised by casting a vote too early if a candidate should die (as was the case with Senator Paul Wellstone in 2002), drop out of the race (like John Edwards during the 2008 primary), or be disqualified in the waning days.

Another form of early voting is "no excuse" absentee balloting—systems under which anyone can vote by mail in advance of the election and the voter does not need to provide a justification for doing so. Although Democrats have been pushing hard for an expansion of no-excuse absentee balloting and vote by mail, the voter inclusion principle pushes back somewhat. Democrats believe that the greater convenience mail balloting provides, and the ability for the party in some jurisdictions to actively encourage loyalists to vote absentee, automatically means it will be helpful to their cause. There is no evidence, however, to suggest that more absentee balloting equals more Democratic votes. Moreover, most research shows that as currently conducted, no-excuse absentee balloting has little impact on voter turnout overall and brings some arguably negative qualities to bear on the democratic process that outweigh some of the benefits.

The overwhelming majority of scholarly study has found that liberalized absentee ballot rules do not increase voter turnout in major elections in any significant way (the evidence is more mixed for more local elections). Rather, they just give people who would have voted anyway another—perhaps more convenient—way to do so. It is a reform that does very little to engage new voters and bring them into the system.[50] There is one caveat to this finding, however. Research also finds that the one circumstance where absentee balloting has a positive impact on turnout is if it is combined with party mobilization. However, once again such activity generally just retains more people who are already likely voters. It is an effective way for parties to turn out their bases early by sending known partisans, where lists of such individuals are available, absentee ballots that are already filled out—then all the voter need do is sign it.[51]

Yet the voter inclusion principle still warns against expanding absentee balloting *without serious safeguards*, for a number of reasons.

First is the issue of fraud. While many claims about voter fraud are largely unfounded, claims about fraud through the absentee ballot process, while exaggerated, have much more credibility. In a report submitted to the U.S. Election Assistance Commission, I and a colleague interviewed two dozen experts and advocates in the field from across the political spectrum and concluded that "there is virtually universal agreement that absentee ballot fraud is the biggest problem."[52] Similarly, in our analysis of six years' worth of news articles on Nexis, absentee ballot fraud was the one area in which there had been a substantial number of official investigations of allegations and charges filed. We also found that in the existing research and literature on the issue of fraud, the opportunity for fraud in absentee balloting was an area of common concern. Numerous scholars and commissions studying elections have pointed out the susceptibility of absentee ballots to fraud, and the anecdotal evidence that this does occur is strong.[53] Such fraud can take place in many ways, the most prevalent being individuals filling out and submitting absentee ballots with fake names or the names of others; paying voters for their absentee vote, which can more easily be done because it is not a secret ballot and can be checked by a third party; and coercion of voters when filling out their absentee ballot— for example voters who are elderly or under pressure from someone with financial or perceived moral authority over the voter (such as an employer or a religious leader of a congregation).

Aside from these more pragmatic considerations, there are other negatives to democracy associated with absentee ballots. Language minorities have a more difficult time completing and having their absentee ballots counted than native English speakers.[54] In addition, having voters voting on dramatically different days—usually starting much farther out from Election Day than when early in-person voting begins—is problematic because it takes away from the idea of having a time of collective democracy.[55] Finally, as with extended in-person early voting, the need for a prolonged get-out-the-vote effort likely results in escalating campaign costs and further damage to the ideal of limiting the influence of money in campaigns.

As a result, in order to come out on the right side of the voter inclusion principle, at a minimum any plan to expand "no excuse" absentee balloting ought to follow guidelines that the organization Common Cause has done an excellent job of assembling. Among these are that citizens should always have the option to vote in person; in order to avoid fraudulent ballots, vote-by-mail programs should adopt the practice of requiring voters to sign ballot envelopes and comparing those signatures to the signatures on the voter's registration file; and workers engaged in signature comparison ought to be fully trained in how to do so accurately. Moreover, mail-in ballots should contain prominent notices that ballots must be filled out privately unless a voter requires assistance, and that it is a felony to offer anything in return for a vote or to coerce any person while that person is filling out his or her ballot. Election officials should contact voters in the case of a lack of a signature match or an overvote and give the voter the opportunity to correct it.[56]

The one exception to the arguments against absentee ballots is, of course, overseas and military voters.[57] Despite recent legislative improvements, such voters, known as UOCAVA voters, for the Uniformed and Overseas Civilian Absentee Voting Act, face enormous challenges in voting, are often disenfranchised and, among civilian voters, have very low participation rates.

While about a million UOCAVA absentee ballots were requested for the 2006 election, sixteen million voters could have applied for such ballots and did not. Moreover, only one-third of those ballots requested were actually cast and counted. In sum, only 5.5 percent of eligible UOCAVA voters actually participated successfully in the 2006 election.[58] Overall, the Overseas Vote Foundation found that one in five UOCAVA voters who sought to vote in the 2006 election were not able to cast a ballot successfully. In 2004, the National Defense Committee did a survey finding that 24 percent of UOCAVA voters were unable to vote successfully in that presidential election. Earlier studies have found that many overseas and military voters did not vote in the 2000 election because they received their absentee ballot too late or never.

In 2009, the U.S. Congress passed the Military and Overseas Voter Empowerment Act (MOVE) to try to address some of these failings. The new law allows for the exchange of materials between election officials and overseas voters electronically, including electronic transmission of ballots, and requires that election officials send blank ballots to overseas voters at least forty-five days before the election.

In its first go-round, the MOVE Act made a small but not insignificant difference. One-third of would-be overseas and military voters attempted to vote but could not, either because they did not receive a ballot on time or did not get it at all. However, this was an improvement over the 50 percent who were unable to vote for these reasons in 2008.[59] According to a survey, overall nearly 11 percent of respondents tried to vote but could not complete the process, and another 12 percent did not try to vote—most often, respondents said, because of a "lack of information." That is, these voters felt that they did not have enough information about the candidates and races to make an informed decision.[60] Use of technology in the transmittal of information and material varied widely by state, and several states were unable to meet the required forty-five-day deadline, leading to effective enforcement actions by the Department of Justice that led in most cases to settlements with the states that would make it more likely that voters would receive and be able to cast their ballot on time.[61]

Since overseas voters are believed to trend Republican[62]—the Republican Party claims that it has a 3-to-1 advantage[63]—it is in the interests of that party to make overseas voting as easy as possible, and it ought to push for effective implementation of UOCAVA and the MOVE Act. The partisan skew is usually attributed to the military being a Republican voting bloc. Yet there are more overseas voters *not* in the military than in the military, and there is some evidence that the military is not the solid bloc it was once thought to be. Therefore this is a group that the Democratic Party should also analyze and strategically target for increased turnout.

Most important, it is also in the American public's interest that Americans living in other countries and serving in the military have high rates of participation. They bring a unique perspective to the process that simply cannot be replicated or represented by domestic voters. Moreover, clearly all Americans support the rights of overseas and military voters to vote and have their votes count. Too often, overseas and military voters are not voting and not having their votes counted. Turning that around is a cause that both parties should champion.

Surely, the Internet and e-mail could be better used to educate overseas voters about how they can cast a ballot and ensure that it is counted. The Federal Voter Assistance Program, the Overseas Vote Foundation (OVF), and other organizations that work on voting issues for overseas voters are trying to build e-mail databases and reach out to more voters. These kinds of efforts need to expand beyond these organizations. All sorts of websites that are frequented by military and overseas voters ought to include a link to voter information for such voters. This includes web versions of international publications, the home pages of websites of government agencies, universities, and nongovernmental organizations that send many Americans overseas, and any blog sites that are geared toward Americans abroad. Moreover, private multinationals that employ Americans abroad have a responsibility to e-mail their employees during election times about their rights and how to vote effectively. This same responsibility applies to institutions that send students on study-abroad programs during election periods.[64]

A trickier topic is sending and submitting ballots online. This raises issues of security, accuracy, privacy rights, and the right to a secret ballot. We must balance these concerns against the multitude of problems overseas voters face in getting their voices heard. A December 2008 report by the National Institute of Standards and Technology found it is relatively safe to e-mail information to voters, including a ballot, but that it is much too risky to cast a vote via the Internet. "E-mail does not provide any guarantee that the intended recipient will receive the message," the report says. "An attack on DNS [Domain Name System] servers could route e-mails to an attacking party. This would not only result in voter disenfranchisement, but also the loss of sensitive voter information." The report also cites the possibility of a denial-of-service attack.[65] The solution may be to move toward giving all overseas voters the *option* of sending and receiving all materials electronically over a secure website *except* the completed ballot itself, provided voters are fully apprised of the potential privacy issues.

According to the OVF survey of overseas voters in the 2006 election, technical and administrative problems were not the only barrier. Nineteen percent of overseas respondents said they did not vote because they did not have enough information on the candidates and/or the issues.[66]

In order to increase interest and participation in the primaries, the parties ought to sponsor an overseas voter debate. Such a debate could be modeled after the Internet debate hosted by Yahoo, the *Huffington Post*, and *Slate Magazine* during the 2008 campaign. In these forums, candidates were able to participate from whatever location they chose, and the program allowed for "real-time questions sent in by the online audience, as well as viewer questions uploaded on video."[67] Only overseas voters would be invited to participate. By taking questions from overseas voters only, the questions would reflect the concerns and issues of importance to this group of voters in particular.

In addition to being on the Internet live and archived online, the debates might be aired in group settings throughout the world, including on military bases. NGOs and the State Department could also host group sites.

Although all the procedural reforms referred to above are critically needed, they cannot operate in a vacuum. As has been noted, it has been demonstrated that election reforms tend to retain existing voters, also necessary and good, but do not always necessarily increase turnout among previous nonvoters.[68] Structural reforms need an assist from the parties and the candidate campaigns, as well civic organizations. This is no less likely to be true in the realm of UOCAVA voters.

In some states, whether a person is overseas is indicated and publicly available on the voter registration list, along with that person's party registration. It is also public information as to who has requested an absentee ballot from overseas.[69] As a result, the parties could be engaging in the same types of get-out-the-vote efforts for overseas voters as they do for absentee voters in the United States. For example, the parties could, at a minimum, target their most loyal members whom they can identify as currently residing overseas and send them e-mail and mail reminders, information on how to effectively cast a ballot, and deadline dates for their state; send them the federal postcard application that they can use to register and request an absentee ballot, which is available online on the FVAP website with state-specific instructions; and even send them and e-mail them copies of the federal write-in absentee ballot (for voters who requested but have not received their state's absentee ballot in time to vote in a general federal election), which is also available for downloading on the FVAP website. As mentioned, such party efforts around absentee voting have been statistically shown to increase participation rates. In addition, the Democratic and Republican parties should have information about how to register and vote as a UOCAVA voter on the home page of their main websites, not just on the websites of Democrats and Republicans Abroad.[70]

On Election Day

Strict voter identification requirements have become the weapon of choice over the last decade to suppress the participation of voters likely to vote Democratic. Such laws patently fail the voter inclusion principle. It is clearly in the interest of electoral fairness and increasing participation that strict voter identification laws—defined as those that require very specific, limited types of identification that some citizens do not possess—be struck down and that no such further laws be enacted.

Numerous studies have demonstrated that huge numbers of people do not have the type of government-issued photo identification many states will now require. One report finds definitively that strict voter identification laws have a "negative impact on the participation of registered voters" relative to other methods of verifying identity, such as a signature match.[71] Far greater numbers of elderly, minority, immigrant, and poor voters lack the requisite documentation.[72]

At the same time, it has been amply demonstrated that the purported justification for voter identification laws—voter fraud—is completely unsupported. Academic studies, government studies, and even data from the U.S. Department of Justice all reveal that in-person polling-place fraud—the only type of fraud that would be addressed by a voter identification requirement—is an invented problem.[73] Indeed, in all the cases brought against states that have enacted stringent identification laws, not one state has been able to produce one substantiated case of polling place fraud. Not one of the amicus briefs filed in the Supreme Court case regarding identification was able to provide an apt example.[74]

Additionally, caging and challenges at the polls do nothing but raise the political acrimony in the midst of what is usually already a contentious election. Both parties should seek to greatly limit this practice. The bottom line is that this can go on because most states make it far too easy to challenge a voter's right to be registered and/or vote.[75] Many states allow any voter to engage in such a practice, or a political party, or any other entity that chooses to do so. States have extremely lenient standards, or no standards at all, regarding the evidence that must be presented in order to challenge another person's right to register or vote. And an ill-motivated challenger risks little if any punishment at all in making an unsupported challenge.[76]

There is simply no place in the democratic process for systematic registration challenges by people and groups outside the election administration system. The parties should support, and Congress should pass, federal legislation banning caging. The proposed Caging Prohibition Act[77] prohibits challenges to a person's eligibility to register or vote based solely on returned mail or a caging list and mandates that anyone who challenges another person's right to vote must set forth the specific grounds for the alleged ineligibility, based on firsthand knowledge, under penalty of perjury.

In addition, states must establish fair standards for challenges. All states should have uniform challenge procedures characterized by transparency and fairness; such procedures must be designed in a way that prevents disenfranchisement or voter deterrence. Ideally, on Election Day, only poll workers—not another voter or a poll watcher—should have the legal authority to challenge a voter. Otherwise, states should enact stringent requirements for when someone can make a challenge at the polls, and the bases upon which such challenges can be made must be narrowly defined. Such challenges should be based on personal knowledge and documentary evidence of lack of eligibility. States should also require pre-election challenges to be filed well ahead of Election Day, and similarly be based on very particularized charges and on personal knowledge and/or documentary evidence. The U.S. Department of Justice should also actively pursue vote caging and polling place challenges clearly based on race or ethnicity.

It is also important for the parties to support activities that make it easier for Americans who are not fluent in English to participate on Election Day. Current political trends indicate that both Democrats and Republicans should seek reforms that increase Latino and Asian voting rates, as well as those of Native Americans, especially where they are the potential margin of difference (such as in South Dakota, New Mexico, and Arizona). Numerous reports have made clear that the Latino population is rapidly increasing and that Latinos are becoming more and more a reliable Democratic voting bloc.[78] At the same time, some Republicans acknowledge the need to reach out to this rapidly growing and increasingly powerful group if their party is to be successful in future elections and in some key swing states.[79]

While limited studies show Asian American voters to be less partisan generally, the recent trend is for Asian Americans to vote Democratic. A major survey of Asian American voters in 2001 showed them identifying as Democrats by a more than 2-to-1 margin. Indeed, Al Gore outpolled George Bush in 2000 substantially among these voters,[80] and a 2008 poll showed Asian American voters favored Obama over McCain by a 3.4-to-1 ratio.[81] Like these other groups, Native Americans also lean heavily toward the Democratic Party[82]—by some estimates, up to 80 percent Democratic.[83]

However, the parties need to capitalize on this to maximize the potential advantage by getting more of these voters to vote. The voting rates of all three of these groups lag behind that of whites, for a variety of reasons, including, of course, continued discrimination and intimidation.[84]

Additionally, however, many Latino, Asian, and Native American voters do not speak English as their first language, potentially diminishing their participation rates. There are 8 million limited English proficiency (LEP) eligible voters; 4.5 million speak Spanish or Spanish Creole, and over 1.5 million speak an Asian language.[85] Native American jurisdictions rank second to Spanish-speaking jurisdictions in the number of places where there must be language translation assistance. Studies have shown that when language assistance is not made available to these voters, they are much less likely to participate. By contrast, where bilingual services are offered, participation rates are higher One study found that in counties covered by Section 203 of the Voting Rights Act and thus required to provide language assistance at the polls, Latino voter turnout was much higher than in noncovered counties—10 to 14 percent higher.[86]

The parties must ensure that Latino, Asian, and Native American voters get the assistance they ought to receive if this is to be a fully participatory democracy. Democrats and Republicans should insist that any new requirements regarding increased voter education efforts, as detailed above, take appropriate account of language minority communities. This means, for example, sending sample ballots in alternative languages and requiring that any free airtime opportunities encourage use of ethnic media. In addition, though many states provide election information and material on their websites in alternative languages, many covered by Section 203 of the Voting Rights Act do not;[87] as web use becomes increasingly prevalent across a wide spectrum of groups, the parties should advocate measures that require states to do so. Jurisdictions in noncovered areas should also be strongly encouraged to provide web-based information and materials, such as registration forms, in alternative languages known to be commonly used. Several states already do this: for example, Minnesota provides voter registration forms in Hmong, Spanish, Somali, Russian, and Vietnamese. Iowa provides forms in Spanish, Vietnamese, Lao, and Bosnian.[88] This is an easy, inexpensive way to get more information and easier access to limited-English speakers and should be done elsewhere.

Implementation of Section 203 requirements that language assistance be available at the polls where needed is spotty at best. Numerous incidents of noncompliance have been documented by civil rights groups, scholarly research shows that jurisdictions repeatedly fail to carry out the mandates of the Voting Rights Act, and the U.S. Department of Justice has filed a number of Section 203 voting rights lawsuits against jurisdictions over the last several years. The most wide-reaching survey of covered jurisdictions found that only 68 percent of jurisdictions visited provided the required registration materials and alternative language staff. One-seventh of the jurisdictions could not offer required alternative language registration materials, and one-fourth did not have the legally mandated language translators available to assist non-English-speaking voters.[89]

Parties must not only be vigilant in ensuring Department of Justice enforcement of these provisions; they must find their own ways to hold jurisdictions responsible and accountable. Implementation is left to the states and then often to the counties. Therefore, once again, action must occur at the state and local level. One element in this should include a required emphasis on the rights of language-minority voters in poll-worker training. Many of the problems occur because poll workers are not educated on how to handle voters who do not speak English well; and occasionally poll workers are overwhelmed and rude to language-minority voters.

Both parties ought also to seek state laws that address the voting needs of language-minority groups who do not meet the threshold for Section 203 coverage. Many states have groups such as these, and some include minority groups that are just shy of the mark. Providing language assistance— just the promise of such assistance in advance of the election—may do much to increase participation among these constituencies.

A few states have already gone in this direction, providing political players a template for reform elsewhere. Under California state law, "LEP voters who live in a county that is not covered under Section 203 have the right to access a copy of the ballot, along with instructions translated into Spanish or another language, 'if a significant and substantial need is found' by the local election official. California's laws also mandate that minority-language sample ballots be provided and posted in polling areas where the Secretary of State determines that three percent or more of the voting age citizens are LEP, or when citizens or organizations provide information supporting a need for assistance. Local clerks in California are required to make reasonable efforts to recruit election officials who are fluent in Spanish and other languages."[90] Under Colorado law, county clerks and registrars in all counties where 3 percent or more of eligible voters are language minorities must hire staff to assist those voters.[91]

Another group of voters almost as big is actually systematically blocked from the polls: people who have prior felony convictions. It is critical that we stop the practice of disenfranchising people who have in the past committed a felony and served their time and paid their dues. Currently 5.3 million Americans are denied the right to vote because of felony convictions. Three-fourths of them are no longer incarcerated, and 2 million have fully completed their sentences. All but two states disenfranchise felons who are incarcerated, and the majority continue to disenfranchise ex-felons while they are on probation or parole, while a few drag it out even further to require ex-felons to go through complicated clemency processes and/or require that they have paid all fees, fines, and restitution before regaining the right to vote. Two states, Kentucky and Virginia, continue to deny the right to ever vote again to people who have been convicted of a felony.[92]

Clearly for some the issue of disenfranchising former felons is a partisan issue, whether they publicly acknowledge that or not. It stands to reason. Based on a reading of the demographics, the likelihood is that loosening of felon disenfranchisement laws will bring more Democratic voters into the system than Republicans. Yet partisan advantage aside, the injustice of disenfranchising former felons so violates the voter inclusion principle that on that basis alone it must fall.

In large part because of the racial skew of the criminal laws and the criminal justice system, felon disenfranchisement systematically excludes minorities and poor people from democracy. Some 1.4 million African American men—13 percent—are disenfranchised, a rate that is seven times the national average.[93] Latinos are also overrepresented. This is not surprising, given the state of the criminal justice system. Nearly half of prisoners are African American, although African Americans represent only 13 percent of the population; and 20 percent of prisoners are Latino, even though Latinos make up only 16 percent of the general populace.[94] Some of this lack of proportion is clearly due to the disparate criminal laws regarding drug crimes, as well as potential bias in the criminal justice system.

Poor people are also hit disproportionately by felon disenfranchisement laws. First, the poor are dramatically overrepresented in the criminal justice system. According to the U.S. Department of Justice in 1997, 68 percent of people in prison had not completed high school, 53 percent earned less than $1,000 a month, and almost half were unemployed or underemployed prior to their arrest.[95] This is compounded by requirements in ten states that ex-felons pay all fines, fees, court costs, restitution, and other legal payments before regaining their rights.[96] This further discriminates against the poor, who may literally never be able to get out from under this debt. It has been called a modern-day poll tax, and surely in effect it is.

Felon disenfranchisement cannot even be justified in principle.[97] It serves to achieve no rational goal, nor does it fulfill any rational need of the criminal justice system. From the perspective of election integrity, if the point is to "cleanse" the electorate of those who are immoral, we would need more than a judge and jury to weed out all those who fit the bill in this country who are not incarcerated. It is true that we are denying felons other rights, such as free movement; but felons—even ones still in jail—enjoy many constitutional rights, such as free speech and free exercise of religion. Why single out this one right?

It is not even good for society to exclude these members of the citizenry. Indeed, in some ways it is counterproductive. Certainly no would-be criminal is deterred from committing a crime because of the threat of loss of voting rights. It strains credulity to believe that felons view loss of such a right as a core element of their punishment, or retribution against them. Disenfranchisement does not serve to rehabilitate the criminal. In fact, there is reason to believe it does just the opposite. If one accepts the argument that participation in itself leads to a greater sense of efficacy and a stronger trust in government, restoring voting rights would aid in the rehabilitation process. It will help to reengage the person in civic society, something that we know can help reduce recidivism.[98]

At the same time, it may be useful to the political system to have the views of these individuals represented. As has been made clear, felons and ex-felons are disproportionately minority and poor. As we have seen, these are groups that persistently lag in voter turnout in general, and thus their views and unique experiences living and working in this country are disproportionally excluded from public debate and consideration. It would behoove society to have more voices from these backgrounds engaged so that our public discourse and policy decisions reflect the true makeup and the true viewpoints and concerns of the American populace.

Another more practical, nuts-and-bolts aspect of working toward reforms impacting Election Day itself to increase turnout is the fair allocation of voting machines and poll workers. As much talk as there has been about the security and reliability of voting machines over the last few years, Democrats' electoral fortunes have likely been affected just as much or even more by poorly allocated voting machines and voting sites. The reports from the 2004 election in this regard are voluminous. Most notorious was Ohio. Several scholars, press investigations, along with the Democratic National Committee and the House Judiciary Committee Democratic staff, determined that there were disproportionately fewer voting machines available in minority and predominantly Democratic jurisdictions, leading to disproportionately long lines, long waiting times, and voters leaving the polling sites without voting, likely deterring other voters who might have been planning on voting from coming out to the polls.[99] It is estimated that 3 percent of voters in Ohio who went to the polls left without voting and did not return.[100] This is also another instance where an extreme negative experience at the polls can lead to a disinclination to participate in the future. None but the most dedicated voters—and the voters who have the work and life flexibility to spend hours in a voting line—will participate in a system that presents so many frustrations and so much inequity.

Thus it is crucial that Democrats, for the sake of the turnout of their voters and for justice in democracy, demand that states identify formulas and create plans for allocation of voting machines that have the best chance of creating an equal playing field and effective voting process on Election

Day. Many states have no requirements at all regarding machine allocation, and in others those rules are extremely vague. Often the decision is
left to the counties, and only some of them have any concrete, discernible
formula for making sure there are enough machines, that they are distributed equitably, and allocated in such a way to ensure minimal wait times.
In the states that do have laws, they are often not enforced.[101] Not only
does this likely diminish participation, but it may well be unconstitutional;
there are machine-allocation disparities within states that could violate the
equal protection clause of the Fourteenth Amendment.

By the same token, we need to be smarter about allocation of poll workers. In some places the parties play a direct role in the appointment of poll
workers, but even where they do not, they should urge election administrators and legislators to take a different approach in this area. A dearth of
poll workers is a perennial problem throughout the country. However, it is
even worse in poorer communities. This is a problem because if there are
too few poll workers operating a polling place, the likelihood of long waits
to vote increases. As wait time increases, the probability that voters will
show up at the polls and walk away without voting also goes up. Sometimes shortfalls in poll workers result in polling sites opening late—or, in
some cases, not opening at all. This occurs all over the country every year.
This failing must deter a great many voters from voting, a number that has
yet to be assessed but must intuitively be high.

There are also troubling disparities in poll-worker allocation that make
addressing this problem more crucial. The U.S. Election Assistance Commission (EAC) Election Day Survey found that jurisdictions with higher-
income voters and more highly educated voters had more poll workers
and fewer staffing problems than poorer and less-educated jurisdictions.[102]
Another EAC study found that "predominantly non-Hispanic, Black jurisdictions reported a greater percentage of polling places or precincts with
inadequate number of poll workers. Predominantly non-Hispanic, Native
American jurisdictions reported the second highest percentage of staffing problems."[103] This clearly violates the voter inclusion principle. It also
makes it more likely that voters in these areas will be deterred from participating because of long lines. As a result, in the same way the parties—
again, especially the Democrats—must ensure at the state level that there
are plans for equitable distribution of machines and polling sites, they
must also insist on the fair allocation of poll workers.

It has long been evident to anyone who has done election work or been a poll worker that in most places there is a rush in the morning before people go to work, a smaller uptick during the lunch hour, and then another rush in the evening when voters are returning home from work. Through more study, we could chart these patterns more precisely and allocate poll workers accordingly. This would also be helpful to recruitment of poll workers in that they would not necessarily need to work sixteen-hour days as is currently the practice. In the meantime, split shifts for poll workers seems to be helpful in those jurisdictions that make use of them, such as Wisconsin.[104]

Counting the Votes

Counting provisional ballots cast in the wrong precinct but the correct jurisdiction is an obvious way to increase the number of votes counted. It is also likely to increase voters' faith that their votes will be counted and thereby boost turnout. Thousands of voters cast provisional ballots only to find out their vote was not counted because they mistakenly went to the wrong place—yet they had made the effort to come out and vote and were eligible voters.[105] Such negative experiences at the polling place can lead to disenchantment with the electoral process and cause voters to simply give up and stay home in the future.

Democrats have favored counting these ballots, while Republicans have fought vigorously against doing so. One possible reason for this is that conventional wisdom holds that Democrats are more likely to move more often, and therefore are more likely to experience mix-ups in where they are supposed to vote.[106] There is some evidence that some demographic groups that trend Democratic are indeed more mobile, perhaps because they are more likely to be home renters rather than homeowners.[107] Moreover, the EAC's Election Day Study found that provisional ballots were cast at a much higher rate in "Section 203" jurisdictions in which there are sizable language minority populations—more likely Democrats. Urban and other high-density areas also had higher rates of provisional ballots.[108] This is likely because precincts are smaller in geographic area in urban centers, thereby increasing the probability of a voter moving over a precinct line without becoming aware of it.[109]

Given demographic realities and strategic political calculations, it is no wonder that Republicans would seek to reduce the number of provisional ballots counted. So far they have been largely successful, regardless of the law itself—for there is a very strong case to be made based both on the statutory language itself and the legislative history that the intent of the Help America Vote Act was to count provisional ballots that may have been cast in the wrong polling site but the correct county.[110]

In any case, not counting such ballots is politically unethical and a drain on democracy, for what is demonstrably evident is that states that exclude ballots cast in the wrong site disenfranchise legitimate voters. In 2004, twenty-eight states did not count out-of-precinct ballots, while seventeen states did.[111] If all states had counted out-of-precinct ballots, it is estimated that nearly 300,000 more votes would have counted in the 2004 election.[112] Overall, one-third of the nearly two million provisional ballots cast were not counted. The second most common reason election administrators reported for rejecting provisional ballots was that the ballots were cast in the wrong precinct. According to a government study, jurisdictions that accepted provisional ballots cast in the wrong precinct counted 71.7 percent of their ballots, while jurisdictions that did not counted only 52.5 percent of their ballots.

While surely it is true that a voter turning up at the wrong polling site and casting a ballot there causes administrative inconvenience, it is not so onerous that it should trump the right to vote. There is also no evidence to suggest that states that do count out-of-precinct ballots had more voters casting provisional ballots than other states. In other words, there was no evidence to suggest that citizens unconcernedly went to random polling places. Moreover, quite often voters will vote in the wrong place through no fault of their own, but rather have not been informed or have been misinformed of their proper polling place, or have had their polling place move without notice.[113]

The election reform that has been proposed in a number of federal bills—to require states to count votes for statewide offices if the ballot was cast in the wrong precinct or polling site but in the correct county—therefore makes sense from an ethical point of view and from a strategic perspective. Boiled down, it makes sense politically that Democrats should favor this reform; evidence suggests that more of their voters than Republican voters are impacted by the more-restrictive rules. But it is also ethically obligatory for both parties to seek this reform—it will increase participation, and none of the arguments against it surmount the injustice of disenfranchisement of legal voters.

At the same time, both parties also have an incentive to do more to ensure that their voters know the proper place to vote. It is absurd that a sizable number of Americans may not vote, or not have their vote counted, because they do not know where to go to cast a ballot.

What the Parties Can Do

For most of our history, political operatives have bent the meaning and intent of election laws in order to suppress the votes of their political foes. They perceived this to be an effective means for winning elections. At times their tactics were illegal, and at others they just skirted the boundaries of the law; often they were, from a democratic standpoint, potentially legal but certainly damaging and against any rules of fairness. While both major parties and minor parties engaged in such endeavors until the mid-twentieth century, the expansion of voting rights and the movement of voters of color to the Democratic Party led the Republicans to be the major users of such tactics after the mid-1960s.

There is another way to use election laws to one side's advantage that does not include excluding some Americans from exercising their right to vote: using these same election laws for the purpose of vote expansion. As has been described, there are many reasons why blocking certain voters from participating is wrong and harmful to our society and democracy. The other side of the coin is that it is healthy for democracy to employ tactics that encourage greater participation among a broader slice of society. There are many ways to accomplish this goal.

Politicians clearly have a dominant role to play in deciding to use these methods instead of suppressing votes. Yet it is also the American voter, regardless of his or her political persuasion, who must demand fair elections that allow for the participation of all eligible citizens. The politicians control the levers of power over laws and procedures—but it is the American people they must answer to as they set the rules of our democracy. We the people must demand better in the elections to come.

EPILOGUE

What Citizens Can Do

As the 2012 presidential campaign got into gear in late 2011, the partisan assault on voting rights showed no signs of abating. The push for more laws requiring government-issued photo identification at the polls was continuing, most notably in the large swing state of Pennsylvania. Referendum campaigns around amending the state constitution to require photo ID were being planned in Missouri and Minnesota. The state legislative sessions of 2012 promised further such efforts, including in some states where legislators had unsuccessfully tried to pass ID laws the previous year, like Nebraska. In Maine, which had for years been able to boast of some of the highest participation levels in the country, the state legislature did away with the state's decades-old Election Day registration law. Maine is a state in which Republicans took control over both chambers of the legislature in 2010.[1]

Perhaps the 2011 season of attacks on student voting rights was the most striking part of the current campaign, and Maine was the epicenter of this phenomenon as well. In that state, the head of the Republican

Party, Charles Webster, decided to undertake his own investigation of student voters, announcing a list of 206 students he claimed to have committed fraud by virtue of their being registered to vote in Maine but hailing from other states, claiming some of them had voted twice. Based on just this proclamation, the Republican secretary of state, Charles Summers, launched his own investigation. He determined that in fact none of these students had engaged in any type of illegal voting.

The story did not end there, however. In September, Summers then proceeded to send a letter, despite his own finding that there had not been illegal voting, to 191 of the students on his original list of 206. In the letter he warned them that they might be violating Maine election and motor vehicle laws if they did not have a Maine driver's license and have their vehicles registered in the state of Maine. In fact, there is no such connection between the right to vote and these motor vehicle laws. Moreover, the letter enclosed a "Voter Request to Cancel Registration"—but not a form to apply for a Maine driver's license or vehicle registration form, suggesting that was the appropriate remedy. Demos, a policy and research center, and the American Civil Liberties Union wrote Secretary Summers a letter in which he was informed that, by targeting students and suggesting that they might be at jeopardy of criminal prosecution, he was violating the Voting Rights Act's prohibition on voter intimidation, among other federal laws.[2]

At the same time, in a heartening sign, organizations and individuals were fighting for voting rights. In Maine, citizens, through the activities of Protect Maine Votes, submitted 70,000 signatures in just four months in order to put repeal of the law eliminating Election Day registration on the ballot. On November 8, 2011, Mainers voted in favor of the repeal measure reinstating Election Day registration by a margin of 60 percent to 40 percent.[3] In Wisconsin, state legislators and members of the Milwaukee City Council were working on passing state and local laws that would waive the $20 fee for residents who need their birth certificates in order to get the "free" photo ID the state was providing for voters.[4] House and Senate Democrats in Tennessee were working to repeal that state's new ID law, and, outside the statehouse, a citizen group called No Barriers to the Ballot Coalition of Tennessee was gathering petitions to present to legislators calling for repeal. Also in Tennessee, legislators and citizens, community, civic, and professional organizations, and churches were coming together to work to ensure that Tennesseans without identification were assisted in obtaining it, including by providing transportation to departments of motor vehicles. Finally, in Florida, Senator Ben Nelson stepped in to work toward the repeal of that state's new package of voting restrictions. He became engaged in this effort after learning that a teacher had been reported to state authorities for violating one of these laws. Her crime was that she provided her students voter registration forms without first registering to do so with the state and then failing to return them within forty-eight hours.

Laws like the Florida "antifraud" measures are being challenged by voting rights groups across the country. Yet, more action needs to be taken against vote suppression, and every interested person in the country should find a way to participate. Much critical work to secure voting rights is done in statehouses and within the official committees of the two main political parties. However, individual citizens have a role to play, and efforts on the part of persons and groups can often be effective in the struggle for voter inclusion.

A place for someone to start is to join one of the local, state, and national organizations working on these issues, many of which are planning efforts to help individual citizens obtain required ID and other documentation. In addition, any citizen can reach out to individual members of communities that disproportionately lack identification and help them obtain it. Signing petitions in the support of the repeal of restrictive laws or starting a petition drive is another positive action. Showing up at public hearings conducted by state legislators and making one's voice heard is a democratic right open to anyone, and in some cases it is possible to submit testimony to legislative bodies.

Joining national efforts to protect voting rights in 2012 is another optimal way to support voter participation. Election Protection—a coalition of voting, civil, and human rights organizations—was started in 2004 to help voters at the polls throughout the country. By means of phone hotlines and the quick deployment of volunteers to poll sites, Election Protection monitors and reports any problems voters might be having, especially those that might be of a systematic nature. On Election Day in November and throughout early voting in 2012, the organization will have comprehensive deployments that include thousands of volunteers to monitor activity at the polling place, assist voters, and solve problems before they lead to mass disenfranchisement. The 2012 effort will be major, and all the organizations involved will need volunteers to help in these nationwide efforts.

The 2012 presidential campaigns will focus attention on the polls and serve as a focal point for voting-rights work. Given the tenor of debate in American politics, we can expect heightened political rhetoric regarding voter fraud, and we should be prepared for campaign strategies that instrumentalize the fear of fraud for partisan ends. The election itself will be a contest between candidates but also between vote suppression and voter inclusion. As I have made clear, work to support the vote and maintain the right to the ballot at the polls is intensive, and it is very much grassroots and occurs at the precinct level. Such work gives American citizens ample opportunity to not only exercise their democratic rights but also to protect the rights of others.

Notes

1. The Voter Inclusion Principle

1. Douglas Hess and Judy Herman, "Representational Bias in the 2008 Electorate," Project Vote, November 2009, p. 2.

2. The Brennan Center for Justice, *League of Women Voters of Florida v. Cobb* (summary), August 6, 2008, http://www.brennancenter.org/content/resource/league_of_women_voters_of_florida_v_cobb/.

3. Frank Cerabino, "Early Voting Change Might Reduce Black Participation," *Palm Beach News*, July 6, 2011; Justin Levitt, "A Devil in the Details of Florida's Early Voting Law," Election Law Blog, May 23, 2011, http://electionlawblog.org/?p=18296#more-18296.

4. Travis Pillow, "Florida Senator's Argument Favoring Elections Bill: Voting Should Not Be Easy," *American Independent*, May 5, 2011; Michael Bennett, "Think We Have It Tough? In Africa, People Walk Up to 300 Miles to Vote, GOP Senator Says," Politifact Florida, *St. Petersburg Times* and *Miami Herald*, May 6, 2011.

5. Bennett, "Think We Have It Tough?"

6. *Wesberry v. Sanders*, 376 U.S. 1 (1964), at p. 17.

7. Eric S. Heberlig, Peter L. Francia, and Steven H. Green, "The Conditional Party Teams of the 2008 North Carolina Federal Elections," in *Change Election: Money, Mobilization, and Persuasion in the 2008 Federal Elections*, ed. David Magleby (Philadelphia: Temple University Press, 2010), 115.

8. "2008 Recap: Same Day Registration and Other Successes," press release, Democracy North Carolina, December 26, 2008, updated March 19, 2009.

9. Ibid.

10. Ibid.

11. Heberlig, Francia, and Green, "Conditional Party Teams of the 2008 North Carolina Federal Elections," 117.

12. See Greg Gordon, "Surge in Minority Voting Pushed Obama over the Top," McClatchey Newspapers, November 19, 2009; CNN Politics.com, Election Center 2008, Local Exit Polls, North Carolina, at http://edition.cnn.com/ELECTION/2008/results/polls/#val=NCP00p1.

13. "2008 Recap: Same Day Registration and Other Successes," press release, Democracy North Carolina, December 26, 2008, updated March 19, 2009.

14. Heberlig, Francia, and Green, "Conditional Party Teams of the 2008 North Carolina Federal Elections," 116.

15. See Douglas Hess and Judy Herman, "Representational Bias in the 2008 Electorate," Project Vote, November 2009; Justin Levitt, "A Citizen's Guide to Redistricting," Brennan Center for Justice, 2010; Ellen S. Miller, "Money, Politics and Democracy," *Boston Review*, March/April 1993; National Voting Rights Institute, "The Wealth Primary," at http://www.nvri.org/about/wealth1.shtml.

16. See Steven J. Rosenstone and John Mark Hansen, *Mobilization, Participation, and Democracy in America* (New York: Pearson Education, 2003); according to U.S. Census reports, voting rates are higher among older, married, more-educated, higher-income, and white citizens. See, for instance, "Voting and Registration in the Election of November 2004, Population Characteristics," United States Census Bureau, March 2006.

17. "Who Votes, Who Doesn't, and Why," Pew Research Center for the People and the Press, October 18, 2006, at http://www.people-press.org/2006/10/18/who-votes-who-doesnt-and-why/.

18. See Rosenstone and Hansen, *Mobilization, Participation, and Democracy in America*.

19. See, for example, Benjamin Highton and Raymond E. Wolfinger, "What If They Gave an Election and Everyone Came?" Public Affairs Report, University of California at Berkeley, July 1999, and "The Political Implications of Higher Turnout," Working Paper 99–5, Institute of Governmental Studies, 1999.

20. Rosenstone and Hansen, *Mobilization, Participation, and Democracy in America*, 247.

21. Ibid.

22. "America Unplugged: Citizens and Their Government," Council for Excellence in Government, July 12, 1999, at http://www.excelgov.org/excel/default.htm/.

23. Tim O'Brien, "If You Don't Care, Then Don't Vote," *Albany (NY) Times Union*, November 3, 2005, p. 1.

24. Drew Avery, "I Don't Care If You Don't Care," *Seattle Times*, July 10, 2004, at http://seattletimes.nwsource.com/html/next/2001975986_nextvoterapathy11.html.

25. Louis Menand, "Fractured Franchise," *New Yorker*, July 9, 2007.

26. Testimony of Karen Snow, Colorado Senate, State, Veterans, and Military Affairs Committee, Hearing on Senate Bill 11–018, 68th General Assembly, 1st sess., January 2011, transcribed from recording.

27. Keith G. Mahalak, *Livingston (MI) Daily Press & Argus*, letter to the editor, August 10, 2007.

28. Adam Berinsky, "The Perverse Consequences of Electoral Reform in the United States," *American Politics Research* 33, no. 4 (July 2005): 471–91.

29. Robert Stein, Chris Owens, and Jan Leighley, "Electoral Reform, Party Mobilization and Voter Turnout" (paper presented at the annual meeting of the American Political Science Association, Washington, DC, September 1, 2005).

30. J. Eric Oliver, "The Effects of Eligibility Restrictions and Party Activity on Absentee Voting and Overall Turnout," *American Journal of Political Science* 40, no. 2 (May 1996): 498–513.

31. Peter L. Francia and Paul Herrnson, "The Synergistic Effect of Campaign Effort and Election Reform on Voter Turnout in State Legislative Elections," *State Politics and Policy Quarterly* 4, no. 1 (Spring 2004): 85.

32. Berinsky, "Perverse Consequences of Electoral Reform," 471–91. Berinsky argues that reform alone does not bring out nonvoters but rather results in existing "transient" voters voting with more frequency. Hence structural reforms that may be meant to expand the electorate really just retain voters.

33. Dennis F. Thompson, *Just Elections: Creating a Fair Electoral Process in the United States* (Chicago: University of Chicago Press, 2002), 25.

34. Ibid., 23.

35. George Washington University Battleground Poll 2008, Tarrance Group and Lake Research Partners, July 2007.

36. See Gerry Mackie, "Why It's Rational to Vote," University of California, San Diego, August 2007, at http://www.social-phil.tcd.ie/downloads/002%20Mackie%20NonparadoxNonvoting.pdf.

37. Eric Plutzer, "Becoming a Habitual Voter: Inertia, Resources, and Growth in Young Adulthood," *American Political Science Review* 96, no. 1 (March 2002): 43.

38. Alan S. Gerber, Donald P. Green, and Ron Schachar, "Voting May Be Habit Forming: Evidence from a Randomized Field Experiment," *American Journal of Political Science* 47, no. 3 (July 2003): 540–50.

39. Plutzer, "Becoming a Habitual Voter."

40. Thompson, *Just Elections*, 20.

41. Ibid., 19.

42. Steven Finkel, "Reciprocal Effects of Participation and Political Efficacy: A Panel Analysis," *American Journal of Political Science* 29, no. 4 (November 1985): 891–913, at 892.

43. Ibid., 908.

44. John Stuart Mill, *On Representative Government* (London: Longmans, Green, Reader and Dyer, 1878), 27.

45. Ibid., 19.

2. The Early Years of Vote Suppression

1. J. Morgan Kousser, *The Shaping of Southern Politics* (New Haven, CT: Yale University Press, 1974), 7–8.

2. See Alexander Keyssar, *The Right to Vote: The Contested History of Democracy in the United States* (New York: Basic Books, 2000).

3. *Crawford v. Marion County Election Board*, 553 U.S. 181 (2008); argued January 9, 2008, decided April 28, 2008; no. 07–21, footnote 11.

4. See, for example, John Fund, "How to Steal an Election," *City Journal*, Autumn 2004, http://www.city-journal.org/html/14_4_urbanities-election.html. "Nowhere did voter fraud have a more notorious record than in Tammany-era New York. Tammany Hall's ruthless efficiency in manufacturing votes—especially during the zenith of its power in the second half of the nineteenth century—is legendary."

5. See, for example, Peter Argersinger, "New Perspectives on Election Fraud in the Gilded Age," *Political Science Quarterly* 100, no. 4 (1985–86): 669–87; Philip E. Converse, "Change in the American Electorate," in Angus Campbell and Philip E. Converse, *The Human Meaning of Social Change* (New York: Russell Sage, 1972), 263–337; Howard W. Allen and Kay Warren Allen, "Vote Fraud and Data Validity," in *Analyzing Electoral History: A Guide to the Study of American Voter Behavior*, ed. Jerome Clubb, William Flanigan, and Nancy Zingale (Beverly Hills, CA: SAGE Publications, 1981), 153–93; W. Dean Burnham, "The Changing Shape of the American Political Universe," *American Political Science Review* 59 (1965).

6. Paul Kleppner, *Who Voted? The Dynamics of Electoral Turnout, 1870–1980* (Santa Barbara, CA: Praeger Publishers, 1982), 59–60.

7. Keyssar, *Right to Vote*, 160–61.

8. Much of this description is drawn from the historical research of Richard Franklin Bensel and J. Morgan Kousser.

9. Richard Franklin Bensel, *The American Ballot Box in the Mid-Nineteenth Century* (Cambridge: Cambridge University Press, 2004), 36–38.

10. Alex Keyssar, "Unions, the Secret Ballot, and American Values," *Huffington Post*, June 26, 2007.

11. Bensel, *American Ballot Box*, 36–38.

12. Ibid., 40–41.

13. The amount of the taxes varied. In Tennessee, Article 2, Section 28 of the state constitution did not specify the amount of the tax on polls but provided that the tax should not be less than fifty cents nor more than one dollar a year. Frank B. Williams Jr., "The Poll Tax as a Suffrage Requirement in the South, 1870–1901," *Journal of Southern History* 18, no. 4 (November 1952): 469–96, n. 22. In South Carolina, the 1895 constitution put the poll tax at one dollar for males between the ages of twenty-one and sixty. Herbert Aptheker, "South Carolina Poll Tax, 1737–1895," *Journal of Negro History* 31, no. 2 (April 1946): 131–39, at 139.

14. David R. Goldfield, *Black, White, and Southern: Race Relations and Southern Culture, 1940 to the Present* (Baton Rouge: LSU Press, 1991), 9.

15. Bensel, *American Ballot Box*, 42.

16. Kousser, *Shaping of Southern Politics*, 58.

17. Laughlin McDonald, *A Voting Rights Odyssey: Black Enfranchisement in Georgia* (Cambridge: Cambridge University Press, 2003), 46.

18. Bensel, *American Ballot Box*, 49.

19. Lewis L. Gould, *Wyoming: A Political History, 1868–1896* (New Haven, CT: Yale University Press, 1968), 102, 117–18.

20. Kousser, *Shaping of Southern Politics*, 125–26.

21. Gunnar Myrdal, *An American Dilemma: The Negro Problem and Modern Democracy* (Piscataway, NJ: Transactions Publishers, 1995), 482.

22. See Steven F. Lawson, *Black Ballots: Voting Rights in the South, 1944–1969* (New York: Lexington Books, 1999), 12–13; Huey Perry and Wayne Parent, *Blacks and the American Political System* (Gainesville: University Press of Florida, 2005), 4.

23. Keyssar, *Right to Vote*, 143–44.

24. *Spencer v. Blackwell*, United States District Court, Southern District of Ohio, Western Division, complaint, case number 1:04CV738, October 27, 2004, p. 4.

25. Bensel, *American Ballot Box*, 143.

26. Ibid.

27. Keyssar, *Right to Vote*, 138.

28. "'Show Your Papers!' Jersey's New Registration Law Works Hardship to Old Voters," *New York Herald*, October 17, 1888, p. 1.

29. Michael J. Klarman, "The White Primary Rulings: A Case Study in the Consequences of Supreme Court Decisionmaking," *Florida State University Law Review* 29, no. 55 (2001).

30. Kousser, *Shaping of Southern Politics*, 52–54.

31. Ibid., 124.

32. Ibid., 127.

33. Ibid., 129.

34. Ibid., 134.

35. Tracy Campbell, *Deliver the Vote: A History of Election Fraud, an American Political Tradition, 1742–2004* (New York: Carroll & Graf, 2005), 98–99.

36. Ibid., 98.

37. Dayna Cunningham, "Who Are to Be Electors? A Reflection on the History of Voter Registration in the U.S.," *Yale Law and Policy Review* 9, no. 2 (1991): 384.

38. Keyssar, *Right to Vote*, 65. Keyssar cites Pennsylvania as an example, saying that "in 1836, Pennsylvania passed its first registration law, which required the assessors in Philadelphia (and only Philadelphia) to prepare lists of qualified voters: no person not on the list was permitted to vote. Although the proclaimed goal of the law was to reduce fraud, opponents insisted that its real intent was to reduce the participation of the poor—who were frequently not home when assessors came by and who did not have 'big brass' nameplates on their doors."

39. Jason P. W. Halperin, "A Winner at the Polls: A Proposal for Mandatory Voter Registration," *NYU Journal of Legislation and Public Policy* 3, no. 69 (1999–2000): 76–79.

40. Kousser, *Shaping of Southern Politics*, 48.

41. Georgia and Kansas followed suit in 2010 and 2011 respectively.

42. Keyssar, *Right to Vote*, 128.

3. Conditions and Consequences of the Voting Rights Act

1. Alexander Keyssar, *The Right to Vote: The Contested History of Democracy in the United States* (New York: Basic Books, 2000), 180.

2. Ibid., 182.

3. See Steven F. Lawson, *Black Ballots: Voting Rights in the South, 1944–1969* (New York: Lexington Books, 1999); Keyssar, *Right to Vote*, 192.

4. Keyssar, *Right to Vote*, 197.

5. See Lawson, *Black Ballots*.

6. See Steven Hahn, *A Nation under Our Feet: Black Political Struggles in the Rural South from Slavery to the Great Migration* (Cambridge, MA: Belknap Press of Harvard University Press, 2003).

7. Nancy J. Weiss, *Farewell to the Party of Lincoln: Black Politics in the Age of FDR* (Princeton, NJ: Princeton University Press, 1983).

8. David Bositis, "Blacks and the Democratic National Convention," Joint Center for Political and Economic Studies, 2008, p. 8.

9. See Andrew Gelman, Lane Kenworthy, and Yu-Sung Su, "Income Inequality and Partisan Voting in the United States," *Social Science Quarterly* 91, no. 5 (December 2010): 1203–19.

10. David Lublin, *The Republican South: Democratization and Partisan Change* (Princeton, NJ: Princeton University Press, 2004), 33.

11. See Isabel Wilkerson, *The Warmth of Other Suns: The Epic Story of America's Great Migration* (New York: Random House, 2010).

12. Kevin Phillips, *The Emerging Republican Majority* (New Rochelle, NY: Arlington, 1969).

13. Merle Black, "The Transformation of the Southern Democratic Party," *Journal of Politics* 66, no. 4 (November 2004): 1001–17, at 1006.

14. According to the USCCR in 1968, "Negro registration now is more than 50 percent of the voting age population in every Southern State. Before the Act this was true only of Florida, Tennessee, and Texas. The biggest gain has been in Mississippi, where Negro registration has gone from 6.7 to 59.8 percent. But there also have been important gains in other States. In Alabama, the percentage has gone from 19.3 to 51.6; in Georgia, from 27.4 to 52.6; in Louisiana, from 31.6 to 58.9; and in South Carolina, from 37.3 to 51.2." United States Commission on Civil Rights, "Political Participation," 1968, p. 12.

15. David Bositis, "Blacks and the 2004 Republican Convention," Joint Center for Political and Economic Studies, 2004, Table 1, p. 13.

16. See Earl and Merle Black, *Politics and Society in the South* (Cambridge, MA: Harvard University Press, 1987), 286.

17. Later on, the minority language provisions were added to the act. These provisions re-quire certain covered jurisdictions to provide bilingual written materials and other assistance to language minority voters, defined as American Indians, Asian Americans, Alaskan Natives, and persons of Spanish heritage.

18. Earl Black and Merle Black, *The Rise of Southern Republicans* (Cambridge, MA: Belknap Press of Harvard University Press, 2002), 2.

19. Charles S. Bullock and Mark Rozell, eds., *The New Politics of the Old South: An Introduction to Southern Politics* (Lanham, MD: Rowan & Littlefield, 2006), 2–3.

20. Fewer than 1 percent of voting-age blacks in Mississippi were registered to vote in 1964. Goldwater received 87 percent of the total state vote. Chandler Davidson, "Republican Ballot Security Programs: Vote Protection or Minority Vote Suppression—or Both?" A Report to the Center for Voting Rights and Protection, September 2004, p. 13; Dewey W. Grantham, *The South in Modern America: A Region at Odds* (New York: Harper Collins, 1994), 247.

21. James L. Sundquist, *Dynamics of the Party System: Alignment and Realignment of Political Parties in the United States* (Washington, DC: Brookings Institution, 1983), 362.

22. Ibid., 363.

23. Joseph A. Aistrup, *The Southern Strategy Revisited: Republican Top-Down Advancement in the South* (Lexington: University of Kentucky Press, 2011), 32–36.

24. Grantham, *South in Modern America*, 285.

25. Sundquist, *Dynamics of the Party System*, 374.

26. Keyssar, *Right to Vote*, 228.

27. Vote dilution methods used for partisan purposes will not be fully explored here, as they did not encompass efforts to actually block certain voters from the ballot box, the focus of this study.

28. Keyssar, *Right to Vote*, 231. See Chandler Davidson, "Minority Vote Dilution: An Overview," in *Minority Vote Dilution*, ed. Chandler Davidson (Washington, DC: Howard University Press, 1989), 4. Examples include such practices as racial gerrymandering and using at-large election districts.

29. See Lisa Handley and Bernard Grofman, "The Impact of the Voting Rights Act on Minority Representation: Black Officeholding in Southern State Legislatures and Congressional Delegations," in *Quiet Revolution in the South: The Impact of the Voting Rights Act, 1965–1990*, ed. Chandler Davidson and Bernard Grofman (Princeton, N.J.: Princeton University Press, 1994), 335.

30. United States Commission on Civil Rights, "Political Participation," 1968, p. 60, http://www.law.umaryland.edu/marshall/usccr/documents/cr12p753.pdf.

31. Ibid., 70

32. United States Commission on Civil Rights, "The Voting Rights Act: Ten Years Later," January 1975, p. 70, http://www.law.umaryland.edu/marshall/usccr/documents/cr12v943a.pdf.

33. Ibid., 84.

34. Ibid., 91.

35. United States Commission on Civil Rights, "The Voting Rights Act: Unfulfilled Goals," September 1981, p. 27, http://www.law.umaryland.edu/marshall/usccr/documents/cr12v944a.pdf.

36. United States Commission on Civil Rights, "The Voting Rights Act: Ten Years Later," 30.

37. United States Commission on Civil Rights, "The Voting Rights Act: Unfulfilled Goals," 65.

38. Ibid.

4. Vote Suppression Goes National—and Republican

1. This included Arizona in particular. According to Chandler Davidson, Latinos made up over 8 percent of the population in Phoenix in 1960, and Democrats "had taken over the state in

the 1930s with the support of new voters and Latinos." Chandler Davidson, Tanya Dunlap, Gale Kenny, and Benjamin Wise, *Republican Ballot Security Programs: Vote Protection or Minority Vote Suppression—or Both?* A Report to the Center for Voting Rights and Protection, September 2004, pp. 16–17.

2. *Spencer v. Blackwell*, United States District Court, Southern District of Ohio, Western Division, complaint, case number 1:04CV738, October 27, 2004, p. 4.

3. Richard Franklin Bensel, *The American Ballot Box in the Mid-Nineteenth Century* (New York: Cambridge University Press, 2004), 143.

4. Joseph P. Harris, *Registration of Voters in the United States* (Washington, DC: Brookings Institution, 1929), 231–32.

5. Justin Levitt and Andrew Allison, "A Guide to Voter Caging," Brennan Center for Justice, June 2007.

6. Ibid.

7. Rick Perlstein, "Operation Eagle Eye," Campaign for America's Future, April 24, 2007, citing "Chairman Bailey Warns against Republican Plans to Intimidate Voters," Democratic National Committee press release, October 27, 1964.

8. Chandler Davidson, Tanya Dunlap, Gale Kenny, and Benjamin Wise, "Vote Caging as a Republican Ballot Security Technique," *William Mitchell Law Review* 34, no. 2 (2008): 533–62, at 559.

9. Memo from director, FBI, to SAC Phoenix and SAC San Diego, July 27, 1986, 77–106904–307.

10. FBI report from Los Angeles office, August 11, 1986, investigation on July 1, 1986, field office file no. 77B-19657.

11. Testimony of Charles Pine, *Nominations of William H. Rehnquist and Lewis F. Powell, Jr.: Hearings before the Committee on the Judiciary, United States Senate, Ninety-second Congress,* 1971, p. 1051.

12. Interview of a "Phoenix Civil Rights Leader" on October 26, 2971, NK 77–12035.

13. David Beckwith and Amy Wilentz, "Through the Wringer," *Time,* August 11, 1986.

14. Transcription of an FBI interview, August 1, 1986, at Washington, DC, file no. 77B-86748.

15. Transcription of an FBI interview, July 28, 1986, SD 77B-5664.

16. "Democrats Charge G.O.P. Poll Watch Today Will Harass the Negroes and the Poor," *New York Times,* November 3, 1964.

17. Cabell Phillips, "GOP Opens Drive to Prevent Fraud," *New York Times,* October 20, 1964.

18. "GOP's 'Operation Eagle Eye' At Polls Stirs Democrats," Associated Press, in *Washington (DC) Evening Star,* November 2, 1964.

19. James MacNees, "Republicans Set Up Program to Check Ballots in Coming Election, Burch Sees Vote Fraud in '60 Race, Plan Will Encompass 'Every Precinct' in the Country," *Baltimore Sun,* October 13, 1964.

20. Frank Wright, "GOP Poll Watchers, Told to Be Partisan When It Helps Party," *Minneapolis Tribune,* October 24, 1964. Emphases in the original.

21. "Challenges in the South," *New York Times,* November 4, 1964.

22. "Eagle Eye Disrupts the Polls," special to the *Miami Herald Tribune,* November 4, 1964.

23. Ibid.

24. Chandler Davidson reports that "According to the *Chicago Daily News,* Operation Eagle Eye had 10,000 poll-watchers for Chicago's 3,552 polling places. Most were to be concentrated in "the so-called 'river wards,' areas close to the Loop where the Democratic machine is traditionally strong." Eagle Eye in Chicago worked in conjunction with the Joint Civic Committee on Elections (2,000 watchers), the Citizens Honest Election Foundation (7,500 watchers), and the Non-Partisan Law Student Committee for Honest Elections (200 watchers paid $15 per day). "250,000

Accredited to Watch City Polls," *Chicago Daily News,* 2 Nov. 1964, 1, 14." Davidson, Dunlap, Kenny, and Wise, *Republican Ballot Security Programs,* note 5, 26.

25. Ibid.

26. Stanley Penn, "Policing the Polls," *Wall Street Journal*, October 22, 1964.

27. Davidson, Dunlap, Kenny, and Wise, *Republican Ballot Security Programs,* 6.

28. Earl Black and Merle Black, *The Rise of Southern Republicans* (Cambridge, MA: Belknap Press of Harvard University Press, 2002), 216.

29. Ibid., 26.

30. Ibid., 34.

31. Ibid., 172.

32. Ibid., 205.

33. *Democratic National Committee v. Republican National Committee*, Civil Action 81–3876 (D.N.J., November 1, 1982) consent order.

34. Laughlin McDonald, "The New Poll Tax," *American Prospect*, December 30, 2002.

35. Patrick Breslin, "New Jersey Voters Were 'Intimidated,' Democrats Charge," Associated Press, November 6, 1981.

36. Settlement Agreement, *Democratic National Committee v. Republican National Committee*, Civil Action 81–3876 (D.N.J. 1981).

37. McDonald, "New Poll Tax."

38. Davidson, Dunlap, Kenny, and Wise, *Republican Ballot Security Programs,* 61.

39. Ibid.

40. Ibid., 60.

41. George Andreassi, "Judge Orders Democrats to Withhold Evidence Embarrassing GOP," UPI, October 20, 1986.

42. "GOP Memo Admits Plan Could 'Keep Black Vote Down,'" *Washington Post*, October 25, 1986.

43. Davidson, Dunlap, Kenny and Wise, *Republican Ballot Security Programs,* 63.

44. Ray Formanek Jr., "Head of Ballot Integrity Defends Tactics, GOP Effort," Associated Press, October 9, 1986.

45. Nicholas M. Horrock, "GOP Turned 60,000 In to FBI," *Chicago Tribune*, October 24, 1986, p. 8.

46. Settlement Stipulation and Order of Dismissal, *Democratic National Committee v. Republican National Committee*, Civil Action 86–3972 (D.N.J. 1986).

47. Davidson, Dunlap, Kenny, and Wise, *Republican Ballot Security Programs,* 73.

48. Thomas B. Edsall, "Bush Takes No Stand on Ballot Plan; Program Targeted N.C. Black Voters," *Washington Post*, November 9, 1990, p. A13.

49. James Rowley, "Senator's Campaign Settles Intimidation Allegation," Associated Press, February 26, 1992.

50. U.S. Department of Justice, "The Civil Rights Division at Thirty-five, A Retrospective," online at http://www.usdoj.gov/crt/overview.html.

51. Simon Tidsall, "Voting Disrupted in Senate Poll," *The Guardian*, November 7, 1990.

52. *Harper v. Virginia Board of Elections*, 383 U.S. 663, no. 48, argued January 25–26, 1966, decided March 24, 1966.

5. The Battle over Motor Voter

1. See Steven J. Rosenstone and Raymond E. Wolfinger, "The Effect of Voter Registration Laws on Voter Turnout," *American Political Science Review* 72, no. 1 (March 1978): 22–45; Ruy Teixeira, *The Disappearing American Voter* (Washington, DC: Brookings Institution, 1992).

2. Jennifer Rosenberg, *Expanding Democracy: Voter Registration around the World*, Brennan Center for Justice, June 10, 2009.

3. "A Summary of the National Voter Registration Act," Project Vote, February 19, 2006, http://projectvote.org/fileadmin/ProjectVote/pdfs/A_20Summary_20of_20the_20National_20Voter_20Registration_20Act1.pdf.

4. Lorraine Minnite, "Securing the Vote: An Analysis of Election Fraud," Demos, 2003, p. 23.

5. Youjin B. Kim and Lisa Danetz, "A Preliminary Analysis of the Public Assistance Agency Data within the Election Assistance Commission's 2009–2010 Biennial NVRA Report," Demos, July 1, 2011.

6. See Jody Herman, Douglas R. Hess, and Margaret Groarke, "A Review of the Existing Literature on the Effectiveness of the National Voter Registration Act," Project Vote, 2009; Frances Fox Piven and Richard A. Cloward, *Why Americans Still Don't Vote* (Boston: Beacon Press, 2000); Reports of the Federal Election Commission and the Election Assistance Commission on the Impact of the National Voter Registration Act on Federal Elections, http://www.eac.gov/registration-data/; Benjamin Highton, "Voter Registration and Turnout in the United States," *Perspectives on Politics* 2, no. 3 (September 2004): 507–15.

7. Tracy Campbell, *Deliver the Vote: A History of Election Fraud, an American Political Tradition, 1742–2004* (New York: Carroll & Graf, 2005), 284.

8. Rebekah Evenson, "Motor Voter in the States," Fairvote, 1995.

9. Piven and Cloward, *Why Americans Still Don't Vote*, 123.

10. Ibid., 135.

11. Ibid., 136.

12. Ibid., 144–45.

13. Ibid., 168.

14. Ibid., 178–79.

15. Ibid., 192.

16. Ibid., 200.

17. S. Rep. No. 103-6 (1993). National Voter Registration Act of 1993: Report of the Committee on Rules and Administration together with minority and additional views (to accompany S. 460) establishing national voter registration procedures for federal elections and for other purposes. United States Congress, Senate Committee on Rules and Administration, Washington, DC: G.P.O., 1993.

18. Teixeira, *Disappearing American Voter*, 61–69.

19. U.S. Senate Committee on Rules and Administration, "Establishing National Voter Registration Procedures for Federal Elections, and Other Purposes," February 25, 1993.

20. Piven and Cloward, *Why Americans Still Don't Vote*, 251.

21. National Voter Registration Act of 1992 (House of Representatives—June 16, 1992).

22. Ibid.

23. Piven and Cloward, *Why Americans Still Don't Vote*, 252.

24. U.S. Senate Committee on Rules and Administration, "Establishing National Voter Registration Procedures for Federal Elections, and Other Purposes," minority report, February 25, 1993.

25. Frances Fox Piven and Richard A. Cloward, "Northern Bourbons: A Preliminary Report on the National Voter Registration Act," *Political Science and Politics* 29, no. 1 (March 1996): 41.

26. *U.S. Code* 42 (1973) gg.

27. Jonathan E. Davis, "The National Voter Registration Act of 1993: Debunking States' Rights Resistance and the Pretense of Voter Fraud," 6 *Temple Political and Civil Rights Law Review* 117 (Fall 1996/Spring 1997): fn. 71.

28. Joan Biskupic, "Court Won't Hear State Challenge to 'Motor Voter Law,'" *Washington Post*, January 23, 1996, p. A1.

29. Stephen Knack and James White, "Did States' Motor Voter Programs Help the Democrats?" *American Politics Quarterly* 26, no. 3 (July 1998): 344.

30. Davis, "National Voter Registration Act of 1993," 136.

31. "Federal Court Approves Agreement Outlining the Way Michigan Will Comply with Voter Registration Law," U.S. Department of Justice, press release, March 6, 1996.

32. *Acorn v. Miller*, 129 F 3d. 833 (6th Cir. 1997).

33. Brett Bursey, "The Long Road to Voters Rights," http://www.scpronet.com/point/9602/p04.html, February 1995.

34. Arlie Porter and Sid Gaulden, "Federal Judge Orders State to Carry Out Motor Voter Law," *Charleston (SC) Post and Courier*, November 22, 1995, p. A1.

35. Ann Scott Tyson, "Illinois Court Drives Motor-Vehicle Debate," *Christian Science Monitor*, May 8, 1995.

36. Testimony of Sonia R. Jarvis, George Washington University, hearing of the U.S. House Oversight Committee, July 25, 1995.

37. Piven and Cloward, *Why Americans Still Don't Vote*, 257.

38. "'Motor Voter' Law Upheld in Virginia," Associated Press, in *Herald*, October 5, 1995.

39. Andrew McCain, "Allen Loses on Voter Mandate; Virginia Must Obey Registration Rules," *Washington Times*, October 4, 1995, p. C3.

40. Elizabeth Caldwell, "Motor Voter Proposal Stalls as House Cries States' Rights," *Arkansas Democrat-Gazette*, February 28, 1995.

41. Thad Slaton, "Motor-Voter Hasn't Turned Out as Predicted," *Greater Baton Rouge (LA) Business Report*, June 25, 1996, p. 25.

42. Testimony of Becky Cain, president, League of Women Voters, before the hearing of U.S. House Oversight Committee, July 25, 1995.

43. Becky Cain, "On the Road with Motor Voter," *Update on Law-Related Education* 20 (Fall 1996): 15–16, at 1–2.

44. U.S. Federal Election Commission, Executive Summary of the Federal Election Commission's Report to the Congress on the Impact of the National Voter Registration Act of 1993, June 1997.

45. John Harwood, "In a Surprise for Everyone, Motor-Voter Law Is Providing a Boost for GOP, not Democrats," *Wall Street Journal*, June 11, 1996, p. A16.

46. U.S. Federal Election Commission, Executive Summary of the Federal Election Commission's Report to the Congress on the Impact of the National Voter Registration Act of 1993, June 1997.

47. Harwood, "Motor-Voter Law Is Providing a Boost for GOP," A16.

48. See Teixeira, *Disappearing American Voter*; Benjamin Highton, "Voter Registration and Turnout in the United States," *Perspectives on Politics* 2, no. 3 (September 2004): 507–15; Benjamin Highton and Raymond E. Wolfinger, "The Political Implications of Higher Turnout," Notes and Comments, *British Journal of Political Science* 31 (2001): 179–223, at 187; Knack and White, "Did States' Motor Voter Programs Help the Democrats?" 344.

49. U.S. Senate Committee on Rules and Administration, "Establishing National Voter Registration Procedures for Federal Elections, and Other Purposes," February 25, 1993.

50. Job Serebrov and Tova Andrea Wang, "Voting Fraud and Voter Intimidation: Report to the U.S. Election Assistance Commission on Preliminary Research and Recommendations," http://www.slate.com/id/2166287/entry/2166282/.

51. The Brennan Center for Justice, "Alleged Registration Fraud," at http://www.truthaboutfraud.org/case_studies_by_issue/alleged_registration_fraud.html#more.

52. Lori Minnite, "Securing the Vote," Demos, 2003, p. 24.

53. Ibid., 25; Job Serebrov and Tova Andrea Wang, draft report, "Voter Fraud and Voter Intimidation," July 17, 2006.

54. Piven and Cloward, "Northern Bourbons," 41.

55. U.S. Senate Committee on Rules and Administration report, "Establishing National Voter Registration Procedures for Federal Elections, and Other Purposes," February 25, 1993.

56. Ibid.

57. Brian Kavanagh, Steve Carbo, Lucy Mayo, and Michael Slater, "Ten Years Later, a Promised Unfulfilled: The National Voter Registration Act in Public Assistance Agencies, 1995–2005," Demos, ACORN, and Project Vote, September 14, 2005, http://archive.demos.org/pub634.cfm.

58. Ibid., 5.

59. "Justice Department's Failure to Enforce National Voter Registration Act Underscored by New Report," *Project Vote News*, Project Vote, July 3, 2007.

60. Ibid.

61. Thom File and Sarah Crissey, "Voting and Registration in the Election of November 2008," U.S. Census, May 2010.

62. See, for example, *Harkless v. Brunner*, 545 F.3d 445 (6th Cir. 2008).

63. Scott Novakowski, "Fulfilling the Promise: Expanding Voter Registration of Low–Income Citizens under the National Voter Registration Act," Demos, July 22, 2010, p. 3

6. The Election of 2000 and Its Fallout

1. See, for example, Abner Greene, *Understanding the 2000 Election: A Guide to the Legal Battles That Decided the Presidency* (New York: NYU Press, 2005).

2. Lorraine C. Minnite, *The Myth of Voter Fraud* (Ithaca, NY: Cornell University Press, 2010), 134. Only one major figure was claiming that vote fraud was a major issue in the 2000 election: Senator Kit Bond, who complained about the process that occurred in Missouri, not Florida. Due to overcrowding and administrative mismanagement in St. Louis, a local circuit judge ordered polls in St. Louis held open an additional three hours, apparently allowing some great number of voters to vote for Democrats. "Bond went on to request formally a federal criminal investigation of the incident. Much to his chagrin, once investigations were complete, not only were charges of voter fraud not brought, but also the U.S. Justice Department concluded that the city election board had improperly purged voters from the rolls ahead of the 2000 election." Charles Stewart III, "What Hath HAVA Wrought? Consequences, Intended and Not, of the Post–*Bush v. Gore* Reforms" (prepared for the conference on "Bush v. Gore, 10 Years Later: Election Administration in the United States," Center for the Study of Democracy, University of California, Irvine, April 16–17, 2011), p. 18. As Minnite describes, Bond also went around the country during the debate over the Help America Vote Act and made numerous claims of fraud in the registration lists, most famously insisting that "Ritzy," a dog, was on the Missouri voter registration list.

3. For example, in 1994, the U.S. Department of Justice found that African Americans in Louisiana were four to five times less likely than white residents to have government photo identification. Letter from Deval L. Patrick, assistant attorney general, Civil Rights Division, U.S. Department of Justice, to Sheri Marcus Morris, Louisiana assistant attorney general (November 21, 1994).

4. "Help America Vote Act of 2002" (HAVA), Pub. L. No. 107-252, 116 Stat. 1666 (2002).

5. *William Crawford et al. v. Marion County Election Board*, United States Court of Appeals for the Seventh Circuit, Nos. 06–2218, 06–2317, January 4, 2007.

6. Kristen Mack, "In Trying to Win Has Dewhurst Lost a Friend?" *Houston Chronicle*, May 18, 2007.

7. Testimony of Jonah H. Goldman, director of the National Campaign for Fair Elections, before the Senate Committee on the Judiciary, May 20, 2008; testimony of John C. Fortier, American Enterprise Institute, for the Committee on House Administration Elections Subcommittee on Expanding and Improving Opportunities to Vote by Mail or Absentee, October 22, 2007; Job

Serebrov and Tova Andrea Wang, Voting Fraud and Voter Intimidation Report to the United States Election Assistance Commission on Preliminary Research and Recommendations, 2006.

8. Sheila Dewan, "In Georgia, Thousands March in Support of Voting Rights," *New York Times*, August 7, 2005.

9. Erik Erickson,"Voter ID Precleared," RedState.com, August 27, 2005, 10:37 a.m.

10. Erik Erickson, "Brown Opposed Voter ID Law," RedState.com, July 28, 2005 8:30 a.m.

11. Section 5 Recommendation Memorandum: August 25, 2005, Factual and Legal Review by U.S. Department of Justice Voting Section Attorneys Recommending Objection to the Submission.

12. Brian Bassinger Morris News Service, "Voter ID Bill Draws Concern," *Augusta (GA) Chronicle*, March 27, 2005.

13. Section 5 Recommendation Memorandum: August 25, 2005, Factual and Legal Review by U.S. Department of Justice Voting Section Attorneys Recommending Objection to the Submission, p. 6

14. M. Kasim Reed, "The Voter ID Debate: A Problematic Solution for a Nonexistent Problem," *Atlanta Journal-Constitution*, April 3, 2005.

15. *Crawford v. Marion County Election Board*, 553 U.S. 181 (2008). Many legal analysts believe one of the major "take aways" from the decision is that the Court will not be inclined to rule in favor of challenges to voting laws as being discriminatory before there are actual plaintiffs before the court demonstrating the extreme burden—an "as applied challenge" as opposed to a "facial challenge." "Once the state has posited its neutral reasons for such a law, the law is to be upheld if it doesn't impose serious burdens on most voters. For those voters who do face serious burdens, they must bring an 'as applied' challenge where they present specific evidence applied to them as to why the law is onerous." Rick Hasen, "Initial Thoughts on the Supreme Court's Opinion in *Crawford*, the Indiana Voter Identification Case," Election Law Blog, April 28, 2008. While the ruling was certainly a defeat for opponents of voter identification laws such as these, the Court did leave the door open for a future "as applied" challenge under the right circumstances.

16. See, for example, Matt A. Barreto, Stephen A. Nuño, and Gabriel R. Sanchez, "The Disproportionate Impact of Indiana Voter ID Requirements on the Electorate," Working Paper, Washington Institute for the Study of Race and Ethnicity, November 8, 2007; R. Michael Alvarez, Delia Bailey, and Jonathan N. Katz, "The Effect of Voter Identification Laws on Turnout," *California Institute of Technology Social Science Working Paper No. 1267R*, January 1, 2008; Matt A. Barreto, Stephen A. Nuño, and Gabriel R. Sanchez, "Voter ID Requirements and the Disenfranchisement of Latino, Black and Asian Voters" (prepared for presentation at the American Political Science Association Annual Conference), September 1, 2007; "Citizens without Proof," Brennan Center for Justice, November 2006; John Pawasarat, "The Driver License Status of the Voting Age Population in Wisconsin," Employment and Training Institute, University of Wisconsin–Milwaukee, June 2005.

17. "Citizens without Proof," Brennan Center for Justice, November 2006.

18. For example, 26 percent of Wisconsin's ninety-one DMVs are open one day a month or less, over half are open on a part-time bases, the state has only one DMV with weekend hours, and three Wisconsin counties have no DMVs. See One Wisconsin Now, "One Wisconsin Now Statements on Walker Signing Voter Suppression Bill," May 9, 2011.

19. "Policy Brief on Voter Identification," Brennan Center for Justice, September 2006.

20. In early 2007, the political world was shaken by what came to be known as the U.S. attorneys' scandal. As a larger picture of the politicization of the Department of Justice emerged, especially the Civil Rights Division, the focal point was the firing and forced resignations of nine U.S. attorneys and the consideration of three more for sudden removal, for apparent political reasons. As it turned out, five of those twelve were targeted because they had not pursued alleged voter fraud accusations with sufficient vigor for the political operatives in the Bush administration. The

case of U.S. attorney for New Mexico David Iglesias was particularly telling. In the midst of a very tight congressional race, Iglesias was pressured by the state's U.S. senator and political operatives in the White House via appointees in the Department of Justice to prosecute more people for alleged incidents of voter fraud in advance of the 2006 election. In fact Iglesias had vigorously pursued the allegations, even setting up a special task force to investigate, and found nothing to prosecute. He was soon after fired. The case of Todd Graves was also notable. In that instance, there was a very tight senatorial race going on. Just after Graves was removed because he did not want to be involved in a Department of Justice effort to purge Missouri's voter rolls in a way that could have disenfranchised eligible voters, he was replaced by one of the architects of the politicization of the Department of Justice, Bradley Schlozman. He went on to bring charges of registration fraud against the group ACORN (considered to be more likely to register Democratic voters) a week before the election, in violation to Department of Justice procedures that warn against bringing voter fraud cases just before an election. When Schlozman filed the charges, ACORN had already fired the workers and turned them over to law enforcement, making the motivation behind bringing the charges seem all the more suspicious. See Dan Eggen and Amy Goldstein, "Voter Fraud Complaints by GOP Drove Dismissals," *Washington Post*, May 14, 2008; Eric Lipton, "Panel Asks Official about Politics in Hiring," *New York Times*, June 6, 2007; Frank Morris, "Attorneys Scandal May be Tied to Missouri Voting," *All Things Considered*, NPR, May 3, 2007.

21. *Crawford v. Marion County Election Board*, 553 U.S. 181 (2008).

22. Stephen Ansolabehere and Nathan Persily, "Voter Fraud in the Eye of the Beholder: The Role of Public Opinion in the Challenge to Voter Identification Requirements," 121 *Harvard Law Review* 1737 (2008).

23. Tova Andrea Wang, "Election 2004: A Report Card," *American Prospect*, January 1, 2005, at http://www.tcf.org/list.asp?type=NC&pubid=824.

24. Ibid.

25. Teresa James, "Caging Democracy: A 50-Year History of Partisan Challenges to Minority Voters," Project Vote, September 2007, p. 16.

26. *Order of U.S. District Court*, District of New Jersey, Civ. No. 81–3876(DRD), November 1, 2004.

27. Spencer Overton and Daniel Tokaji, "Profiling at the Polls in Ohio: Presence of Partisan Challengers a Threat to Our Democracy," *Dayton Daily News*, October 31, 2004.

28. Testimony of Judith Brown-Dianis, co-director of Advancement Project, Hearing on Voter Caging and Voter Challenges before the Senate Committee on Rules and Administration, February 13, 2008.

29. Abby Goodnough and Don Van Natta, "Bush Secured Victory in Florida by Veering from Beaten Path," *New York Times*, November 7, 2004.

30. "Conference Call: The New Voter Suppression and the Progressive Response," Progressive States Network, June 12, 2008.

31. Jason Leopold and Matt Renner, "Emails Detail RNC Voter Suppression in Five States," *Truthout*, July 26, 2007.

32. Alexander Keyssar, *The Right to Vote: The Contested History of Democracy in the United States* (New York: Basic Books, 2000), 271.

33. For a more thorough analysis of this question, see Stewart, "What Hath HAVA Wrought?"

34. Ibid., 34.

35. Ibid., 16.

7. A Slight Upswing

1. E-mail exchange between the author and Bob Phillips, executive director, Common Cause North Carolina, November 18, 2008.

2. Art Levine, "Was Clinton Campaign Targeting Black Voters with Deceptive Calls?" *Huffington Post*, May 5, 2008.

3. Meredith Decker, "Iowa Caucus Ruckus," *The Nation*, December 13, 2007.

4. Ed Brayton, "Obama Campaign Files Suit over Voter Foreclosure Plans," *Michigan Messenger*, September 16, 2008.

5. Settlement agreement at http://s3.amazonaws.com/propublica/assets/docs/settlement_agreement_081020.pdf.

6. See Advisory 2008–25, Voting Rights of Persons Facing Foreclosure, Ohio secretary of state, September 24, 2008.

7. According to the U.S. Election Assistance Commission, "More than 2.1 million provisional ballots [were] reported cast nationwide. . . . More than 600,000 provisional ballots, or 28.2 percent, were rejected, most commonly because it was determined that the voter was not properly registered." U.S. Election Assistance Commission, "2008 Election Administration and Voting Survey," November 2009, p. 4.

8. "Pa. GOP Sues ACORN, State, Alleging Voter Fraud," Associated Press, October 17, 2008.

9. Ian Urbina, "States' Actions to Block Votes Appear Illegal," *New York Times*, October 8, 2008.

10. Justin Levitt, Wendy R. Weiser, and Ana Munoz, "Making the List: Database Matching and Verification Processes for Voter Registration," Brennan Center for Justice, March 24, 2006; Kim Zetter, "Voter Database Glitches Could Disenfranchise Thousands," *Wired*, September 17, 2008.

11. Steve Bousquet, "New Voter Registration Law Snares Mostly Minorities," *St. Petersburg (FL) Times*, October 17, 2011.

12. According to the Florida director of Common Cause, Ben Wilcox, the county administrators of the following counties agreed to process IDs at early voting sites to allow voters to cast regular ballots: Alachua Bay, Broward, Calhoun, Citrus, Clay, Columbia, Gilchrist, Gulf, Hardee, Hendry, Highlands, Marion, Pasco, Pinellas, Monroe, Nassau, Okaloosa, Palm Beach, Polk, Santa Rosa, Washington, Jackson, Jefferson, Leon, Liberty, Manatee, St. Johns, and Wakulla. Internal field report, October 24, 2008.

13. E-mail exchange between the author and Derek Cressman, Common Cause, Washington, DC, November 3, 2008.

14. See American Civil Liberties Union, "Georgia's Voter Registration Procedures Discriminate and Should Be Permanently Blocked, Civil Rights Coalition Argues," press release, May 24, 2010.

15. Ibid.

16. *State of Georgia v. Holder*, Response to Plaintiff's and Defendant's Joint Motion to Dismiss by Defendant-Intervenors Brooks et al., Georgia Association of Latino Elected Officials, and Organization of Chinese Americans Georgia Chapter et al., no. 1:10-CV-01062, p. 9, citing May 29, 2009, objection letter.

17. Mary Lou Pickel, "Long-time Voters Also Being Checked by Georgia," *Atlanta Journal-Constitution*, October 16, 2008.

18. Mary Lou Pickel, "Nearly 5,000 Challenge Ballots Cast," *Atlanta Journal-Constitution*, November 8, 2008.

19. Zachary Roth, "Georgia's 'Non-Citizen' Voting Controversy: A Recap," Talking Points Memo (TPM), November 12, 2008, http://tpmmuckraker.talkingpointsmemo.com/2008/11/georgias_non-citizen_voting_co.php.

20. *State of Georgia v. Holder*, 1:10-cv-01062 (D.D.C.).

21. *Jennifer Brunner, Ohio Secretary of State v. Ohio Republican Party et al.*, 129 S. Ct. 5 (2008), per curiam, no. 08A332, on application for stay [October 17, 2008].

22. Todd Hartman, "Judge Orders Coffman to Stop Voter Purge," *Denver Rocky Mountain News*, October 31, 2008.

23. It should be noted that while the turnout was historic, at between 62 and 63 percent, we must at the same time wonder what kind of system breakdown would ensue should we ever achieve the turnout levels that are routine in most countries around the world where participation rates are in the 75–94 percent range. See http://www.idea.int/publications/vt/upload/Voter%20 turnout.pdf.

24. Election Protection, "Michigan Alert: Long Line Plagues Polling on East Side of Detroit," press release, November 4, 2008; Ian Urbina, "Voters Find Long Lines but No Catastrophes," *New York Times*, November 5, 2008.

25. R. Michael Alvarez, Thad Hall, Stephen Ansolabehere, Adam Berinsky, Gabriel Lenz, and Charles Stewart III, "2008 Survey of the Performance of American Elections," CalTech/MIT Voting Technology Project, p. 42.

26. Ibid., 2.

27. Democratic National Committee, "Democracy at Risk: The 2004 Election in Ohio," 2005, p. 5.

28. They Want to Make Voting Harder? *New York Times* editorial, June 5, 2011.

29. Susan Page, "Poll: Young Voters Hint at Electoral Shift," *USA Today*, October 6, 2008.

30. *Symm v. United States*, 439 U.S. 1105, no. 77–1688, January 15, 1979.

31. U.S. Census Bureau, "Voting and Registration in the Election of November 2008" (May 2010). Available at www.census.gov/prod/2010pubs/p20–562.pdf.

32. See Young Voter Strategies, "Voting Is a Habit," Graduate School of Political Management at the George Washington University, February 2007.

33. Tamar Lewis, "Voter Registration by Students Raises Cloud of Consequences," *New York Times*, September 7, 2008.

34. "Virginia Officials Blocking Eligible Student Voters," Brennan Center for Justice, press release, October 31, 2008; Jennifer S. Rosenberg, "The Postman Always Rings My Dorm Room Twice," Brennan Center for Justice, October 2008.

35. Naomi Zeveloff, "El Paso County Democrats Claim Voter Disenfranchisement," *Colorado Independent*, September 25, 2008.

36. Avni Patel, "'Tis the Season of Election Dirty Tricks: Scaring Student Voters," ABC News, October 6, 2008.

37. Josh White, "Hoax Voting E-Mail Targets George Mason Community," *Washington Post*, November 4, 2008.

38. David Broockman, Yale University, and Ethan Roeder, New Organizing Institute, "Hispanics Are the Future of Progressive Strength in America: A Systematic Quantitative Analysis of Where, When, and How Investing in the Latino Vote Will Make the Difference between Victory and Defeat for Democrats Nationwide," New Organizing Institute, September 2010, p. 6.

39. Cristina Silva, "Nevada Senate Race Turns Uglier with Hispanic Ad," Associated Press, October 20, 2010.

40. Andrea Nill Sanchez, "GOP Candidate's Claims That Mexicans Are Being Bused In to Vote Dismissed by AZ Secretary of State," *Think Progress*, October 29, 2010.

41. Sean McCaffrey, "Correction: Email from B.A.N. President Sean McCaffrey," BanAmnestyNow.com, October 29, 2010.

42. Stephen Clark, "Justice Department to Send Election Observers to Arizona as Concern Rises about Illegal Voters," Fox News, October 30, 2010, http://www.foxnews.com/politics/2010/10/29/justice-dept-send-election-observers-arizona-group-seeks-crack-illegal-voters/#ixzz1ULuvI1JS.

43. "The Myth of Widespread Noncitizen Voting," Mexican American Legal Defense and Education Fund, August 20, 2008.

44. Angela Maria Kelley, Marshall Fitz, Gebe Martinez, and Vanessa Cárdenas, "Latinos Make Their Mark," Center for American Progress, November 9, 2010.

45. See *Crawford v. Marion County*, in the Supreme Court of the United States, brief for amicus curiae, Mexican American Legal Defense and Educational Fund in Support of Petitioners, p. 25.

46. Matt A. Barreto, Stephen A. Nuño, and Gabriel R. Sanchez, "Voter ID Requirements and the Disenfranchisements of Latino, Black and Asian Voters" (prepared for presentation at the 2007 American Political Science Association Annual Conference, September 1, 2007).

47. Gabriel R. Sanchez, Stephen A. Nuño, and Matt A. Barreto, "The Disproportionate Impact of Photo ID Laws on the Minority Electorate," Latino Decisions, May 24, 2011, http://latinodecisions.wordpress.com/2011/05/24/the-disproportionate-impact-of-stringent-voter-id-laws/.

8. Effects on Election Outcomes

1. J. Morgan Kousser, *The Shaping of Southern Politics: Suffrage Restriction and the Establishment of the One-Party South, 1880–1910* (New Haven, CT: Yale Historical Publications, 1974).

2. Ibid., 61.

3. Ibid., 55.

4. Ibid., 68.

5. Ibid., 91.

6. "Negroes Must Be Barred; White Supremacy Demanded by the South Carolina Convention," *New York Times*, September 12, 1895.

7. Kousser, *Shaping of Southern Politics*, 91.

8. Ibid., 92.

9. Ibid., 101.

10. Ibid., 102, Table 4.9.

11. Ibid., 110.

12. Ibid., 122.

13. Ibid., 116.

14. Ibid., 118.

15. United States Commission on Civil Rights, "Political Participation," 1968, p. 12.

16. Ibid.

17. Ibid.

18. Ibid.

19. The Central Arkansas Library System, the *Encyclopedia of Arkansas History and Culture*, http://www.encyclopediaofarkansas.net/encyclopedia/entry-detail.aspx?entryID=593.

20. United States Commission on Civil Rights, "Political Participation," 14.

21. Ibid., 15.

22. United States Commission on Civil Rights, "The Voting Rights Act: Ten Years Later," January 1975, p. 41.

23. Ibid., 40–41.

24. Ibid., 41.

25. Ibid., 46.

26. Ibid., 49.

27. United States Commission on Civil Rights, "The Voting Rights Act: Unfulfilled Goals," September 1981, p. 11.

28. Ibid., 54.

29. The Sentencing Project, "Felony Disenfranchisement Laws in the States," March 2011.

30. "Felon Disenfranchisement," *Ford Reports* 37, no. 3 (2008).

31. Eddie Hailes, "It's Time to Give Felons Back Their Right to Vote," *Washington Post*, July 27, 2008.

32. Stevens's conviction was ultimately set aside.

33. Brennan Center for Justice, "An Unhealthy Democracy," editorial memorandum, July 2, 2002.

34. Senate Amendment 2879, "To Secure the Federal Voting Rights of Certain Qualified Persons Who Have Served Their Sentences," amendment to S. 565 (107th Congress) "Martin Luther King, Jr., Equal Protection of Voting Rights of 2002," offered February 14, 2004, by Senator Harry Reid (D-NV).

35. A number of Democrats also voted against the bill, many people believe, because it threatened to derail the entire underlying comprehensive election reform bill.

36. The term "ex-felon" is often used with different meanings, depending on the circumstances. It is sometimes used to describe persons who have completed their prison sentences, regardless of whether they may still be on parole or probation. Most commonly it refers to a person who has fully completed his sentence, including any post-incarceration punishment.

37. See ACLU, "Voting Rights for People with Criminal Records: 2008 State and Legislative Changes," http://www.aclu.org/votingrights/exoffenders/statelegispolicy2008.html.

38. See Spencer Overton, *Stealing Democracy* (New York: W. W. Norton, 2006), esp. 59; Alexander Keyssar, *The Right to Vote: The Contested History of Democracy in the United States*, rev. ed. (New York: Basic Books, 2000), 276.

39. However, using survey data of self-reported voting behavior, researchers at the Pew Hispanic Trust have questioned Manza and Uggen's results, reporting that "Uggen and Manza (2002) estimate voter turnout and voter choice on the basis of the *known* characteristics of the disenfranchised individuals, including: gender, race, age, income, labor force status, marital status, and education. It is important to note that these characteristics are just a subset of the controls included in our analysis. However, as our results indicate, differences in the voting behavior of criminals still exist, even when controlling for these known characteristics. Thus, it is likely that this previous research overestimates the rate at which disenfranchised felons would turn out to vote and, thus, the political impact of changes in disenfranchisement laws." Randi Hjalmarsson and Mark Lopez, "The Voting Behavior of Young Disenfranchised Felons: Would They Vote If They Could?" Pew Hispanic Center, May 2008, p. 6. However, most book critics and experts in the field praised the work, and Uggen and Manza's work is cited in many reports and publications. From the *New York Review of Books*, for example: "Surprised at how little was known about the practice of disenfranchisement, Manza and Uggen, sociologists at Northwestern University and the University of Minnesota, set out to investigate it. Exacting and fair, their work should persuade even those who come to the subject skeptically that an injustice is at hand. . . . Manza and Uggen write with an appealing evenhandedness, searching out arguments that challenge their own. They find few people articulating the case for felon disenfranchisement, which appears to thrive more as practice than theory. . . . The authors warn against overestimating felon apathy." Jason DeParle, "The American Prison Nightmare," *New York Review of Books* 54, no. 6 (April 12, 2007).

40. Jeff Manza and Christopher Uggen, "Punishment and Democracy: Disenfranchisement of Nonincarcerated Felons in the United States," *Perspectives on Politics* 2, no. 3 (September 2004): 491–505, at 497.

41. See Kenneth Bridges, *Twilight of the Texas Democrats* (College Station: Texas A&M University Press, 2008).

42. Senator Mitch McConnell, WhoRunsGov.com.

43. Jeff Manza and Christopher Uggen, *Locked Out: Felon Disenfranchisement and American Democracy* (New York: Oxford University Press, 2006), 194. See also Manza and Uggen, "Punishment and Democracy," 491–505.

44. Manza and Uggen, *Locked Out*, 192.

45. Ibid., 197.

46. "An Unhealthy Democracy: Florida Court Case Highlights Felon Disenfranchisement Crisis in U.S.; National Effort to Restore Voting Rights to Ex-Felons Grows," editorial memorandum, Brennan Center for Justice, July 2, 2002.

47. U.S. Commission on Civil Rights, "Voting Irregularities in Florida during the 2000 Presidential Election," June 2001, chap. 1, http://www.usccr.gov/pubs/vote2000/report/ch1.htm.

48. Ibid., chap. 5, http://www.usccr.gov/pubs/vote2000/report/ch5.htm.

49. John Lantigua, "How the GOP Gamed the System in Florida," *The Nation*, April 12, 2001.

50. U.S. Commission on Civil Rights, "Voting Irregularities in Florida," chap. 5, http://www.usccr.gov/pubs/vote2000/report/ch5.htm.

51. Ibid.

52. Ibid.

53. Ibid.

54. Gregory Palast, "Florida's Disappeared Voters: Disenfranchised by the GOP," *The Nation*, January 18, 2001.

55. Ibid.

56. Scott Hiaasen, Gary Kane, and Elliot Jaspin, "Felon Purge Sacrificed Innocent Voters," *Palm Beach Post*, May 27, 2001.

57. Lantigua, "How the GOP Gamed the System in Florida."

58. U.S. Commission on Civil Rights, "Voting Irregularities in Florida," chap. 5, http://www.usccr.gov/pubs/vote2000/report/ch5.htm.

59. U.S. Federal Election Commission, "2004 Election Results," at http://www.fec.gov/pubrec/fe2004/tables.pdf.

60. *Preserving Democracy: What Went Wrong in Ohio; Status Report of the House Judiciary Committee Democratic Staff*, January 5, 2005, p. 4.

61. Ibid., 47.

62. Robert F. Kennedy Jr., "Was the 2004 Election Stolen?" *Rolling Stone*, June 1, 2006.

63. "Democracy at Risk: The 2004 Election in Ohio," Democratic National Committee Voting Rights Institute, 2005, Section II, Executive Summary, p. 5

64. Ibid., 7.

65. Ibid., 9.

66. See Brennan Center for Justice, Policy Brief on Voter Identification, September 2006, at http://www.brennancenter.org/content/resource/policy_brief_on_voter_identification/; Dr. Robert Pastor, Robert Santos, Alison Prevost, and Vassia Gueorguieva, "Voter IDs Are Not the Problem: A Survey of Three States," American University, January 9, 2008. This report also points out that "State officials have also given various estimates for the number of voters without ID but have released little if any information on how these estimates were derived. In Michigan, the Secretary of State's office estimated the number of registered voters without ID at 370,000, about 5% of the state's total, while the Secretary of State in Missouri estimated that between 170,000 and 190,000 voters, or about 3 to 3.2% of the state's total population, lacked ID. In Georgia, numerous estimates have been made. . . . A 2006 analysis by the then Georgia Secretary of State office estimated the number of registered voters without photo ID at 675,000, based on a comparison of the voter registration rolls to the state's Department of Driver Services database. . . . A more recent estimate by the new Secretary of State identified 198,000 voters who may not have a driver's license or state ID by comparing voter registration rolls with records from the Department of Driver Services" (p. 5).

67. Robert S. Erikson and Lorraine C. Minnite, "Modeling Problems in the Voter Identification–Voter Turnout Debate," *Election Law Journal* 8, no. 2 (2009): 85–101. In this article, Erickson and Minnite examine three different methodologies used to assess impacts on voter turnout and conclude that "the existing science regarding vote suppression [i]s incomplete and inconclusive. This is not because of any reason to doubt the suppression effect but rather because the

data that have been analyzed to date do not allow a conclusive test" (p. 98). The authors suggest that having more elections to look at in the future may make such studies more possible, and that in the interim researchers do more analysis of aggregate data within and between states.

68. Matt A. Baretto, Stephen A. Nuño, and Gabriel Sanchez, "Voter Identification Requirements and the Disenfranchisement of Latino, Black and Asian Voters" (prepared for presentation at the 2007 American Political Science Association Annual Conference, September 1, 2007), p. 6.

9. How to Increase Participation

1. CNN.com Election 2004 poll at http://www.cnn.com/ELECTION/2004/pages/results/states/US/P/00/epolls.0.html.

2. "A Remarkable Statistic from Obama's Victory (Voting and Income)," *Daily Kos*, November 8, 2008.

3. Michael Alvarez, Morgan Llewellyn, and Thad Hall, "How Hard Can It Be: Do Citizens Think It Is Difficult to Register to Vote?" Caltech/MIT Voting Technology Project Working Paper no. 48, July 2006, p. 13.

4. Ibid.

5. See Alan Gathright, "Motor Voter System a Work in Progress," *San Francisco Chronicle*, October 18, 2003; "Minnesota: Some Voters Still Question Why They Weren't Registered," *Grand Forks (ND) Herald*, November 13, 2004; "Why Does DMV Have Trouble Properly Registering Voters?" *San Joaquin (CA) News Service*, November 7, 2004.

6. Letter to Christopher Coates, acting chief, and T. Christian Herren Jr., acting deputy chief, Voting Section, Civil Rights Division, U.S. Department of Justice, from Demos, December 4, 2008.

7. Annie Linskey, "Nearly 25 Percent of MVA Voter Registrations Fail," *Baltimore Sun*, February 20, 2011.

8. "Policy Brief on Restrictions on Third Party Voter Registration Drives," Brennan Center for Justice, September 2006.

9. Groups have included Project Vote, League of Women Voters, People for the American Way, Redeem the Vote, Focus on the Family, Priests for Life, and the Christian Coalition.

10. One liberal-leaning organization's volunteers have allegedly filled out registration forms with false names, while conservative groups have been accused of jeopardizing the tax-exempt status of churches.

11. "Restricting Voter Registration Drives," Project Vote, January 9, 2006, p. 7.

12. See, for example, Craig Leonard Brians and Bernard Grofman, "Election Day Registration's Effect on Voter Turnout," *Social Science Quarterly* 82, no. 1: 170–83, 2001; Mark J. Fenster, "The Impact of Allowing Day of Registration Voting on Turnout in U.S. Elections from 1960–1992," *American Politics Quarterly* 22 (1994): 74–87; Benjamin Highton, "Easy Registration and Voter Turnout," *Journal of Politics* 59, no. 2 (1997): 565–75; Stephen Knack, "Election-Day Registration," *American Politics Research* 29, no. 1 (2001): 65–78; Michael Alvarez and Stephen Ansolabehere, "Expanding the Vote: Election Day Registration in California," Demos, March 11, 2002; Michael Alvarez, Jonathan Nagler, and Catherine H. Wilson, "Making Voting Easier: Election Day Registration in New York," Demos, April 20, 2004.

13. Alvarez, Nagler, and Wilson, "Making Voting Easier," p. 7.

14. "High 2004 Turnout for States with Election Day Registration," Demos Fact Sheet, available at http://www.demos.org/page18.cfm.

15. "Voters Win with Election Day Registration: A Snapshot of Election 2006," Demos, January 31, 2007.

16. Michael McDonald, "Unofficial 2008 Voter Turnout," United States Election Project at George Mason University, at http://elections.gmu.edu/preliminary_vote_2008.html.

17. Sam Roberts, "In Shift, 40% of Immigrants Move Directly to the Suburbs," *New York Times*, October 17, 2007.

18. Kei Kawashima-Ginsberg, Amanda Nover, and Emily Hoban Kirby, "State Election Law Reform and Youth Voter Turnout," Center for Information and Research on Civic Learning and Engagement, July 2009.

19. The Center for Information and Research on Civic Learning and Engagement, Youth Vote, "2010 Midterm Elections," at http://www.civicyouth.org/quick-facts/youth-voting/.

20. See www.futuremajority.com, "2008 Youth Vote in Context."

21. Michael Alvarez, Stephen Ansolabehere, and Catherine H. Wilson, "Election Day Registration in the United States: How One-Step Voting Can Change the Composition of the American Electorate," Caltech/MIT Voting Technology Project, June 2002, p. 16.

22. "Universal Voter Registration: A Way to Empower and Engage All Californians," New America Foundation, October 30, 2006, p. 8.

23. Michael McDonald, "Voter Pre-Registration Programs," George Mason University, November 20, 2009.

24. "Policy Brief on Student Voting," Brennan Center for Justice, March 8, 2006.

25. "Partisanship: A Lifelong Loyalty That Develops Early," Young Voter Strategies, February 2007, available at http://www.youngvoterstrategies.org/index.php?tg=fileman&idx=get&inl=1&id=1&gr=Y&path=Research&file=Partisanship+is+a+Habit.pdf.

26. Ibid.

27. "Youth Turnout Rate Rises to at Least 52%," CIRCLE, November 7, 2008, at http://www.civicyouth.org/?p=323.

28. See "An Agenda for Election Reform," at http://www.federalelectionreform.com/pdf/Federal%20Agenda.pdf.

29. See Tova Andrea Wang, A Citizen from Day One, Demos, July 2010.

30. Jeffrey S. Passel, "Growing Share of Immigrants Choosing Naturalization," Pew Hispanic Center, March 28, 2007, p. 2.

31. Jackie Calmes, "Republican Forecast: Cloudy," *Wall Street Journal*, September 5, 2007, p. A8.

32. Jane Junn and Kerry L. Haynie, eds., *New Race Politics in America: Understanding Minority and Immigrant Politics* (Cambridge: Cambridge University Press, March 2008), p. 22.

33. "Cardin, Schumer to Introduce Bill to Prohibit Voter Intimidation and Voter Suppression," press release, December 13, 2011.

34. See, for example, John Wagner, "Md. Robo-Calls: Ehrlich Aide, Consultant Accused of Trying to Suppress Black Vote," *Washington Post*, June 17, 2011.

35. Dennis F. Thompson, *Just Elections: Creating a Fair Electoral Process in the United States* (Chicago: University of Chicago Press, 2002), 59–60.

36. *To Assure Pride and Confidence in the Electoral Process*, National Commission on Federal Election Reform, August 2001, additional statement.

37. Raymond E. Wolfinger, Benjamin Highton, and Megan Mullin, "State Laws and the Turnout of the Registered" (paper prepared for presentation at the 2002 annual meeting of the Midwest Political Science Association, Chicago, April 25–28), p. 9.

38. Raymond E. Wolfinger, Benjamin Highton, and Megan Mullin, "Between Registering and Voting: How State Laws Affect the Turnout of Young Registrants" (paper prepared for presentation at the 2002 annual meeting of the American Political Science Association, Boston, August 29–September 1); "Key Election Laws Can Boost Youth Voter Turnout," Center for Information and Research on Civic Learning and Engagement, June 21, 2004.

39. See Common Cause, "Much at Stake for Democracy in the Transition to Digital TV: The Decisions Congress Makes This Fall Will Affect Us All," August 19, 2005, at http://

www.commoncause.org/atf/cf/{fb3c17e2-cdd1–4df6–92be-bd4429893665}/common%20cause%20editorial%20memo%20on%20digital%20tv%20transition1.pdf.

40. Paul Taylor and Norman Ornstein, "The Case for Free Air Time: A Broadcast Spectrum Fee for Campaign Finance Reform," New America Foundation, Spectrum Series Issue Brief no. 5, June 2002.

41. See Tova Andrea Wang, "Increasing Voter Participation," The Century Foundation, June 2006, p. 12.

42. Henry Milner, "Civic Literacy: How Informed Citizens Make Democracy Work," Tufts University, 2002, p. 44.

43. See Paul Gronke and Eva Galanes-Rosenbaum, "Getting Out the Early Vote: Lessons for Progressives" (report prepared for the Progressive Targeting Conference, Center for American Progress, August 31, 2005).

44. Robert Stein, Chris Owens, and Jan Leighley, "Electoral Reform, Party Mobilization and Voter Turnout" (paper presented at the annual meeting of the American Political Science Association, Marriott Wardman Park, Omni Shoreham, Washington Hilton, Washington, DC, September 1, 2003), p. 19.

45. See Martin Sieff, "Early Voting Revolution Transforms U.S. Campaign Strategies," United Press International, October 31, 2008; Stephen Ohlemacher, "Democrats Dominate Voting in Early States," Associated Press, October 29, 2008; Dan Balz, "Obama's Early Vote Push," *Washington Post*, October 30, 2008.

46. Christopher D. Kilpatrick, "Early Voting a Big Winner; Nearly 2 in 3 Votes Were Cast before Tuesday, Making Election Day Easy for Precincts in North Carolina," *Charlotte Observer*, November 5, 2008.

47. Robert Stein, e-mail interview with author, July 27, 2007; Stein, Owens, and Leighley, "Electoral Reform, Party Mobilization and Voter Turnout."

48. John P. Katosh and Michael Traugott, "Costs and Values in the Calculus of Voting," *American Journal of Political Science* 26, no. 2 (May 1982): 371; Wolfinger, Highton, and Mullin, "State Laws and the Turnout of the Registered."

49. See Paul Gronke, "Early Voting Reforms and American Elections" (paper presented at the annual meeting of the American Political Science Association, Chicago, September 2–5, 2004).

50. For an extended discussion of these studies see John C. Fortier, *Absentee and Early Voting: Trends, Promises, and Perils* (Washington, DC: AEI Press, 2006); see also the many articles by Paul Gronke at http://earlyvoting.net/resources.html.

51. J. Eric Oliver, "The Effects of Eligibility Restrictions and Party Activity on Absentee Voting and Overall Turnout," *American Journal of Political Science* 40, no. 2 (May 1996): 498–513.

52. Tova Andrea Wang and Job Serebrov, "Voting Fraud and Voter Intimidation: Report to the U.S. Election System on Preliminary Research and Recommendations," July 2006, p. 7.

53. See *Balancing Access and Integrity: The Report of The Century Foundation Working Group on State Implementation of Election Reform*, The Century Foundation, 2005; *To Assure Pride and Confidence in the Electoral Process: Task Force Reports to Accompany the Report of the National Commission on Election Reform*, Miller Center for Public Affairs and The Century Foundation, August 2001; Fortier, *Absentee and Early Voting*; John Fund, *Stealing Elections: How Voter Fraud Threatens Our Democracy* (New York: Encounter Books, 2004); "Building Confidence in U.S. Elections: Report of the Commission on Federal Election Reform," September 2005, Center for Democracy and Election Management, American University.

54. Michael Alvarez, Thad Hall, and Betsy Sinclair, "Whose Absentee Votes Are Counted: The Variety and Use of Absentee Ballots in California," CalTech/MIT Voting Technology Project, July 2005. However, there is anecdotal evidence that some language minorities prefer the

option of being able to complete the ballot in their homes, where they can more easily get the assistance of their choosing.

55. Thompson, *Just Elections*, 35.

56. "Getting It Straight for 2008: What We Know about Vote by Mail Elections and How to Conduct Them Well," Common Cause, January 2008, p. 2.

57. Although they are commonly referred to as "overseas voters," this includes any out-of-country voter.

58. "Uniformed and Overseas Citizens Absentee Voters Act: Survey Report Findings," U.S. Election Assistance Commission, September 2007, p. 4.

59. Overseas Vote Foundation, "Moving Forward: 2010 OVF Post Election UOCAVA Survey Report and Analysis, February 2011," p. 2.

60. Ibid., 11.

61. United States Department of Justice Uniformed and Overseas Citizens Absentee Voting Act, "Annual Report to Congress 2010," at http://www.justice.gov/crt/about/vot/misc/move_act_report.pdf.

62. See Jason Dempsey, "The Army Vote and the Military Times Surveys," Pollster.Com, Guest Pollster, October 20, 2008.

63. Brian Whitmore, "Both Parties Reaching for Votes from Abroad," *Boston Globe*, May 3, 2004. There is little hard data on the partisanship of overseas voters, although conventional wisdom is that military voters are certainly disproportionately Republicans.

64. Marina Mecl, Overseas Vote Foundation, phone interview with author, October 1, 2007.

65. Grant Gross, "NIST Finds Security Problems with Overseas E-Voting," *Network World*, December 24, 2008.

66. "Overseas Vote Foundation 2006 Post Election Survey Results," Overseas Vote Foundation, February 8, 2007, p. 18.

67. "Yahoo!, the Huffington Post and Slate to Host First-Ever Online-Only Presidential Debates, Moderated by Charlie Rose," press release, April 23, 2007, Yahoo! Press room, at http://yahoo.client.shareholder.com/press/ReleaseDetail.cfm?ReleaseID=239007.

68. Adam Berinsky, "The Perverse Consequences of Electoral Reform in the United States," *American Politics Research* 33, no. 4 (July 2005): 471–491.

69. Paul Gronke, Reed College, e-mail interview with author, November 1, 2007.

70. It should be noted that Republicans Abroad is not directly affiliated with the Republican National Committee but rather is a "527 organization."

71. R. Michael Alvarez, Delia Bailey, and Jonathan Katz, "The Effect of Voter Identification Laws on Turnout," Caltech/MIT Voting Technology Project, January 2008.

72. "Citizens without Proof," Brennan Center for Justice, November 2006; Matt Barreto, Stephen A. Nuño, and Gabriel R. Sanchez, "Voter ID Requirements and the Disenfranchisement of Latino, Black and Asian Voters" (paper presented at the annual meeting of the American Political Science Association, September 1, 2007).

73. See, just for example, Lorraine C. Minnite, "The Politics of Voter Fraud," Project Vote, March 13, 2007; Justin Levitt, "The Truth about Voter Fraud," Brennan Center for Justice, 2007; testimony submitted by Lorraine C. Minnite, U.S. House Committee on the Judiciary, Subcommittee on the Constitution, Civil Rights, and Civil Liberties, Oversight Hearing on Voter Suppression, February 26, 2008; testimony delivered at the Senate Rules and Administration Committee Hearing, In Person Voter Fraud: Myth and Trigger for Disenfranchisement? March 12, 2008.

74. Justin Levitt, "Analysis of Alleged Fraud in Briefs Supporting *Crawford* Respondents," Brennan Center for Justice, December 31, 2007.

75. See Tova Andrea Wang, "Voting in 2008: 10 Swing States," Common Cause, The Century Foundation, September 17, 2008.

76. Ibid.

77. H.R. 103: Caging Prohibition Act of 2009, http://www.govtrack.us/congress/bill. xpd?bill=h111-103.

78. See Mark Hugo Lopez, "Latinos and the 2010 Elections," Pew Hispanic Center, October 5, 2010.

79. See, for example, Michael O'Brien, "GOP Messaging Lousy on Hispanics," *The Hill*, May 12, 2011; Jeb Bush, "Conservative Movement Must Commit to a Long-Term Outreach Strategy," *Miami Herald*, January 9, 2011.

80. Taeku Lee, "Asian Americans and the Electorate," American Political Science Association, at http://www.apsanet.org/print/printer_content_5154.cfm.

81. Stephen Chan, "AALDEF: The Asian American Vote," *Asians in America Magazine*, October 3, 2008.

82. David Melmer, "American Indian Voters Face Hostility in South Dakota," *Indian Country Today*, September 26, 2005; Paul McClain, *Can We All Get Along? Racial and Ethnic Minorities in American Politics* (Boulder, CO: Westview Press, 2001), 79.

83. Laura Flanders, "Bottom Up Power," *The Nation*, April 6, 2007.

84. See Jack Citrin and Benjamin Highton, "How Race, Ethnicity and Immigration Shape the California Electorate," Public Policy Institute of California, 2002; Editors, "Educate, Then Get Native American Voters to the Polls," *Indian Country Today*, August 13, 2001; Daniel Kraker, "The Tribal Vote," *High Country News*, August 25, 2004.

85. Jocelyn Friedrichs Benson, "Su Voto Es Su Voz! Incorporating Voters of Limited English Proficiency into American Democracy," *Boston College Law Review* 48, no. 2 (March 2007): 251–329, at 263.

86. Michael Jones-Correa and Israel Waismel-Manor, "Getting into the Voting Rights Act: The Availability of Translated Registration Materials and Its Impact on Minority Voter Registration and Participation" (paper presented at the annual meeting of the American Political Science Association, August 30–September 2, 2007).

87. "Translating the Vote: The Impact of the Language Minority Provision of the Voting Rights Act," Electionline.org, October 2006, p. 10; "Voting in 2010: Ten Swing States," Demos and Common Cause, September 2010.

88. "Translating the Vote: The Impact of the Language Minority Provision of the Voting Rights Act," Electionline.org, October 2006, p. 12.

89. Jones-Correa and Waismel-Manor, "Getting into the Voting Rights Act," 13.

90. Friedrichs Benson, "Su Voto Es Su Voz!" 305.

91. Jones-Correa and Waismel-Manor, "Getting into the Voting Rights Act," 11

92. "Felony Disenfranchisement Laws in the United States," Sentencing Project, April 2007.

93. Ibid.

94. Erika Wood and Neema Trivedi, "The Modern Day Poll Tax: How Economic Sanctions Block Access to the Polls," *Clearinghouse Review Journal of Poverty Law and Policy*, May–June 2007: 31, citing Marc Mauer, *Race to Incarcerate* (New York: New Press, 2006), 32; U.S. Census Bureau: State and County QuickFacts. Data derived from Population Estimates, American Community Survey, Census of Population and Housing, Small Area Income and Poverty Estimates, State and County Housing Unit Estimates, County Business Patterns, Nonemployer Statistics, Economic Census, Survey of Business Owners, Building Permits, Consolidated Federal Funds Report. Last Revised October 13, 2011, http://quickfacts.census.gov/qfd/states/00000.html.

95. Wood and Trivedi, "The Modern Day Poll Tax."

96. Ibid.

97. More and more states have been coming to this realization and, sometimes even putting partisan advantage to the side, have reformed their laws. Since 1997, sixteen states have loosened

restrictions on voting rights for ex-felons. See Jeff Manza and Christopher Uggen, *Locked Out: Felon Disenfranchisement and American Democracy* (New York: Oxford University Press, 2006), 248–50.

98. See Jeffrey Reiman, "Liberal and Republican Arguments against the Disenfranchisement of Felons," *Criminal Justice Ethics*, Winter/Spring 2005.

99. See Benjamin Highton, "Long Lines, Voting Machine Availability, and Turnout: The Case of Franklin County, Ohio, in the 2004 Presidential Election," PS Online, January 2006; Walter R. Mebane Jr., "Voting Machine Allocation in Franklin County, Ohio, 2004: Response to U.S. Department of Justice Letter of June 29, 2005," July 7, 2005; Daniel Tokaji, "Race and Ohio's Machine Shortage," *Equal Vote* blog, July 24, 2007; Theodore Allen and Mikhail Bernshteyn, "Mitigating Voter Waiting Times," *Chance*, vol. 19, no. 4, 2006; "Preserving Democracy: What Went Wrong in Ohio," Status Report of the House Judiciary Committee Democratic Staff, January 5, 2005; "Democracy at Risk: The 2004 Election in Ohio," Democratic National Committee, 2005; Michael Powell and Peter Slevin, "Several Factors Contributed to 'Lost Votes' in Ohio," *Washington Post*, December 15, 2004; James Dao, "Voting Problems in Ohio Spur Call for Overhaul," *New York Times*, December 24, 2004.

100. "Democracy at Risk: The 2004 Election in Ohio," Democratic National Committee, 2005.

101. For a full discussion of this see "Voting in 2006: Have We Solved the Problems of 2004?" The Century Foundation, Common Cause, and the Leadership Conference for Civil Rights, October 2006.

102. Election Assistance Commission, "2004 Election Day Survey: How We Voted: People, Ballots, & Polling Places, Part 2 Survey Results, Poll Workers," September 27, 2005, http://archives.eac.gov/program-areas/research-resources-and-reports/copy_of_docs/eds2004/eds-2004-part-2-chapter-12/attachment_download/file.

103. "Report to the U.S. Election Assistance Commission on Best Practices to Improve Provisional Voting," submitted by the Eagleton Institute and the Moritz College of Law, Ohio State University, June 28, 2006, p. 16.

104. Tova Andrea Wang, Sam Oliker-Friedlander, Melissa Riess, and Kristen Oshyn, "Voting in 2008: Ten Swing States," Common Cause and The Century Foundation, September 16, 2008, p. 22.

105. Wendy R. Weiser, "Are HAVA's Provisional Ballots Working?" Brennan Center for Justice, March 29, 2006.

106. Associated Press, "Ohio Court: Provisional Ballots outside Voter's Precinct Not Valid," October 24, 2004.

107. See Walter R. Mebane Jr., "Inferences from the DNC Provisional Vote Ballot Survey," April 27, 2005. About 60 percent of the provisional ballots cast in Cuyahoga County, Ohio, were cast by those who either were voting in Ohio for the first time or who had previously voted in the state but since moved: "15% of those who said they had previously voted in Ohio said they had since moved. Among those voters, 11.4% cast a provisional ballot, compared to just 1.7% of those who said they had not moved since the last time they voted." However, in the case of this county, Mebane found that these votes were evenly split between Republicans and Democrats. He also found that older voters were much less likely than younger voters to cast a provisional ballot.

108. Leonard Shambon and Keith Abouchar, "Trapped by Precincts? The Help America Vote Act's Provisional Ballots and the Problem of Precincts," *New York University Journal of Legislation and Public Policy* 10, no. 1 (2006–7): 176.

109. Leonard Shambon, e-mail interview with author, August 15, 2007.

110. See Shambon and Abouchar, "Trapped by Precincts?"

111. "Solution or Problem? Provisional Ballots in 2004," Electionline.org, April 2005, p. 6.

112. "Report to the U.S. Election Assistance Commission on Best Practices to Improve Provisional Voting," Eagleton Institute and Moritz College of Law, 14.

113. "Are HAVA's Provisional Ballots Working?" presentation by Wendy R. Weiser, Brennan Center for Justice, at NYU School of Law, March 29, 2006, at http://www.american.edu/ia/cdem/usp/hava_papers/Weiser.pdf.

Epilogue

1. Patrick Caldwell, "Who Stole the Election?" *American Prospect*, October 11, 2011.

2. Letter to Charles E. Summers Jr., secretary of state of Maine, Demos, ACLU Voting Rights Project, ACLU of Maine, October 17, 2011.

3. Eric Russell, "Mainers Vote to Continue Election Day Registration," *Bangor Daily News*, November 8, 2011.

4. Larry Sandler, "Fee Waiver Pushed for Copies of Birth Certificates," *Milwaukee Journal Sentinel*, October 3, 2011.

ACKNOWLEDGMENTS

I am so pleased to be able to publicly thank my colleagues at The Century Foundation, whom I call my second family. This especially includes Jason Renker, whose input, guidance, and support I could not have lived without during the process of producing this book, as well as Greg Anrig, Christy Hicks, Laurie Ahlrich, Carol Starmack, along with former president Richard Leone, who gave me the most important opportunities of my professional life, and new president Janice Nittoli, who recognizes the true importance of this issue. My family at The Century Foundation, with whom I have had an association since I was in law school in 1993, has taught me so much and helped me believe in my own abilities; I owe a great deal personally and professionally to this amazing group of people.

Alexander Keyssar has been a wonderful mentor and friend to me, and his input and guidance throughout the writing process was invaluable beyond words. Chandler Davidson provided me his infinite wisdom and support from start to finish, for which I am grateful. My thanks go to Michael McGandy, who took this book under his wing so that it could find its true home at Cornell University Press. I am also extremely thankful to Sheri Englund, who helped me through one of the most difficult parts of the process and is simply an extraordinary editor.

My democracy program colleagues at Demos have also been tremendously supportive, and Miles Rapoport, Brenda Wright, and the organization have given me the amazing opportunity to continue to work on the issues I care deeply about while surrounded by an outstanding team.

I owe a great deal of gratitude to all of my friends and colleagues from academia and the voting rights community who have helped me with innumerable issues and questions I had along the way, and for all of the great collaborative efforts we have undertaken together over the last decade. Laughlin McDonald and Daniel Tokaji were particularly generous in their time and in helping me shape the book over the course of many years. Others who were kind enough to provide me critical input include Michael Alvarez, Thad Hall, Douglas Hess, Lorraine Minnite, Paul Gronke, Dennis Thompson, Terri Ao Minnis, Robert Stein, and Spencer Overton.

Many interns and co-workers also helped me research a number of the topics covered in the book, and I am very thankful for the work they did, which often put my own skills to shame. I would especially like to thank Melissa Riess, Sam Oliker-Friedland, and my former TCF colleague Kristen Oshyn. Paul Kerlin also provided me with a number of smart thoughts that had a great impact on my thinking.

My sister, Melissa Fisher, was also a constant source of support and the occasional much needed pep talk.

Most of all I thank and express my love to my husband, Jeff Vogt, who truly makes anything possible.

INDEX

absentee balloting: and fraud, xvii, 71, 80, 81, 140; military and overseas voters and, 141; "no excuse," 139–40; party mobilization efforts and, 9; voter inclusion principle and, 14, 139–41

ACORN, 93, 94–95, 173n20

African Americans: 19th-century vote suppression of, 19–20, 109–12; 20th-century vote suppression of, 30, 31, 37, 38–39; in 2000 election, 119; in 2004 election, 123; in 2008 election, 5, 91–92, 101; 2012 election cycle and, xv; caging targeting, 56–58; challenging at the polls, 51; Civil Rights Act of 1964 and political allegiance of, 35–36; civil rights movement and, 31–32; deceptive practices targeting, 135; Democratic Party leanings of, 30, 32; early voting and, 3; felon disenfranchisement and, 114, 115, 119,

121, 150; New Deal and political allegiance of, 30–31, 33, 42; poll worker allocation disparities and, 152; voter ID requirements and, 80, 81, 83, 171n3; voter registration drives and, 2; Voting Rights Act of 1965 and, 33, 112–14, 165n14

Alabama: black voter turnout in, 19th-century, 110; felon disenfranchisement in, 114; secret-ballot laws in, 110; Voting Rights Act of 1965 and, 113, 114

Allen, George, 68

American Civil Liberties Union, 157

Americans for Legal Immigration, 105

Arizona: 1964 election in, 44, 45–49; 2010 elections in, 105; Latinos in, 166n1; proof-of-citizenship requirements in, 26, 87

Arkansas: school integration in, 32; secret-ballot laws in, 22–23, 110
Asian Americans voters, 146, 147
Avery, Drew, 7

Bachus, Spencer, 65
Baesler, Scotty, 116
Barr, Charles, 50
Bayh, Birch, 48
Beasley, David, 67
Bennett, Michael, 3
Black, Earl and Merle, 53
Black, Hugo, 4
Blackwell, Kenneth, 121, 122
Bond, Kit, 77, 171n2
Brennan Center, 83
Brown, Robert, 80
Browning, Kurt, 95, 96
Bruder, George, 119–20
Brunner, Jennifer, 93
Buchanan, Pat, 76
Bunning, Jim, 116
Burch, Dean, 50
Burmeister, Sue, 81
Bush, George H. W., 61–62, 65
Bush, George W.: in 2000 election, 75, 147; in 2004 election, 85, 121, 127; Latino vote for, 104
butterfly ballot, 76, 89

caging, 44; in 1960s and 1970s, 44, 47, 48, 50, 51; in 1980s, 54–58; in 2004 election, 85; in 2008 election, 94; impact on election outcomes, 109; proposed ban on, 146; states' laws on, 145
California, minority voters in, 149
Campbell, Carroll, Jr., 67
Caplan, Bryan, 7
Cardin, Ben, 135
Carter, Jimmy, xv, 53
challenging at the polls: in 19th-century elections, 19, 20–21, 26; in 20th-century elections, 43–52, 54–59; in 2004 election, 85–86, 122; in 2008 election, 94; detrimental impact of, 43, 59, 145–46; evolution of, 58

Civil Rights Act of 1964, 32; antidiscrimination provisions of, 34; passage of, 35; Reagan's opposition to, 53; southern political transformation after, 35–37
civil rights movement, 4, 31–32, 36
Clinton, Bill, 64, 66, 104
Clinton, Hillary, 93
Coffman, Michael, 99–100
college students, voting rights of, 132–33; attacks on, 102, 156–57
Colorado: 2008 election in, 99–100; minority language assistance in, 149; student voting in, 103
Common Cause, 96, 141, 173n1, 174n12
Condon, Charlie, 67
Conyers, John, 122
Crawford v. Marion County Election Board, 17, 84, 172n15

Davidson, Chandler, 45, 52, 166n1, 167n24
DBT Online, 119–20
Deceptive Practices and Voter Intimidation Prevention Act of 2011, 135
Democratic Party: absentee balloting and, 139; African American vote and, 30, 32; Asian American vote and, 147; Civil Rights Act and transformation of, 32, 35; deceptive practices targeting constituencies of, 135; disenfranchising laws of 19th century and, 109, 110, 111–12; early voting and, 5, 138; election reforms used for political gain by, xiv; felon disenfranchisement and, 116, 149; immigrant voters and, 20, 21; Latino vote and, 134, 146; lawsuits against Republican vote suppression tactics, 55, 57, 58; military and overseas voters and, 142; and multiracial coalitions, 33, 54; National Voter Registration Act (NVRA) and, 127–28; Native American vote and, 147; nonvoters identifying with, 6; provisional ballots and, 153, 154–55, 184n107; and registration reform, 127; and

same-day registration, 130–31; and
secret ballot, 22–23; southern, and
African American vote suppression,
19–20, 37, 39; in southern states, election politics until 1980s, 31, 53–54;
and voter education, 136; on voter
ID requirements, 79; and voter participation advocacy, xviii; and voter
registration requirements, 24; vote
suppression by, 19th-century tactics,
19–20, 22, 25; vote suppression by,
20th-century tactics, 33, 37, 155; voting machine/site allocation and, 151;
and white primaries, 30; youth vote
and, 131, 132–33
Demos, 73, 128, 157
Department of Justice: and 2010 midterm
elections, 105; authority to supervise
election practices, 32, 34; on citizenship verification, 97, 98; politicization
of, 172n20
DePass, Rusty, 67
Dreier, David, 65

early voting, 137–45; in 2008 election,
4–5, 91–92, 102, 137, 138; African
Americans and, 5; party mobilization
efforts and, 9; Republican attempts to
reduce, 101–2; states' laws restricting,
3; and voter turnout, 9, 138
Edgar, Jim, 67
education. *See* voter education
Edwards, John, 139
eight-box law, 110–11
Eisenhower, Dwight D., 32
Election Assistance Committee, 78
Engler, John, 67
Erickson, Erik, 80
Erikson, Robert S., 124, 178n67
ethnicity: vote suppression based on, 16,
17. *See also* minorities
Evans, Terrence T., 79, 80

Fahrenkopf, Frank, 57
Faircloth, Lauch, 54
Fairvote, 132

Federal Voter Assistance Program, 143,
144
felon disenfranchisement, 114–17, 177n39;
in 1970s, 40; in 2000 election, 76, 89,
116, 117, 119, 121; impact on election
outcomes, 109, 116–17; limiting of,
149–51
Fifteenth Amendment, 3–4
Florida: 1964 election in, 51; 2000 election in, 12, 71, 75–76, 89, 118–21;
2004 election in, 86; 2008 election
in, 95–96; 2012 election cycle and,
1–3; disenfranchising laws of late
19th century, 110, 111; felon disenfranchisement in, 76, 89, 114, 116,
117; National Voter Registration Act
(NVRA) and, 69; work toward repeal
of voting restrictions in, 158
Florio, James, 54
Ford, Gerald, xv
Fourteenth Amendment, 3, 32, 152
fraud, voter: in 19th century, 17; in 2000
election, claims regarding, 76, 77, 89,
171n2; absentee ballots and, xvii, 71,
80, 81, 140; NVRA and charges of,
62, 65, 67–68, 70; in polling places,
chances of, 80, 84, 145; Republican
charges of, xvi, xvii, 55, 56–57,
64–66, 79; secret ballot and, 23; U.S.
attorney scandal involving, 172n20;
voter ID requirements claiming to
reduce, 84, 145; voter registration
requirements claiming to reduce,
27–28

Gantt, Harvey, 57
Georgia: 2008 election in, 97–98; black
voter turnout in, 19th-century, 110;
felon disenfranchisement in, 116;
National Voter Registration Act
(NVRA) and, 69; voter ID require-
ments in, 79, 80–82; Voting Rights
Act of 1965 and, 114
Gheen, William, 105
Gilmore, James S., 68
Goldwater, Barry, 35–36, 49

Gore, Al, 75, 117–18, 147
Gramm, Phil, 54
Griffith, Lanny, 56

Handel, Karen, 97
Harris, Katherine, 71, 89
Hawke, Jack, 57
Helms, Jesse, 54, 57
Help America Vote Act (HAVA), 78;
    debate over, 76–78; on felon disen-
    franchisement, 115; flaws in, 88–90,
    95, 106; manipulation of, 78–85, 88;
    positive outcomes of, 90; on provi-
    sional ballots, 78, 88, 89, 90, 154; and
    same-day registration, 90; on voter
    education, 136
Hollings, Ernest, 113
Huddleston, Walter, 116
Humphrey, Hubert, 36, 50

ID requirements. *See* voter identification
    requirements
Iglesias, David, 173n20
Illinois, NVRA in, 67–68
immigrants: voter ID requirements and,
    106; voter registration reform and,
    133–34; vote suppression in 19th cen-
    tury, 17, 20–21; vote suppression in
    20th century, 43, 105, 106
income: and ID possession, 83; and voting
    patterns, 31, 64. *See also* low-income
    voters
Indiana, voter ID requirements in, 79
Internet: overseas voters and, 143–44;
    voter information on, 147–48
intimidation: in 19th-century elections,
    18, 19; in 20th-century elections, 43,
    57–58; in 21st-century elections, 157;
    and election outcomes, 108. *See also*
    challenging at the polls
Iowa: felon disenfranchisement in,
    114; minority language assistance
    in, 148; presidential election of 2008
    in, 93

Johnson, Lyndon B., 32, 36, 49

Kaltenbacher, Philip, 55
Kansas, voter ID requirements in, 79
Kean, Thomas, 54
Kelly, Jesse, 105
Kennedy, John F., 32, 49
Kennedy, Robert F., Jr., 123
Kentucky, felon disenfranchisement in,
    116, 149
Kerry, John, 85, 104, 123, 127
Keyssar, Alexander, 29, 37, 38
Kousser, J. Morgan, 22, 111, 112, 164n8
Krueger, Robert, 116

Landon, Alf, 31
language translation assistance, 146,
    147–49, 166n17
Latinos: felon disenfranchisement laws
    and, 150; language assistance and,
    147; in presidential election of 2008,
    xv, 104, 134; and voter ID problems,
    96; voter registration drives and, 2;
    vote suppression targeting, xv, 104–6;
    voting patterns among, 104, 134,
    146–47
Latinos for Reform, 105
Lawyers Committee for
    Civil Rights, 73
League of Women Voters, 2, 134
literacy tests, 18–19, 20, 25; ban on, 32, 37,
    58; and election outcomes, 108; in pri-
    maries, attempts to use, 39; voter ID
    requirements compared to, 80; and
    vote suppression in 1960s, 45, 46
Livingston, Robert, 65
Louisiana: 1964 election in, 52; 1986 elec-
    tion in, 56; 2010 elections in, 105; Af-
    rican American voters in, 110, 171n3;
    secret-ballot laws in, 110; Voting
    Rights Act of 1965 and, 113, 114
low-income voters: registration for,
    NVRA and, 72–74; vote suppression
    tactics targeting, xv, 31, 127, 150

Maggiore, Vincent, 47
mail: returned, and challenging of voting
    rights, 44; sample ballots distributed

through, 136; voter registration by, 61, 70, 72, 124–25; voting by, 139

Maine, 2012 campaign in, 156–57

Manza, Jeff, 116, 117, 177n39

Maryland, voter registration in, 128

Masset, Royal, 79

McCain, John, 5, 92, 102

McConnell, Mitch, 116

Meyers, Susan Lacetti, 81

Michigan, NVRA and, 67

midterm elections: of 1986, 56; of 1990, 57; of 2006, 124–25, 141, 143; of 2010, xvi, 105

military and overseas voters, 14, 141–45, 182n63

Military and Overseas Voters Empowerment Act (MOVE), 14, 141–42

Mill, John Stuart, 13

Minnesota: 1964 election in, 50–51; 2012 campaign in, 156; minority language assistance in, 148

Minnite, Lorraine C., 124, 178n67

minorities: felon disenfranchisement and, 150; language assistance for, 147–49, 166n17; photo ID requirements and, 81; provisional ballots used by, 153; vote suppression tactics targeting, 42–43, 52, 123–25; voting machine allocation in districts with, 151; voting patterns among, 146–47. *See also specific minorities*

Mississippi: 2000 election in, 171n2; felon disenfranchisement in, 114; Voting Rights Act of 1965 and, 113, 114

Missouri: 2012 campaign in, 156; voter registration in, 73

Mitchell, Emmett, 120

Mondale, Walter, 63

motor vehicle departments (DMVs): voter identification at, 83, 99; voter registration at, 61, 64, 69–70, 71, 72, 127, 128

motor voter law. *See* National Voter Registration Act (NVRA)

multiracial coalitions, 33, 54

National Commission for Federal Election Reform, xv, 136

National Voter Registration Act (NVRA), 60–62; barriers to registration before, 62–64; congressional debates on, 64–66; DMV provision of, 61, 64, 69–70, 71, 72, 127, 128; fraud charges regarding, 62, 65, 67–68, 70; implementation issues, 71–74; mail-in provision of, 61, 124–25; partisan impacts of, 69–70; passage of, 66; public agency provision of, 63, 64, 70–74, 127; recommendations for future utilization of, 127–28; safeguards against fraud in, 70–71; Section 7 provision of, 72–74; state challenges to, 66–68; success of, 68–69, 74; on voter purging, 99

Native Americans: poll worker allocation disparities and, 152; reforms to increase voter participation by, 146; voter ID requirements and, 87; voting patterns among, 147

Nebraska, 2012 campaign in, 156

Nelson, Ben, 158

Nevada, 2010 elections in, 105

New Deal, and African American political allegiance, 30–31, 33, 42

New Jersey: 19th-century elections in, 21, 24; gubernatorial contest of 1981 in, 54–55

New Mexico, felon disenfranchisement in, 114

Nineteenth Amendment, 4, 28, 29

Nixon, Richard M., 35, 36–37

nonvoters: vs. transient voters, election reforms aimed at, 9, 163n32; vs. voters, ideological differences between, 6

North Carolina: 2004 election in, 87; 2008 election in, 4–5, 9, 91–92, 93; voter registration in, 25, 73–74; Voting Rights Act of 1965 and, 114

Obama, Barack: in 2008 election, xv, 5, 92, 93, 102; African American vote for, 5;

Obama, Barack *(continued)*
  on deceptive practices, 134–35; early or
    absentee votes for, 5, 138; Latino vote
    for, 104, 134; youth vote for, 102, 133
O'Brien, Tim, 7
Ohio: 2004 election in, 85–86, 87, 121–23;
    2008 election in, 98–99, 101; voter
    registration in, 73
Operation Eagle Eye, 44, 49–52, 86; lead-
    up to, 45–49; poll watchers in, 44,
    49–52, 167n24
Oregon, mail registration in, 70
Ornstein, Norman, 133, 136
Overseas Vote Foundation (OVF), 143
overseas voters. *See* military and overseas
    voters

Packard, Ronald, 65
Patrick, Deval L., 171n3
Pennsylvania: 2008 election in, 95; 2012
    campaign in, 156; first voter registra-
    tion law in, 165n38
People's Party, 20
Pine, Charles, 46
poll hours, proposal for reform, 138
polling place information, 136
poll taxes, 18, 20, 164n13; ban on, 29, 32,
    37, 58; and black voter participation,
    110; and election outcomes, 108;
    "time tax" compared to, 101; voter
    ID laws compared to, 80, 82, 83
poll watchers, 20; in 1964 election, 50–51,
    52, 167n24. *See also* challenging at
    the polls
poll workers: in 19th century, 18; in 21st
    century, training of, 148; fair alloca-
    tion of, need for, 151, 152–53
Populists (People's Party), 20
Posner, Richard, 67–68
presidential campaign of 2012, 156–59; en-
    couraging work in, 157–58; lessons of
    history and, xvi; worrying signs for,
    xv, 1–2, 156–57
presidential election of 1868, 17
presidential election of 1880, 110
presidential election of 1964, 35–36; Oper-
    ation Eagle Eye in, 44, 49–52, 167n24

presidential election of 1968, 114
presidential election of 1980, 35, 53
presidential election of 1984, 63
presidential election of 2000, 75–76; after-
    math of, 76–78, 88; Asian American
    vote in, 147; author's involvement in,
    xv; charges of voter fraud in, 76, 77,
    89, 171n2; felon disenfranchisement
    in, 76, 89, 116, 117, 119, 121; irregu-
    larities in, 12, 71, 76, 89–90, 117–21;
    military and overseas voters in, 141
presidential election of 2004: lowest-
    income voters in, 127; manipulation
    of, 85–88, 121–23; out-of-precinct
    ballots in, 154; poorly allocated vot-
    ing machines/sites in, 151; same-day
    registration in, 130; voter registration
    groups in, 128–29, 179n9
presidential election of 2008, 91–104;
    Asian American vote in, 147; early
    voting in, 4–5, 91–92, 102, 137, 138;
    Internet debate in, 144; Latino vote
    in, 104, 134; litigation prior to, 92–93,
    94; long lines in, 100–102; lowest-
    income voters in, 127; manipulation
    of, 93–104; military and overseas
    voters in, 142; registration issues in,
    94–100; same-day registration in, 4, 5,
    91–92; voter turnout in, xv, 4–5, 9, 91,
    100, 175n23; youth vote in, 102–4, 131
Project Vote, 73
proof-of-citizenship requirements: in 19th
    century, 21, 26; in 21st-century, 26,
    87, 97–98
provisional ballots: in 2008 election, 94,
    174n7; counting of, 153–55; demo-
    graphic characteristics of voters
    using, 184n107; Help America Vote
    Act (HAVA) on, 78, 88, 89, 90, 154;
    problems with, 2, 83
public ballot, 22, 27
public service agencies, voter registration
    at, 63, 64, 70–74, 127
punch-card ballots, 76, 78, 90

racism: and challenges at the polls, 43; and
    literacy tests, 18–19

radio, and voting, 136–37
Reagan, Ronald: in 1980 election, 53; in
    1984 election, 63; appeal to white
    southern voters, 53; election as presi-
    dent, 41; political realignment after
    presidency of, 53–54
redistricting: vote dilution through, 38;
    Voting Rights Act of 1965 and, 33, 34
registration. *See* voter registration
Rehnquist, William, 45, 46–48
Republican Party: caging by, 44, 47, 48,
    50, 51, 54–58; challenging at the
    polls by, 43–52, 54–59; disenfran-
    chising laws of 19th century and,
    109–12; early voting and, 138; elec-
    tion reforms used for political gain
    by, xiv; and felon disenfranchise-
    ment laws, 115–16, 149; Latino vote
    and, 105, 106, 134, 146–47; military
    and overseas voters and, 142; and
    National Voter Registration Act
    (NVRA), attempts to block, 64–68,
    69; and National Voter Registra-
    tion Act (NVRA), DMV provision
    of, 69, 127; provisional ballots and,
    153, 154–55, 184n107; same-day
    registration and, 130; in southern
    states, 31–32, 33–34, 35–37, 41, 53,
    54; voter fraud charges by, xvi, xvii,
    55, 56–57, 64–66, 79; and voter ID
    requirements, 1, 79, 84; and voter
    registration organizations, 129; and
    voter registration requirements, 24;
    and vote suppression, xvi, xvii, 25,
    33–34, 41, 42–52, 54–58, 94, 155;
    youth vote and, 133
residency requirements, 37
right to vote: vs. privilege of voting, 1, 3–4;
    relationship to democracy, xviii, 10
Roberts, Barbara, 70
robo-calls, 93
Rockefeller, Winthrop, 113
Roosevelt, Franklin Delano, 30–31

same-day registration, 130–32; African
    Americans and, 5; Help America
    Vote Act (HAVA) and, 90; in Maine,

fight over, 156, 157; National Voter
    Registration Act (NVRA) and, 127;
    in presidential election of 2008, 4, 5,
    91–92; and voter turnout, 9, 130
sample ballots, 136, 147
Scholzman, Bradley, 173n20
Schumer, Charles, 135
secret ballot: motives behind introduction
    of, 22–23, 110, 111; pros and cons of,
    14, 26–27
Shipley, Carl, 52
Smith v. Allwright, 30
South: Civil Rights Act of 1964 and
    political transformation in, 35–37;
    complex dynamics since 1960s, 33;
    desegregation in, 31–32; disenfran-
    chising laws of late 19th century,
    109–12; literacy tests in, 18–19; Re-
    publican dominance in, after 1960s,
    31–32, 33–34, 35–37, 41, 53, 54; vote
    suppression in, 19th-century tactics,
    16–18, 20, 21, 22, 25, 29; vote suppres-
    sion in, 20th-century tactics, 30, 31,
    33–34, 37–41; Voting Rights Act of
    1965 and, 33, 113–14, 165n14; white
    primaries in, 22
South Carolina: black voter turnout in,
    19th-century, 110; eight-box law in,
    111; National Voter Registration Act
    (NVRA) and, 67; poll tax in, 164n13;
    voter ID requirements in, 79; Voting
    Rights Act of 1965 and, 113, 114
South Dakota, 2004 election in, 87
states: 2011 elections, assault on voting
    rights in, xv, 1; and felon disenfran-
    chisement, 149, 183n97; laws on
    challenges at polling places, 145–46;
    and minority language assistance,
    148; National Voter Registration Act
    (NVRA) challenges in, 66–68; and
    provisional ballots, counting of, 154;
    same-day registration in, 130; voter
    ID requirements enacted by, 79–82,
    84–85; and vote suppression, early
    years of, 16–17; and voting machine
    allocation, 151–52; voting systems in,
    75, 78. *See also specific states*

Staton, Cecil, 80
Stevens, John Paul, 17, 84
Stevens, Ted, 115
Stevenson, Adlai, 35
Stewart, Charles, 89
Summers, Charles, 157
Sundquist, James L., 36
Supreme Court: on 2000 election, 75, 76, 117; on public school segregation, 31–32; on voter ID requirements, 82, 84, 172n15; on white primaries, 22, 30

Taylor, Paul, 136
television, and voting, 136–37
Tennessee: disenfranchising laws in, 111–12; poll tax in, 164n13; voter ID requirements in, 79; work toward repeal of voting restrictions in, 157–58
Texas: early voting and voter turnout in, 9; felon disenfranchisement in, 116; voter ID requirements in, 79, 82
Thompson, Dennis, 10–12, 135
Thurmond, Strom, 54
Tower, John, 116
transient voters, election reforms aimed at, 9, 163n32

Uggen, Christopher, 116, 117, 177n39
Uniformed and Overseas Civilian Absentee Voting Act (UOCAVA), 141, 142
United States Commission on Civil Rights (USCCR), 38, 39, 40, 41; on Florida election of 2000, 118–19, 121
universal registration, 132–33

Vermont, secret ballot in, 23
Virginia: felon disenfranchisement in, 114, 149; student voting in, 103; voter registration at public assistance agencies in, 74; Voting Rights Act of 1965 and, 114
vote buying, xvii, 18, 19, 22, 80
vote dilution, 38, 40–41
voter education: Internet and, 143; for language minority communities, 147–48; need for, 135–37

voter identification requirements: and African Americans, 80, 81, 83, 171n3; arguments in support of, 8, 84; and college students, 133; Help America Vote Act (HAVA) and, 78, 79; impact on election outcomes, 109, 124, 178n66, 178n67; and Latinos, 106; presidential campaign of 2012 and, 156; presidential election of 2000 and, 77; vs. signature match, 145; state elections of 2011 and, 1; states and, 79–82, 84–85; Supreme Court on, 82, 172n15; vote suppression through, 82–84, 145
voter inclusion principle, 5, 109, 126; 19th-century violations of, 25–28; absentee balloting and, 14, 139–41; and analysis of election reform, 13–14; benefits of, 14–15; challenges of voters as violation of, 43, 145–46; citizens' role in protecting, 158–59; and college students, 102; deceptive practices violating, 134–35; early voting and, 137; felon disenfranchisement and, 149–50; language assistance and, 147; Latino participation and, 106; mobilization tactics and, 63, 129; and NVRA, 62, 74; and registration reform, 127–34; voter education and, 135–37; voter ID requirements and, 145; voter registration requirements and, 100; voting machine and poll worker allocation disparities and, 151–52
voter participation: absentee balloting and, 139–40; advocacy for, xvii–xviii; approaches to increasing, 8–10; benefits of increased level of, 10–13; early voting and, 9, 138; knowledge and, 137; mobilization in 1980s, 63–64; NVRA's contribution to, 61; in presidential election of 2008, xv, 4–5, 9, 91, 100, 175n23; same-day registration and, 9, 130; voter ID laws and, 124, 178n67

voter registration: at DMVs, 61, 64, 69–70, 71, 72; efforts to simplify, 60; local barriers to, 63, 64; at public service agencies, 63, 64, 70–74; reforms needed in, 127–34; universal, 132–33. *See also* National Voter Registration Act (NVRA); same-day registration; voter registration requirements

voter registration drives: in 1980s, 63; in 2004 election, 128–29, 179n9; fraud through, 70–71; restrictions on, 2

voter registration lists, abuse of, 71; in 1970s, 40; in 2000s, 71, 94–100

voter registration requirements: Help America Vote Act (HAVA) and, 95; in late 19th to early 20th century, 23–25, 40; and vote suppression, 27–28; Voting Rights Act of 1965 and, 34

voters, demographic profile of, 6, 162n16

vote suppression: in 19th century, 16–28, 109–12; in 20th century, 29–30, 37–41, 42–52; in 21st century, 123–25; in 2000 election, 12, 71, 76, 89–90, 117–21; in 2004 election, 85–88, 121–23; in 2008 election, 93–104; deceptive practices and, 134–35; detrimental impact of, 5–8, 109, 125; and election outcomes, 108; electoral reforms and, xiii–xiv, 155; first national effort toward, 44, 52; HAVA manipulation and, 78–85, 88; impact on minorities, 123–25; political campaigns and, 6–7; voter ID requirements and, 82–84, 145; voter registration requirements and, 27–28

voting machines: electronic, debate on, xvii; failure in communities of color, 76; fair allocation of, need for, 151–52; HAVA and increased accuracy of, 78, 90; malfunctions in 2004 election, 87;

range used throughout country, 77; shortages in 2004 election, 122

Voting Rights Act of 1965, 4, 32; antidiscrimination provisions of, 34; arguments used against, 67; extensions in 1970s, 54; impact in South, 33, 165n14; impact on election outcomes, 112–14; minority language provisions in, 147–48, 166n17; passage of, 35, 109; Reagan's opposition to, 53; USCCR report on effectiveness of, 38, 39, 40, 41; voter registration after, 62; vote suppression strategies after, 37–39

voting rights groups: 2008 election and, 92, 93, 96, 97, 99, 104; 2012 election cycle and, xv, 157–58; Florida law restricting activities of, 2

Wallace, George, 36, 53

Warren, Francis, 19

Washington, DC, 1964 election in, 52

Webster, Charles, 157

Webster, William, 46

Wellstone, Paul, 139

Wesbury v. Sanders, 4

white primaries, 22, 30

Wilcox, Ben, 174n12

Wisconsin: 2004 election in, 86; poll workers in, 153; voter ID requirements in, 79, 82; work toward repeal of voting restrictions in, 157

Wolfe, Kris, 56

women's suffrage, 4, 28

Women's Voices Women's Votes, 93

Wyoming, felon disenfranchisement in, 114

young people: new electoral laws affecting, xv; in presidential election of 2008, 102–4, 131; proposals for increased participation of, 132–33. *See also* college students